"Biblical evangelicalism must alwa[...] [...] today cannot avoid being denominational. And denominational evangelicalism is a spiritual smorgasbord, offering more spiritual wealth and wisdom than any one person can possibly take on board. In these pages, evangelical leaders become tour guides, each to his own denominational heritage. Authoritative? Yes. Absorbing? That too. Enriching? Very much so. Taste and see."

J. I. Packer, Board of Governors' Professor of Theology,
Regent College

"The editors have assembled a strong lineup of contributors to explain why they are both evangelicals and members of their specific denominations. The result is a sparkling presentation of the very best in a number of Protestant traditions, but also a welcome prompt to think about denominationalism itself. The book is for those who value history, biblical interpretation, Christian witness, and theology—that is, for nearly everyone."

Mark A. Noll, Francis A. McAnaney Professor of History,
University of Notre Dame

"The contributors to *Why We Belong* remind us that the strength of American evangelicalism is its unity-in-diversity. Their personal stories help us understand the importance of both our common evangelical faith and our respective denominational distinctives. This twin emphasis avoids narrow sectarianism, on the one hand, and lowest-common-denominator theology, on the other. As a movement, evangelicalism is richer because of the unified diversity displayed in the chapters of this commendable book."

George O. Wood, General Superintendent, Assemblies of God;
Chairman, World Assemblies of God Fellowship;
Executive Committee member, National Association of Evangelicals

"These essays reflect the wonderful unity *and* diversity that exist in the body of Christ. Thus, they show evangelicalism at its best. Written by practitioners of irenic Christian cooperation and conviction, this book will instruct young believers in the true purposes of evangelicalism. It will also remind older believers why evangelicalism is worth preserving."

Paul House, Professor of Divinity, Beeson Divinity School;
President Emeritus, Evangelical Theological Society

"The authors of *Why We Belong* argue for a robustly evangelical ecumenism—one that does not downplay the importance of doctrine or paper over theological differences, but instead recognizes those differences for what they are and moves forward in authentic Christian unity. Highly recommended."

Bruce Riley Ashford, Provost, Dean of Faculty,
and Associate Professor of Theology and Culture,
Southeastern Baptist Theological Seminary

"The gospel brings life, and that life finds expression in a myriad of institutional forms. This important book shows how evangelicalism, with its gospel-centeredness, transcends any particular denominational form and yet links those who share in the new life that Christ brings. More than that, this work offers a positive theology of denominationalism that is simply refreshing."

Graham Cole, Anglican Professor of Divinity, Beeson Divinity School

"If you find yourself standing over the funeral of either denominationalism or evangelicalism with a smile on your face, then you owe it to yourself to read this book. With biblical wisdom and theological insight (and humor, too) the editors and contributors chart a beautiful path between appreciating all that is good in denominationalism and embracing all that is good in evangelicalism. To put it succinctly, we belong to our churches *and* we belong to each other—and both of these are good for us."

Stephen J. Nichols, Research Professor of Christianity and Culture,
Lancaster Bible College

"Many of us have long felt that a passion for Christian unity does not mean the abolition of denominational distinctives. Finally, here is a book that supports loyalty to both the unique mission of one's church and the larger unity of the people of God. We learn in its pages that the future strength of evangelicalism depends on a passion for both. A must read."

Frank D. Macchia, Professor of Systematic Theology,
Vanguard University

"This book promotes a healthy Christian unity by showing how and why God's family is much larger than any one denomination."

Andy Naselli, Assistant Professor of New Testament and Biblical
Theology, Bethlehem College and Seminary, Minneapolis

WHY WE BELONG

WHY WE BELONG

EVANGELICAL UNITY *and* DENOMINATIONAL DIVERSITY

Edited by

ANTHONY L. CHUTE,
CHRISTOPHER W. MORGAN,
and ROBERT A. PETERSON

 CROSSWAY

WHEATON, ILLINOIS

Trade paperback ISBN: 978-1-4335-1483-8
Mobipocket ISBN: 978-1-4335-1485-2
PDF ISBN: 978-1-4335-1484-5
ePub ISBN: 978-1-4335-2459-2

Library of Congress Cataloging-in-Publication Data

Why we belong : evangelical unity and denominational diversity /
edited by Anthony L. Chute, Christopher W. Morgan, and Robert A.
Peterson.
    pages cm
 Includes bibliographical references and index.
 ISBN 978-1-4335-1483-8
 1. Evangelicalism. 2. Christian biography. 3. Christian sects. I. Chute,
Anthony L., editor of compilation.
 BR1643.A1W49 2013
 280'.042—dc23   2013003481

Crossway is a publishing ministry of Good News Publishers.

VP		25	24	23	22	21	20	19	18	17	16	15	14	13
15	14	13	12	11	10	9	8	7	6	5	4	3	2	1

To Robert J. Dunzweiler,
Jeff Kennedy,
and John Woodbridge,

who have encouraged us
to embrace Christian convictions
while modeling Christlike charity

Contents

Acknowledgments

We want to thank the following for their help:

Our team at Crossway, for their commitment to and embodiment of this project;

California Baptist University's trustees and administration, for their belief in and support of this project;

Covenant Theological Seminary's librarians James Pakala and Steve Jamieson, for fast, courteous, and professional help;

Thom Notaro and Elliott Pinegar, for competently editing the entire manuscript;

Connie, Shelley, and Mary Pat, for supporting us in our ministries;

Amos, Joelle, and Chelsey, for adding joy to our lives.

Introduction:
Are Denominations Dead?
Should They Be?

Anthony L. Chute

In the Charles Schulz classic *It's the Great Pumpkin, Charlie Brown*, an interesting exchange takes place as Linus pens his annual letter to the Great Pumpkin. "When are you going to stop believing in something that isn't true?" inquires Charlie, to which Linus shoots back, "When you stop believing in that fellow with a red suit and white beard who goes 'Ho, Ho, Ho'!" Charlie Brown looks at the camera and says dryly, "We are obviously separated by denominational differences."

For most outside the church, and increasingly many inside the church, denominational differences are viewed as nothing more than petty disagreements between strong-willed religious partisans. Studies on denominational identity rarely reflect an upward trend, and pastors who reach evangelical stardom hardly do so by clinging to denominational coattails. Americans in particular tend to choose a church because of the people who attend rather than the polity it embraces, and few ever think "Southern Baptist" when they hear the name Billy Graham or Rick Warren.

Opposition to denominational Christianity ranges anywhere from the sophisticated to the simple, yet the negative feelings are generally the same. H. Richard Niebuhr argued that denominations were a moral failure of Christianity since they were based on ethnic, class, and racial divisions more than theological or other principled matters. On a lighter note, yet somewhat of a confirmation of Niebuhr's concern, humorist Garrison Keillor explained his Lutheran conclave in a song:

We sit in the pew where we always sit,
And we do not shout Amen.

> And if anyone yells or waves their hands,
> They're not invited back again.[1]

And while statistics may provide helpful scientific analysis regarding the level of interest in denominations, the casual observer who sees multiple churches with various names on the same street is often convinced that Christians cannot get along with each other.

The divide is not merely external. Denominations are often plagued by internal divisions, necessitating the use of adjectival qualifiers in order to distinguish themselves from others who are almost like them. It is hardly enough, for example, to say that one is Presbyterian. Does such a person belong to the Presbyterian Church in America or the Presbyterian Church USA; or the Evangelical Presbyterian Church, the Evangelical Covenant Order of Presbyterians, the Orthodox Presbyterian Church, or the Reformed Presbyterian Church of North America? The most recent edition of Mead's *Handbook of Denominations in the United States* outlines the origins and beliefs of twenty-nine Baptist denominations, twenty-five Pentecostal movements, and eleven different types of Lutheranism, a list that editor Craig Atwood notes is not comprehensive! And a quick glance at the table of contents shows that even peace-loving Mennonites find themselves estranged from one another.[2]

The proposed solution to such divisions is more visible unity, but historically speaking, attempts at establishing visible unity have failed. In the eighteenth century George Whitefield famously asked whether there were any Presbyterians, Methodists, or Baptists in heaven. Playing the role of father Abraham, Whitefield answered himself by saying, "No, there are only Christians up here." And yet, he and his erstwhile preaching partner John Wesley were not on speaking terms owing to a disagreement in doctrine. In the nineteenth century Alexander Campbell used common sense realism to promote Christian unity, attempting to break down barriers between denominations by returning to a simple reading of the Bible. Yet, his desire to speak only where the Bible speaks

---

[1]Cited in Nancy T. Ammerman, "New Life for Denominationalism," *The Christian Century*, March 15, 2000, 302–3. The rendition quoted here is from Garrison Keillor, "I'm a Lutheran," 1999, accessed January 22, 2013, http://prairiehome.publicradio.org/programs/19991002 /lutheran.htm.
[2]Frank S. Mead, Samuel S. Hill, and Craig D. Atwood, *Handbook of Denominations in the United States*, 13th ed. (Nashville: Abingdon, 2010).

and to be silent when the Bible is silent later gave rise not to one or two but to three distinct movements. In the twentieth century, Chuck Smith's remarkable ability to connect the gospel with hippies in Southern California led to the formation of Calvary Chapel, a network of churches now ranging in the thousands. Yet even his attempt to avoid denominational division has not been realized, since Calvary Chapel churches have their own "distinctives" that set them apart from other Christian groups.

In spite of the perennial predictions of the death of denominations, the fact remains that evangelical Christians typically have core beliefs that lead them to identify with other like-minded Christians. Given the plausibility of continued division, is there a way in which evangelical Christians can maintain their distinctive doctrinal beliefs while communicating to the church and the world that they have much more in common? We believe there is, and such is the purpose of this book. *Why We Belong* addresses how denominational affiliation can be natural without being negative, and how evangelical identity can help rather than hinder Christian unity.

How This Book Came About

The idea for this book presented itself in a couple of ways. During my academic excursions through Beeson Divinity School and Trinity Evangelical Divinity School, I (a Southern Baptist) came under the tutelage of professors from various denominational backgrounds. Seeing evangelicals work together as colleagues during the week while worshiping in separate churches on the weekend provided a sense of balance between cooperation and conviction. This seemed to be missing in other places where theology was downplayed for the sake of unity or where peripheral issues had become so central that isolationism was the result.

Chris and Robert were especially interested in this topic because they were already collaborating on numerous academic projects in spite of their denominational differences. They found it both frustrating and humorous when people asked whether it is difficult for a Baptist (Chris) and a Presbyterian (Robert) to work together on such projects. Like many engaged evangelicals, they simply took for granted how much they have in common.

The three of us agreed that people who have not witnessed evangelicals working together while maintaining their denominational identities could benefit from a book that presents how both can cohere. We also took note that Roman Catholicism and Eastern Orthodoxy give the outward appearance of being unified, leading some evangelicals to convert in hopes of demonstrating visible unity in the body of Christ. Yet, if Christian unity is predicated on the gospel first, as we believe, then the pursuit of visible unity at the expense of core convictions is merely a semblance of unity.

In short, the following chapters give a personal side to the reasons why our contributors belong: why they belong to Christ, why they belong to each other in Christ, and why they belong to denominations that seek to be faithful to Christ. The decision to invite the authors to share their "stories" was intentional as it gives a different flavor to the discussion than would a mere doctrinal defense of each one's denominational preference. Differences between denominations are too often discussed in the abstract, as if Methodists are totally unaware of passages proof-texted by Baptists regarding believer's baptism! Consequently, one will readily note that the reasons our contributors belong to a particular tradition also include matters unique to their lives. We suspect our readers will have similar instances in their own backgrounds when they gradually came to see value in their traditions due to both theological and personal factors.

What This Book Is Not

This book is not an attempt to corral readers into a particular denomination, nor is it meant to show the superiority of one denomination over another. Instead, it is designed to demonstrate that godly, thoughtful, and kindhearted Christians have significant reasons for identifying with a denomination, and the Christians represented here have done so in full recognition that God's family is much larger than their own traditions. They recognize that unity in the church occurs on many levels. So it may be helpful to read each of their stories with the following questions in mind: Why has this person chosen to identify with his particular denomination? Does he see anything that I or others seem to have missed? How much does he hold in common with the other contributors? In what ways does his vision of unity operate on a denominational and transdenominational level?

We have chosen six denominations, each of which has played a key role in the development of the Christian faith. To be sure, more denominations could be included, more stories could be told, more reasons for unity could be expounded, and more interaction with thorny issues could be offered. But we could not include more without changing the nature of the book. We also recognize that no contributor can speak for his denomination as a whole. As mentioned above, there are divisions within denominations that prevent any one person from representing the entire group. Still, each contributor is an active participant in a local church that identifies with a denomination, and each contributor has a history of working across denominational lines in an evangelical context.

Summary of Chapters

Why We Belong begins with a presentation of the theological basis of church unity, using Ephesians as our guide. Chris Morgan notes in his opening chapter that God is using the church to display his glory to both the world and cosmic powers, and therefore unity among fellow believers is both a current characteristic and a perennial pursuit. In chapter 2, I offer a historical overview of the rise of the denominations covered in this book. The people who started these denominations were not as interested in founding something new as they were in recovering something old, something they felt their traditions had neglected or missed.

The next six chapters tell the individual stories of why each contributor has chosen his denominational tradition and how he views this position in light of the call for unity in the church. The denominations are presented in alphabetical order. In addition to explaining why he is an Anglican, Gerald Bray discusses in chapter 3 the difficulties associated in defining Anglicanism and the importance of liturgical and organizational structure in the Anglican Church, and he makes crucial observations regarding its relationship with the Roman Catholic and Eastern Orthodox communions. In chapter 4 Timothy George proposes a "hierarchy of ecclesial identity" in his efforts to explain what it means to be a Protestant, evangelical, and Baptist. As dean of Beeson Divinity School, he demonstrates with ease how a Baptist with theological particularities can be a thoroughgoing evangelical ecumenist. In chapter 5, Doug Sweeney, professor of church history at Trinity Evangelical Divinity School, discusses his upbringing in a Baptist home and his studies at Wheaton College as background for his journey to Lutheranism. Bringing an academic theological distinction down to the most basic level, Sweeney describes how Luther's high christology brought him comfort as he learned what Word and sacrament accomplish objectively.

Timothy Tennent, president of Asbury Theological Seminary, reminds us in chapter 6 how the theological teachings and practical emphases of John Wesley transcend time. While admitting that evangelical mainstays such as God's grace, conversion, discipleship, and a global perspective may not be emphasized in all Methodist churches today, Tennent demonstrates that there are many who continue to embrace their founder's godly vision. In chapter 7 Byron Klaus, president of Assemblies of God Theological Seminary, describes the stigma that has long been associated with being Pentecostal and how he has personally experienced such ridicule from others. Nevertheless, in spirited fashion he provides an explanation of Pentecostal belief and practice in a way that defies the typical charges of shallow emotionalism or inane experimentalism, namely, by carefully tying in contemporary Pentecostalism with traditional evangelical emphases. Chapter 8 is from Bryan Chapell, president emeritus of Covenant Theological Seminary. Chapell describes how the providence of God, itself a central doctrine in Presbyterian thought, led him to consider this tradition as a viable possibility. Using a historical and theological approach, Chapell then demonstrates how Presbyterian theology, polity, and worship provide a comprehensive sweep that informs the Christian life.

A concluding chapter, titled "Denominationalism: Historical Developments, Contemporary Challenges, and Global Opportunities," is provided by David Dockery, president of Union University. The chapter provides a recapitulation of the discussion while still pushing the conversation forward. Dockery recognizes the value of renewal movements within the church but warns that over time even they have a tendency to become purveyors of denominational bureaucracy. Moreover, he notes that a weak ecclesiology has too often led evangelicals to elevate parachurch movements over the importance of the local church. His call for a transgenerational and transcontinental approach to the Christian faith, all within the boundaries of orthodoxy, is a fitting close to this book.

Toward a Theology of the Unity of the Church

Christopher W. Morgan

After a worship service one Sunday, I stood in the foyer to greet the church family. In a span of less than thirty minutes, prayer needs abounded: a key leader's mother who is stricken with Alzheimer's has to be placed in a nursing home; some terrific children are stuck in the middle of a messy divorce; missionaries to the Middle East are sorting out how to proclaim the gospel in the midst of a tricky social transition; a solid family has allowed disagreement to create disharmony among them; a deacon, who as a police officer was shot during a seemingly routine traffic stop, still struggles with an excruciatingly painful hip; a nearby church remains embattled by leaders who seem more interested in advancing their agendas than in embodying the love of Christ; the tears and tender hug from a recent widow disclose her continued grief. Add to these the unstated concerns of the people that day—bankruptcy, loneliness, arthritis, barrenness, restlessness, regret, fear, shame, and guilt—and we may safely conclude that we are not in heaven yet!

Not only do our prayer needs remind us that all is not right in the world, but watching the evening news also points to this, as wars, disasters, disease, murder, suicide, starvation, homelessness, and political wrangling fill the hour. Even the seemingly insignificant peace T-shirts and "all we need is love" songs suggest that things are not the way they're supposed to be. Indeed, our longings for peace and love reveal that we do not have peace and love in its fullness; these longings also show that we believe that peace and love are good and right, the way things ought to be.

The Bible acknowledges the rightness of these deep-seated longings and even offers a historical narrative that frames how we understand them. The narrative begins with God's creating everything in a way that pleases him and benefits his creatures (Genesis 1–2). The goodness of God and the goodness of his creation are highlighted by the creation account's refrain, "And God saw that it was good" (see 1:4, 10, 12, 18, 21, 25, 31). By creating humanity in his image, God distinguishes us from the rest of creation and establishes a Creator-creature distinction. Genesis 1–2 depicts all this as good, as Adam and Eve are blessed with an unhindered relationship with God, intimate enjoyment of each other, and delegated authority over creation.

But rather than submitting to God and finding their pleasure in him, Adam and Eve rebel against God, wanting ultimate autonomy. Genesis 3:6 records the fall in a rapid fashion: "she saw," "she took," "she ate," and "she gave," culminating in "he ate." The couple immediately feels shame, realizing they are naked (v. 7), estranged from God (vv. 8–10), and fearful (vv. 9–10). Their alienation from each other also emerges, as the woman blames the serpent and the man blames the woman and even God (vv. 10–13)! Pain, sorrow, and relational disruption also arise (vv. 15–19). Even worse, the couple is banished from Eden and God's glorious presence (vv. 22–24).

In sum, through their disobedience, sin entered and disrupted their relationship to God, to each other, and to creation. Adam's sin, while personal and historical, is also corporate and cosmic, plunging all humanity into sin (Rom. 5:12–21) and resulting in a creation that longs for freedom (8:18–28). So disorder and disunity exist—personally, communally, and cosmically.

Thankfully, the biblical story continues and recounts how God is intent on bringing peace out of the disorder through a mission of reconciliation. His plan is astonishing—to glorify himself through a full-scale restoration of cosmic unity. As we will see, the church and its unity are central in this plan. The biblical material on this is massive, but Paul's letter to the Ephesians emphasizes the church and its unity. Therefore, we will use Ephesians as our guide as we set forth the contours of the theology of church unity.

The Unity of the Church Showcases God's Purpose of Cosmic Unity

Disorder and disunity will not last forever. God is on a mission to bring about cosmic unity. Whereas sin has resulted in disharmony, God's eternal plan for reconciliation brings peace and wholeness.

God's Purpose of Cosmic Unity

This plan addresses the personal, communal, and cosmic consequences of the fall by bringing all things together in Christ—uniting people to him, uniting people to one another, and even uniting the cosmos in Christ. And the church plays a central role in this plan.

The essence of God's plan, which is set forth in Christ, is "to unite all things in him, things in heaven and things on earth" (Eph. 1:10). Notice that "all things" are specified as "things in heaven and things on earth." This is comprehensive language for an eschatological uniting of the cosmos in Christ (cf. Rom. 8:18–30; 2 Cor. 5:14–21; Col. 1:15–20). Peter O'Brien explains: "The emphasis now is on a universe that is centered and reunited in Christ. The mystery which God has graciously made known refers to the summing up and bringing together of the fragmented and alienated elements of the universe ('all things') in Christ as the focal point."[1]

Accomplishing this eternal plan in history through his saving work, Christ is even called "our peace":

> But now in Christ Jesus you who once were far off have been brought near by the blood of Christ. For he himself is our peace, who has made us both one and has broken down in his flesh the dividing wall of hostility by abolishing the law of commandments expressed in ordinances, that he might create in himself one new man in place of the two, so making peace, and might reconcile us both to God in one body through the cross, thereby killing the hostility. (Eph. 2:13–16)

In proclaiming Christ as our peace, Paul puts forward three participles that show how Christ has acted to bring peace: *making* both Jews and

---

[1] See Peter T. O'Brien, *The Letter to the Ephesians*, Pillar New Testament Commentary (Grand Rapids: Eerdmans, 1999), 112–13. He adds: "Chrys Caragounis claims that as Paul proceeds to amplify and explain throughout the letter the meaning of bringing all things together, he concentrates on the two main representatives of these spheres, namely, the powers representing 'the things in heaven,' and the church (particularly the unity of Jews and Gentiles in the body of Christ), representing 'the things on earth.' He further suggests that the two obstacles which need to be overcome before the divine purpose of bringing everything into unity with Christ can be fulfilled are: (a) the rebellion of the powers, and (b) the alienation of Jews from Gentiles (2:11–22, as well as the estrangement of both from God, 2:16). Much of the rest of Ephesians is given over to explaining, with reference to each of these two spheres, the steps in the process that God has taken in order to achieve this supreme goal" (ibid.). The reference is to C. C. Caragounis, *The Ephesian* Mysterion: *Meaning and Content* (Lund: Gleerup, 1977), 144–46.

Gentiles one, *destroying* the barrier between them, and *abolishing* the hostility. What is this peace? O'Brien explains:

> The term "peace" in both Old and New Testaments came to denote well-being in the widest sense, including salvation, the source and giver of which is God alone. "Peace" was used for harmony among people (Acts 7:26; Gal. 5:22; Eph. 4:3; Jas. 3:18) and especially for the messianic salvation (Luke 1:79; 2:14; 19:42). The term could describe the goal and content of all Christian preaching, the message itself being called "the gospel of peace" (Eph. 6:15; cf. Acts 10:36; Eph. 2:17). The biblical concept of peace has to do with wholeness, particularly with reference to personal relationships. Peace describes an order established by the God of peace (1 Cor. 14:33; cf. Rom. 15:33; 16:20; Phil. 4:9). Christ himself is the mediator of that peace (Rom. 5:1; Col. 1:20). He gives peace to believers (2 Thess. 3:16); indeed, he himself is that peace.[2]

Christ's objective accomplishment of this peace is subjectively applied to us by the Holy Spirit through our union with Christ, which addresses the three spheres: personal, communal, and cosmic. In Christ, we as individuals are linked to Christ's death and resurrection and thus receive salvation (Eph. 1:3–14; 2:1–10). In Christ, we are together linked to Christ's death and resurrection and thus are united to each other and become God's people, the church (2:11–22; 3:1–6). And in Christ, the whole cosmos is linked to Christ's saving work and is being reconciled (1:9–10; 3:9–11).

The Church and God's Purpose

God's new creation—including the church—is related to all three spheres of God's plan for cosmic unity. First, the church is composed of believers who were alienated from God but through the saving work of Christ have been united to him by the Holy Spirit (Eph. 2:1–10). The church consists of believers who no longer live in separation from God but are united to Christ and live with full access to God. Ephesians 1:3–14 depicts the church as the new covenant people of God. We are God's chosen people; we are God's holy people; we are God's worshiping people; we are the children of God, adopted into his family; we are the redeemed people;

---

[2]O'Brien, *Letter to the Ephesians*, 193.

we are heirs with an inheritance. So, foundationally, the church is the new covenant people who are reconciled to God.

Second, the church is also the people of God reconciled to each other (Eph. 2:11–22). To be united to Christ also means we are united to one another. The reconciliation of the Jews and Gentiles is described as the creation of one new humanity (vv. 13–16). Christ our peace removes the hostility between Jews and Gentiles, and out of the formerly divided peoples he creates a new and unified humanity. Paul has already used new-creation language in verse 10. There it primarily refers to the salvation of believers, but may also include the larger sphere of the church. Here in verses 13–16 the new-creation language clearly refers to the church. As the focal point and inaugurator of the new creation, Christ, the Son of God, bears the divine image and is also "the one who by virtue of his death and resurrection is now re-creating a people into that same image."[3] Gordon Fee explains:

> For here is the one who is himself the "image" of God, who is the Father's own "firstborn," and by virtue of his resurrection the "first-born" with regard to the new creation, is now the one who "re-creates" broken and fallen humanity back into the divine image that he himself has perfectly borne. The Creator of the first creation, who himself bears the Father's image, now is seen as the Creator of the new creation, as he restores his own people back into the divine image.[4]

Because of Christ's saving work, and through our union with him, we as the church are now the image of God. We are the one new people, the new humanity, the people called to display God to the world—the new creation in the image of God, called to reflect Christ and embody God's holiness (Eph. 2:14–16; 4:13, 24). As this one new humanity, Jews and Gentiles together form God's nation, God's family, and God's temple:

> So then you are no longer strangers and aliens, but you are fellow citizens with the saints and members of the household of God, built on the foundation of the apostles and prophets, Christ Jesus himself being

---

[3] Gordon D. Fee, *Pauline Christology: An Exegetical-Theological Study* (Peabody, MA: Hendrickson, 2007), 515. See also Richard B. Gaffin Jr., "The Glory of God in Paul's Epistles," in *The Glory of God*, ed. Christopher W. Morgan and Robert A. Peterson, Theology in Community 2 (Wheaton, IL: Crossway, 2010), 127–52.

[4] Fee, *Pauline Christology*, 515.

the cornerstone, in whom the whole structure, being joined together, grows into a holy temple in the Lord. In him you also are being built together into a dwelling place for God by the Spirit. (2:19–22)

Third, the church plays a key role in the cosmic dimension. As the people reconciled to God and to each other, the church showcases God's plan of cosmic reconciliation. Paul portrays this astonishing purpose of the church:

> To me, though I am the very least of all the saints, this grace was given, to preach to the Gentiles the unsearchable riches of Christ, and to bring to light for everyone what is the plan of the mystery hidden for ages in God who created all things, so that through the church the manifold wisdom of God might now be made known to the rulers and authorities in the heavenly places. This was according to the eternal purpose that he has realized in Christ Jesus our Lord. (Eph. 3:8–11)

So the current existence of the one new people, the church, testifies that God is on a project to create unity; the reality of the unity of Jews and Gentiles together as the one new humanity is an amazing testimony of God's broader purposes. Notice that the intended audience of this showcase is here described as the rulers and authorities in the heavenly realms, likely referring to both angels and demons. The point seems to be that the beings in the heavenly realms are put on notice: God is going to do cosmically what he has already done for individuals in Christ; and God is going to do cosmically what he has done corporately with the Jews and Gentiles. All things in heaven and on earth will be brought together in Christ; all things will highlight Christ as the focal point of the cosmos. So not only is Christ the Savior of sinners and the Head of the church; he is the goal of the entire cosmos! Paul's idea here is similar to that of Colossians 1:16, where he instructs us that all things are created by Christ and for Christ.

Amazingly, it is the church as God's visible exhibition that proclaims these cosmic purposes. In a sense, the church preaches Christ not only to humanity in the verbal proclamation of the gospel, but also to the entire cosmos through the visible display of unity. Bryan Chapell captures Paul's astounding point:

This grafting of the redeemed is so amazing that it was God's intent to use it to display his wisdom to the heavenly beings. Thus Paul's words create a celestial stage to display the wonders of grace. . . . In union with other sinners made perfect, and as members of one body, we who come from every tribe and nation, people and personality, are on display as a church before the heavenly hosts as a testimony to the wisdom of God. . . . Just as Paul's sin makes the grace of God more apparent, the uniting of sinners in the body of Christ makes the grace of God more brilliant—even to the hosts of heaven. By our unity in Christ's body, the church, we are preaching to the angels about the power, wisdom, and glory of God who made us.

This is the apex of Paul's thought about the church. . . . Here we learn that the church is intended not only to transform the world but also to transfix heaven.[5]

Thus, as the church we showcase God's purposes not just to each other and to the world, but according to Ephesians 3:9–12, even to the heavenly realms! And as we showcase God's eternal purpose of cosmic unity to the world, we are demonstrating that the kingdom of God has already broken into history. Certainly, there is a "not yet" aspect of the kingdom still to come. God's eternal purpose of cosmic reconciliation is not perfectly realized yet—sin and injustice still occur. But sin will not have the last word; disorder and division will not last forever. Though the present age can still be characterized as not the way things are supposed to be, God will bring about a new creation.

And what is so striking is that the apostle Paul asserts that God's new creation is already under way—in the church! The church is the firstfruits of the ultimate new creation that is still to come; as the firstfruits, we are both the genuine reality of the new creation and the foretaste of more to come. Thus, as the church, we are the new humanity, new society, new temple—a new creation. We are a foretaste of heaven on earth, a genuine embodiment of the kingdom, a glimpse of the way things are supposed to be, and a glimpse of the way the cosmos ultimately will be; we are a showcase of God's eternal plan of cosmic unity.

---

[5]Bryan Chapell, *Ephesians*, Reformed Expository Commentary (Phillipsburg, NJ: P&R, 2009), 144–45.

The Unity of the Church Displays the Unity of God

God creates the church as the one new humanity not only to display his eternal plan of cosmic reconciliation, but also to display himself and thus glorify himself. God has eternally planned to glorify himself by displaying himself through the church. In other words, God creates the church in order to display himself, and as he displays himself, he glorifies himself.

In the creation of the cosmos, God communicates himself (Ps. 19:1–6). And in the formation of Israel, God displayed himself. Israel was called to embody God's holiness. Israel's holiness was essential not only to their proper worship of God, but also to their mission; they accurately reflected the true God to the nations only when they lived in a way that reflected him (Ex. 19:5–6; Deut. 28:9–10). As a kingdom of priests, Israel was to be committed to the ministry of God's presence throughout the earth; and as a holy nation, Israel was "to be a people set apart, differ-ent from all other people by what they are and are becoming—a display people, a showcase to the world of how being in covenant with Yahweh changes a people."[6]

In the new creation of the church, God also displays himself. The church too is rightly described as "a display people, a showcase to the world of how being in covenant with Yahweh changes a people."[7] In Ephesians, Paul often underscores that God saves and creates the church to display himself, for example:

> . . . so that in the coming ages he might show the immeasurable riches of his grace in kindness toward us in Christ Jesus. (2:7)

> For we are his workmanship, created in Christ Jesus for good works, which God prepared beforehand, that we should walk in them. (2:10)

> . . . so that through the church the manifold wisdom of God might now be made known to the rulers and authorities in the heavenly places. (3:10)

---

[6]John I. Durham, *Exodus*, Word Biblical Commentary (Waco, TX: Word, 1987), 263. I first noticed this quote in Graham A. Cole, *God the Peacemaker: How Atonement Brings Shalom*, New Studies in Biblical Theology, ed. D. A. Carson (Downers Grove, IL: InterVarsity, 2009), 94.
[7]Durham, *Exodus*, 263.

Ephesians demonstrates how the church showcases God in several ways. Even in the basic structure of the exhortations in Ephesians, Paul calls attention to how God's people are to "walk" or "live." Before knowing Christ, we walked according to the world, the flesh, and Satan (Eph. 2:1–3). But God graciously steps in and rescues us through the saving work of Christ. Through uniting us to Christ, God makes us alive (vv. 4–7). In turn, our entire "walk" has been transformed (v. 10). We used to bear resemblance to the way of the world, but now we walk in good works, in a way that bears family resemblance with our good God. We have been re-created by God to display his goodness to the world and are now exhorted to walk in ways that reflect God and his purposes. We are to walk in unity (4:1–3), in holiness (vv. 17–24), in love (5:2), in the light (v. 8), and in wisdom (v. 15). In so doing, we serve as God's "display people": our salvation glorifies God by displaying his grace (1:6, 12, 14; 2:7); our existence as the church glorifies God by displaying his wisdom (3:10); our love glorifies God by displaying his love (3:14–19; 4:11–16; 5:2, 22–33); our holiness glorifies God by displaying his holiness (1:4; 4:24; 5:25–27).

In the same way, our unity as a church glorifies God by displaying his oneness. In Ephesians 4:1–6, Paul powerfully shows this link:

> I therefore, a prisoner for the Lord, urge you to walk in a manner worthy of the calling to which you have been called, with all humility and gentleness, with patience, bearing with one another in love, eager to maintain the unity of the Spirit in the bond of peace. There is one body and one Spirit—just as you were called to the one hope that belongs to your call—one Lord, one faith, one baptism, one God and Father of all, who is over all and through all and in all.

That God is one and not many means that he is the only God and is alone worthy to receive worship (Deut. 6:4–5). Being the only God also means that he deserves to be worshiped universally. The sheer diversity of human beings would make it appear unlikely that unity would characterize God's people. But in God's eternal plan, he actually displays his oneness through the unity of his church, which is united to Christ and to each other (see also John 17:20–23). Our church unity is grounded in and declares the fact that there is one God, who is over all, through all, and in all. The truth that the church is one body is grounded in and declares the fact that there is one Lord, one Spirit, one faith, one hope, one baptism. The church's oneness also points to its inherent universality, which also results from and displays God's universality.

The Unity of the Church Is Both a Current Characteristic and a Perennial Pursuit

We have seen that the unity of the church not only showcases God's cosmic purpose of unity, but also displays the unity of God. In addition, the unity of the church is both a current characteristic and a perennial pursuit.

Church Unity as a Current Characteristic

As we saw in Ephesians 2:11–22, the unity of the church is a reality. God has created one new people. The one church is one with Christ and with one another.

It is important to remember that while recounting our union with Christ and our manifold resultant privileges, Paul also maintains that Christ possesses a unique identity, retains ultimate and universal authority, and is the sole Head of the church (Eph. 1:20–23). As Michael Horton reminds us, "The church is always on the receiving end in its relationship to Christ; it is never the redeemer, but always the redeemed; never the head, but always the body."[8] So, as much as we are united to Christ, we are distinguished from Christ.

Yet there is a real unity between Christ and his church, as well as the corollary: the unity of the church itself. John Stott points this out as he comments on Ephesians 4:3–6:

> We must assert that there can only be one Christian family, only one Christian faith, hope and baptism, and only one Christian body, because there is only one God, Father, Son and Holy Spirit. You can no more multiply churches than you can multiply Gods. Is there only one God? Then he has only one church. Is the unity of God inviolable? Then so is the unity of the church.[9]

Thus, unity marks the church as a whole, or what is often called the universal church. Unity also marks the local church. As we previously

---

[8] Michael S. Horton, *People and Place: A Covenant Ecclesiology* (Louisville, KY: Westminster John Knox, 2008), 31.

[9] John R. W. Stott, *The Message of Ephesians: God's New Society*, 2nd ed., The Bible Speaks Today (Downers Grove, IL: InterVarsity, 1992), 151.

noted, the reconciliation of Jews and Gentiles into one new people is across a vast scale. It is sweeping, salvation-historical, and global, and it requires belief in some sort of universal church. Yet the very fact that the reconciliation of Jews and Gentiles into this one new people serves as a showcase of God's eternal purposes of cosmic unity also requires the church's visibility, and thus the local church.

Church Unity as a Perennial Pursuit

What is so peculiar, though, is that while the church is already one, it is exhorted to maintain unity (Eph. 4:1–3). Thus, the unity of the church is both a current reality and a perennial pursuit.

This means that the unity of the church bears witness to "the already and not yet" of the kingdom. Because of its location in salvation history as a part of, an agent of, the community of, and a display of Jesus's messianic kingdom, the church is necessarily characterized by the nature of the kingdom, including its already-and-not-yet tension. Other attributes of the church also reflect this tension, as Donald Bloesch observes:

> The church is already one, but it must become more visibly one . . . in faith and practice. The church is already holy in its source and foundation, but it must strive to produce fruits of holiness in its sojourn in the world. . . . The church is already apostolic, but it must become more consciously apostolic by allowing the gospel to reform and sometimes even overturn its time-honored rites and interpretations.[10]

Even more, the exhortation to maintain this unity is grounded in the reality of its existent unity. Using what some refer to as "the indicative and the imperative," Paul teaches that what the church is drives how the church should behave. Thus, he urges the church toward specific behaviors and grounds those exhortations on the theological realities of the church's identity.

Ephesians regularly points to these already-and-not-yet and indicative-imperative aspects of the church. The church is currently the fullness of Christ (1:23), but Paul prays that it will be filled with the fullness of Christ (3:19), and the church is to attain to the measure of the stature

---

[10]Donald Bloesch, *The Church* (Downers Grove, IL: InterVarsity, 2002), 103.

of the fullness of Christ (4:13).[11] The church is currently the one new humanity (2:14–18), but it is to attain unto a mature humanity (4:13) and put on the new humanity (4:20–24). The church is under its Head, Christ (1:22–23), but is to grow up into Christ, who is the Head (4:15). The church is now holy (2:19–22), but it is also to walk in holiness, put on the new humanity and holiness, become more and more holy, and one day be ultimately presented to Christ as holy (4:20–24; 5:2–21, 27). The church is already grounded in truth and built on Christ as the cornerstone, with the apostles and prophets as the foundation (2:19–22), yet the church is to teach truth, speak truth in love, walk in truth, and stand firm as an army with truth (4:5, 11, 14–15, 21; 6:10–18). The church is glorious now, as the fullness of Christ (1:22–23), but one day it will be presented to Christ as fully glorious (5:25–28).

In the same way, the church already is one, united in Christ (2:12–22; 4:4–6), yet the church is also to be eager to maintain the unity of the Spirit, as Ephesians 4:1–3 states: "I therefore, a prisoner for the Lord, urge you to walk in a manner worthy of the calling to which you have been called, with all humility and gentleness, with patience, bearing with one another in love, eager to maintain the unity of the Spirit in the bond of peace." Note that Paul calls the church not to create unity but to maintain the unity of the Spirit, thus living out visibly the reality of its inherent unity.

The Unity of the Church Fosters and Is Itself Fostered by Love and Humility

To recap, God has eternally purposed to restore his fallen creation. He will bring about cosmic unity through Christ, and he has already taken steps toward this end by Christ's reconciling work. Christ has broken down the wall of hostility and has become our peace, bringing us into a right relationship with God and also bringing all believers—Jews and Gentiles—into unity with each other. We are now one body, one temple, one family. God has purposed that the church give a foretaste of this ultimate cosmic unity. The church is to display unity, and as it does so it showcases God and his plan for cosmic unity to the world.

---

[11]For how the "already and not yet" relates to the church as temple, see the insightful work by G. K. Beale, *The Temple and the Church's Mission: A Biblical Theology of the Dwelling Place of God*, New Studies in Biblical Theology, ed. D. A. Carson (Downers Grove, IL: InterVarsity, 2004), 392–93.

But on this side of heaven, unity is hard to come by. It is much easier to bring disunity than unity. So Paul urges the church to prioritize unity—to live in unity, to prize it, to be eager to maintain it, and to avoid doing, thinking, and saying things that undercut it. He does this strategically and often.

So how does the church visibly display this unity? John Stott comments perceptively, "Too many start with structures (and structures of some kind are indispensible), but the apostle starts with moral qualities."[12] Indeed, a large portion of Paul's moral exhortations in Ephesians relates to living in unity. Two passages in Ephesians prominently underline this. Both are in chapter 4, which begins and ends with an emphasis on promoting church unity.

In Ephesians 4:1–3, Paul exhorts the church to live out its unity through humility, gentleness, and patience, its members bearing with one another in love and being eager to maintain the unity of the Spirit in the bond of peace. Therefore, in keeping with the church's already-and-not-yet aspect, unity both fosters love and humility among God's people and is itself fostered by their love and humility.

It is important to note that in 4:1–6, unity does not emerge through theological vagueness, theological minimalism, or a lack of doctrinal conviction. Rather, church unity is built upon the theological foundations of the one God, one Lord, one Spirit, one faith, and so forth. And Paul's emphases on love, humility, and patience do not point to an epistemic uncertainty about core components of the Christian faith. Instead, Paul clarifies that such unity simultaneously requires both doctrinal truth and love. As the people of God love one another, they value each other and subdue their own egos. They refuse to treat others with roughness but are gentle and considerate, willing to give up their agendas for the sake of others. They put up with each others' faults, realizing they too need the patience of others. Because they prize the church, they uphold the truth and make every effort to promote its health and unity.

In Ephesians 4:17–32, Paul continues this emphasis. The church is to put off the old ways, be renewed, and put on the new ways (vv. 20–24). How does Paul characterize this new way, the way of the new humanity, the church? He stresses that being united to one another means that we must speak truth to each other (not using spin and manipulation), refuse

---

[12]Stott, *Message of Ephesians*, 148.

to nurse anger, give generously to others, refrain from using words to hurt, build others up, and avoid grieving the Spirit via disunity (vv. 25–30). Indeed, he urges church unity as he commands the Ephesians to put away bitterness, wrath, anger, clamor, slander, and malice, and instead to be kind to one another, tenderhearted, and forgiving. For Paul, the unity of the church is a theological reality and a perennial pursuit. Therefore, he consistently strives to promote love, humility, patience, self-control, and forgiveness. Indeed, he summarizes this section by exhorting the church to live in love (5:1–2; see also 1 Corinthians 12–14; Gal. 5:18–25; Phil. 2:1–4).

The Unity of the Church Is Both an Important Doctrine and an Important Praxis

Because of all this, it is crucial that we see the unity of the church as both an important doctrine and a day-to-day practical challenge (Eph. 4:1–6).

Church Unity as a Doctrine

That the unity of the church is itself a doctrine is frequently forgotten.[13] This is significant because too often the unity of the church is thereby viewed as a nice additive to the church, something to be preferred but not necessarily something formative. Ephesians makes it clear that the opposite is the case. As we have seen, the unity of the church is itself a doctrine and is linked to God's ultimate end of glorifying himself, to God's eternal purpose of cosmic reconciliation, to union with Christ, and to the doctrine of the church. And as Ephesians makes plain, the unity of the church is highlighted by the images of being one body, one temple, one nation, one people, one new humanity, one bride, and so on.

But clarification is in order: though the unity of the church is a formative part of the doctrine of the church, it does not exhaust biblical ecclesiology. After all, unity is not the only attribute of the

---

[13]Unfortunately, even some significant confessions of faith neglect the doctrine of the unity of the church. For example, "The Baptist Faith and Message 2000" (along with its 1925 and 1963 predecessors) does not speak to the doctrine of the unity of the church under "The Church" but only addresses "Christian unity" as a practical matter under "Cooperation." Interestingly, "The London Baptist Confession of Faith" (1677 and 1689) and "The Philadelphia Baptist Confession of Faith" (1742) each include in their ecclesiology sections a reference to the church's being one.

church.[14] Indeed, as the Nicene Creed states, "We believe in one holy, catholic and apostolic Church." Or, in the language of Ephesians, the church is one, holy, and grounded in the teachings of the apostles. As such, Ephesians stresses that the church is marked by oneness, universality, holiness, truth, and love, and it must therefore walk in unity, holiness, truth, and love.

Even more foundational, church unity is a meaningful concept only in terms of genuine Christianity. The Christian church is created in and through the gospel; it is not and cannot be united with those who deny the gospel, the deity of Christ, or any other core truths of the faith (cf. Gal. 1:6–10). Any approach to ecumenism that seeks church unity by minimizing the gospel may promote some sort of amorphous religious unity—but not authentic *church* unity. Such sentiments are too generic and stand contrary to biblical theology, historic Christianity, and even the very doctrine of the unity of the church. True church unity exists among, and can only be found among, true Christians. It presupposes a biblical understanding of the church itself—as the new covenant people of Jesus (Eph. 2:11–22).

The Doctrine of Church Unity Shapes Church Praxis

The doctrine of church unity shapes the church's praxis. This is clear from what we have seen in Ephesians 4:1–6, 17–32. Similarly, Romans is laden with how the unity of the church relates to our theology and praxis. Romans 14:1–15:13 is particularly instructive as it shows how the doctrine of church unity functions in relationship to other doctrines and practices. In this passage, Paul entwines a matrix of concerns that shape ethical decision making, including the unity of the church, the good of others, conscience, culture and tradition, love for others, what is appropriate for the kingdom, God's global mission, truth, the example of Jesus, the uniqueness of God and his judgment, Christian liberty, the eschatological inclusion of Gentiles and Jews into one body, and the glory of God. In an incredible way, Paul weaves in and out of some major cultural issues and points the church at Rome in a healthy direction based on such ethical guidelines. Paul addresses the unity of the church as both an important doctrine and an important practice, and he promotes the unity of the church through his explanation of truth. The doctrine and practice of

---

[14]And the attributes of the church are a part of a larger set of topics in ecclesiology, which also includes the nature, images, place in salvation history, marks, structure, ordinances, and purposes of the church.

the unity of the church are directly tied to theology and are particularly related to salvation history, the reality of the new covenant, the example of Jesus, the uniqueness of God and his right to judge, the nature of Christian liberty, the nature of the kingdom and what is consistent with it, the nature and mission of the church, the greater significance of the covenant community than the individual, and more.

It is precisely *because* of the unity of the church and these truths that the church lives with certain differences of opinion on culture and tradition. Indeed, in this particular case, Paul deems such biblical teachings as freedom from food laws and the freedom of the conscience as less important than the unity of the church. Thus, the doctrine of church unity is of greater importance than many (other) doctrines, cultural norms, and personal preferences.[15]

Note also that church unity can exist even *in the midst of* certain differences of opinion. It is striking that Paul never urges the church at Rome to agree on the particulars of food laws and custom, but urges them to worship God with one voice despite such differences: "May the God of endurance and encouragement grant you to live in such harmony with one another, in accord with Christ Jesus, that together you may with one voice glorify the God and Father of our Lord Jesus Christ. Therefore welcome one another as Christ has welcomed you, for the glory of God" (Rom. 15:5–7). Amazingly, church unity can and does exist amid some theological and cultural differences, so long as the church practices deference, patience, mutual acceptance, love, and shared mission.[16]

Church Unity as Praxis

So Ephesians underlines the theological realities of God's oneness, of cosmic unity, and of church unity, in part, to stress the importance of living out the realities of such unity. The day-to-day practice of such unity is shown in Christian relationships to the church as a whole and to individual believers.

---

[15]When faced with a divisive issue, we would be wise to ask, is the topic of our disagreement more or less important than the doctrine of the unity of the church? If it is not more important, then why would we divide over it?

[16]Though, as my previous discussion stressed, there cannot be differences on core issues like the gospel, the deity of Christ, etc.

As we noted, Paul's words in Ephesians 4:1–6, 17–32 connect living out this church unity to the following:

- valuing others
- being gentle, not rough, with others
- being patient with others
- putting up with quirks in others
- eagerly promoting the peace and unity of the community more than oneself or one's own way
- genuinely telling the truth rather than manipulating through deception
- refusing to nurse anger
- working hard, not to accumulate wealth but to share with others who need it
- refusing to speak negatively about the church or others but using words to strengthen one another and to build up the church
- putting away bitterness, anger, slander
- showing kindness to others
- being tenderhearted
- forgiving one another

Paul then summarizes these: walk in love (5:1–2).

Note also that Paul assumes here that unity is hard to maintain and that Christians will face challenges in getting along with others. Paul assumes that Christians will be hurt, be offended, and need to work hard to relate appropriately to others—yes, even in (and especially in) the church.

Paul later shows how the holiness (5:3–18) and worship of the church (vv. 18–21) are also to display God and church unity. As the church lives out its holy calling, it displays the kingdom of light as one temple, blessed with and characterized by God's holy presence. As the church worships, the people of God demonstrate their oneness with God and one another, genuinely addressing one another in psalms, singing to the Lord, giving thanks to God in the name of Christ, and submitting to one another out of reverence for Christ (vv. 18–21).[17] These "one another" responsibilities flow from and lead to church unity.

---

[17]The unity of the church is similarly portrayed through baptism (Eph. 4:4–6), communion (1 Corinthians 10–11), and the sharing of resources (Acts 2:42–47; 4:34–37).

Such unity is also expressed in Christian families or households. For example, the husband and wife relate to one another in a way that reflects Christ and his bride, the church. Love, self-sacrifice, submission, respect, and holiness characterize marriage, which, in and of itself, testifies to the unity of Christ and the church (vv. 21–33).

The parent-child relationship is also to reflect such unity. As the children obey their parents, and as the parents raise their children with patient love and careful instruction, God's families display God's purposes (6:1–4).

Church unity is also to be expressed in extended household relationships, even those of a master and bondservant. As the bondservant works hard, respects authority, and serves sincerely as unto Christ the preeminent Lord, he honors Christ with his vocation. The master, too, is to live out such unity as he treats the bondservant with respect, refuses to bully, and recognizes that he will also stand before his Master, the Lord Jesus—who is not impressed with his position and will judge without any partiality (6:5–9).

Conclusion

So, in Ephesians, Paul addresses church unity from the macro to the micro level. He teaches us that church unity showcases God's purpose of cosmic unity, displays the unity of God, is both a current characteristic and a perennial pursuit, fosters and is fostered by love and humility, and is an important doctrine and important praxis, especially affecting church relationships, from the use of words to community worship, and household relationships, from the approach to marriage and parenting to even a view of work.

But questions naturally arise: If this is the biblical teaching on the unity of the church, then how do we minimize the disunity sometimes exacerbated by denominations? How do we avoid the pride, narrowness, self-promotion, and myopia that too often characterize denominations? Can denominations play a role in advancing the unity of the church? Can Christians committed to the unity of the church promote such unity from within denominations? *How do we prize and promote the unity of the church in our world of denominations?* The following chapters address these and other questions.

One Lord, One Faith,
but Many Expressions

DENOMINATIONS AND THEIR STORIES

Anthony L. Chute

I am a Christian and a Baptist. I became a Christian by faith, following Christ to his cross. I became a Baptist by sight, following a Baptist girl to a Baptist church. I have no regrets with either, though I have found better reasons for the latter. Not the girl, mind you, as we have been married for twenty-two years at the time of this writing. As for being a Baptist, however, I became convinced over time that this expression of the Christian faith is better than the alternatives. An inauspicious start to be sure, but my brief testimony points to the basic truth that one's choice of denominational affiliation is something of a mix between theological and personal factors. So even though I am a Baptist by conviction, I have sometimes wondered whether other alternatives would have appealed to me more if the one I love had gone to a Methodist or a Presbyterian church. In short, one's story matters.

For some the mere existence of denominational alternatives seems to complicate rather than complement the Christian faith. Why not just call ourselves Christians? Ultimately we shall, but for now such labels help to explain what kind of Christians we are, since the word itself means different things to different people. Roman Catholics, Protestants, and Mormons have little in common with each other when it comes to biblical authority and the way of salvation, matters that are central to what it means to be a Christian. Even nondenominational churches have core beliefs that set them apart from other Christian traditions, as every congregation must adopt a form of church government, a standard for church membership, and a position on the ordinances (sacraments), the very issues that give rise to denominations in the first place. Denominational labels may be unwanted, but they are not necessarily unwarranted.

The purpose of this chapter is to tell the story of the founders of the six traditions covered in this book, with the aim of helping readers appreciate that denominations are not inherently divisive. The factors that led to each person's breaking away from a tradition he embraced, a separation done in hopes of capturing fundamental truths he believed were too significant to omit, must be considered. Without exception the reasons were much better than mine when I first walked into a Baptist church, and without a doubt the various founders had much more to lose when they made up their minds to leave one denomination for another. Before I share their stories, it will be helpful to place the discussion of Christian unity in its larger historical context, and once their stories have been told, I will make some concluding observations concerning how denominations foster rather than forsake unity.

Church Life before Denominations

The story of denominational beginnings emerges outside the Bible, but that is not to say that denominations are unbiblical. It is to say, on the one hand, that John was not a Baptist in the modern sense of the word, and that Paul's mention of the churches of God in Christ was in reference to Judea and Thessalonica, not Tennessee or Indiana (1 Thess. 2:14). Indeed, anyone who said, "I follow Paul," or, "I follow Apollos," was rightly rebuked for focusing on servants of God rather than the Son of God (1 Cor. 1:12–13). On the other hand, it is clear that Christians in the New Testament had differences of opinion on a number of matters, which led to divisions in the church. Paul and Barnabas had a nasty falling out when they could not agree on whether Mark was missionary material (Acts 15:36–41), and the Christians at Corinth were unable to appreciate how the food they ate affected the faith of their friends (1 Corinthians 8).[1] More disturbing is the fact that some believed they were Christians without believing in the resurrection, and others

---

[1]Most denominations do not begin over such questions as whom to take on a mission trip or what food to buy from the market, but such issues can still lead to strong feelings on both sides. For example, can women take the lead in planting a church? And can Christians drink wine with their

claimed they knew God without confessing their sin (1 Cor. 15:12–19; 1 John 1:5–10).

Christians ever since have struggled with these and other issues, with the result that divisions sometimes occur. Prior to the advent of denominations, there was no such thing as a friendly departure. Virtually all separations from the church were categorized as schismatic, hardly a term of affection for people following their consciences. Of particular importance in maintaining Christian unity has been the need to safeguard the faith passed on by Jesus and his apostles. For this reason Christians in the early church made a distinction between orthodox and heretical teachings, treating the latter as unacceptable aberrations, whereupon the promoter of false teaching was dismissed from the congregation of the faithful.

Heresy was often defined as novelty, reflecting the early Christians' concern to remain connected to a larger tradition than one local church or geographic location could claim. For example, one of the earliest heretical movements in the church was Gnosticism, which claimed that secret teachings had been passed on by Jesus through the apostle John to a select few within the Christian movement. Not only did Gnostics fail the test of orthodoxy regarding their understanding of God (whom they believed was not the Creator of this world), but they also threatened the unity of the church by pitting one disciple against the original group, and a subset of Christians against the larger family of God.

The idea that we can simply call ourselves Christians with equal clarity works well in a world where heretics do not exist, but from the early church onward such a luxury has not been available. The question then arises, who is the arbiter of orthodoxy? This is a complex question because orthodox and heretical groups all claim to have the angle on truth. Jehovah's Witnesses do not introduce themselves as the local cult when knocking on the door! Indeed, they believe they are labeled as such because they are misunderstood by "heretical" Christians. Historically speaking, however, the arbiters of orthodoxy were those most closely connected to the apostles. Though Gnosticism was theologically suspicious from the start, it met a fateful end when Irenaeus of Lyons

---

meat? Christians generally have an opinion either way and will normally find a church home among Christians of like minds.

argued against it as one who was instructed by Polycarp, who was himself discipled by the apostle John.[2]

As effective as that notion was in exposing the inherent novelty in questionable movements, it proved to be damaging in the long run as the idea of apostolic authority gave way to apostolic succession. Those who once protected the church from false teachings introduced new teachings of their own under the auspices of acting on behalf of the long-deceased apostles. Questions that the Bible did not address or alluded to only vaguely were given official pronouncement by bishops presiding over councils that often comprised a minority of the church's leaders. Even a small matter could become an issue of great importance if one bishop attempted to unify the church in accordance with his own practice. For example, Christians in the second century found themselves celebrating Easter on different days. Christians living in the eastern portion of the Roman Empire followed the practice of dating Easter on the same day as the Jewish Passover, regardless of the day of the week on which it fell. Christians living in the western portion of the Roman Empire adopted the practice of observing Easter on the Sunday following the Jewish Passover. Attempts by a Roman bishop to enforce a single date for all the churches were viewed as bullying by Christians in the East, not because they devalued Christian unity but because they were the ones who had to compromise if unity was to be realized. This seemingly minor point should not be overlooked—unity always requires compromise, which is no small feat when two opposing sides both believe they are correct.

Questions continued to reverberate throughout the medieval church as Christians attempted to come to terms on what kind of bread to eat for the Eucharist (leavened in the East, unleavened in the West), whether or not a priest should be allowed to marry (affirmed in the East, prohibited in the West), and whether a beard was optional for a bishop (not optional in the East, optional in the West).[3] The fact that agreements were reached

---

[2]For a discussion of heresy in the early church, see Alistair McGrath, *Heresy: A History of Defending the Truth* (New York: HarperOne, 2010). For a critique of the view that categories of heresy and orthodoxy fail to appreciate the inherent diversity in the early church, see Andreas Köstenberger and Michael Kruger, eds., *The Heresy of Orthodoxy: How Contemporary Culture's Fascination with Diversity Has Reshaped Our Understanding of Early Christianity* (Wheaton, IL: Crossway, 2010).
[3]It is easy to surmise at this point that these are not issues dealing with the core of the Christian faith, so allowances should have been made for different approaches. However, such matters seem small only to Western readers who prize their freedom and value their identity as individuals. And,

along, but not across, geographical lines reveals that unity was elusive for reasons beyond mere theology. Christians living in the East submitted more readily to the teachings of their bishops (or patriarchs) but were hesitant to change their ways for the sake of a single bishop in the West. For his part, the Western bishop (the pope) believed that he was the sole successor of Saint Peter, the one who received the keys to the kingdom of heaven from Christ himself. Supporters of the papacy viewed its role not as a power play over pretentious issues but as a matter of faithfully shepherding the entire flock of God.

Not surprisingly, the most prominent division prior to the advent of denominations occurred when Christians separated into the Eastern Orthodox and Roman Catholic churches. Their story is instructive for understanding the reason for and the value of denominations as it demonstrates how social factors can shape theology and expose differences between churches. It also underscores the hindrances that can occur when one tradition claims to be in sole possession of the history and direction of the church.[4]

The common faith between Eastern and Western Christians was overshadowed by their speaking different languages (mainly Greek in the East, mostly Latin in the West), which resulted in their reading different Bibles (Greek in the East, Vulgate in the West). The Roman Catholic Church claimed superiority for the Vulgate and developed its theology accordingly. As we will observe shortly, the Protestant Reformation took place in part because of Roman Catholic doctrines that were based on poorly translated portions of the Vulgate. There was no corresponding reformation in the Eastern Orthodox tradition inasmuch as the East had no need of a translated New Testament and was therefore less liable to be misguided by textual inaccuracies.[5]

However, Christians in the East had a different set of problems as decisions for their churches were made collectively by patriarchs in con-

---

since the quest for Christian unity is by definition a collective effort, the very decision to bypass smaller matters is, ironically, a form of imposing one's beliefs on how others should understand the Christian life.

[4]Not surprisingly, such divisions result in competing historiographies. For a sympathetic but fair presentation of the history of the Eastern Orthodox Church, see Timothy Ware, *The Orthodox Church*, 2nd ed. (New York: Penguin, 1993); from the Roman Catholic perspective see Thomas Bokenkotter, *A Concise History of the Catholic Church* (New York: Doubleday, 2004).

[5]Diarmaid MacCulloch, *The Reformation: A History* (New York: Viking, 2003), 80.

junction with the emperor. An aberrant translation of the Bible is most unfortunate, but a powerful emperor whose concerns are more political than theological can also have negative ramifications on the direction of the church. When Emperor Leo III prohibited the use of icons in 730, he was not primarily concerned that God might be angry over a violation of the second commandment; rather he issued the decree out of fear that Muslims were recruiting jihadists based on their belief that only infidels worship images. Christians in the East and West believed that Leo's concern over border security trumped the use of icons as an essential aspect of worship. Christians in the West, who were living far enough away to dismiss the emperor's concerns, used the term "caesaropapism" to describe his influence. It was their way of saying that Christians in the East had a pope of their own in the person of the emperor who, by the way, was not a successor to any of the apostles.

Questions over doctrine and decision making created suspicions between the two traditions such that the smallest of matters threatened to become a breaking point. In fact, it may be said that the insertion of one word in the Nicene Creed signaled the end of their relationship for the next one thousand years. This was an ironic turn of events since the Nicene Creed marked a triumph for orthodoxy as both Eastern and Western Christians regularly confessed their faith in the triune God and celebrated their unity as "one holy catholic and apostolic Church." It is not clear when or how the word was introduced, but by the ninth century Western Christians began using the Latin word *filioque* to describe the procession of the Holy Spirit. Originally the creed affirmed that the Holy Spirit was sent by the Father, but the addition of *filioque* indicated that the Holy Spirit also proceeded "from the Son." Western Christians felt they were on solid biblical ground since Jesus told his disciples, "if I go, I will send him to you" (John 16:7), but their diplomatic grounds were considerably more shaky. According to Eastern Christians, the Nicene Creed was not the West's to change, even if the pope had given his permission to do so.

Once more, issues of doctrine and decision making posed a threat to Christian unity. Eastern Christians were concerned that adding *filioque* to the creed diminished the person of the Holy Spirit, whereas Western Christians were concerned that removing the word from the creed diminished the role of the pope. This lingering disagreement permeated all future discussions to the point where mutual excommunications were issued in 1054. This "Great Schism" gave rise to the Eastern Orthodox and Roman Catholic churches, neither of which viewed the other as a genuine expression of the Christian faith. Each tradition claimed to be the one true church while deeming the other a false church, a stigma that was not officially removed until both sides recanted their anathemas in 1965.

At this point it should be evident that Christian unity, while good and admirable, is quite difficult to achieve. In each case mentioned above, efforts to make amends were made by calling either heretics to repent or brothers in the faith to reconsider. However, differences in doctrine and decision making, combined with obstacles of language and culture, often proved too formidable. With these realities in mind, we can observe that denominations give but an appearance of disunity. Indeed, one of the advantages the concept of denominations has brought to the Christian church is that divisions between Protestant Christians seldom reach the level of orthodoxy versus heresy. Therefore, condemnations and excommunications of entire church bodies are quite rare in a denominational age. Belonging to a different denomination does not mean that one belongs to another faith. It provides an environment for Christians to worship with like-minded believers.

Lutheran Beginnings

Of all the denominations discussed in this book, the Lutheran tradition is the only one named for its founder, a somewhat fitting tribute as Martin Luther was a larger-than-life personality.[6] It is also an ironic twist of history because Luther derided the idea of a movement bearing his name:

> The first thing I ask is that people should not make use of my name, and should not call themselves Lutherans but Christians. What is Luther? The teaching is not mine. Nor was I crucified for anyone. . . . How did

---

[6]For a detailed examination of the life and writings of Martin Luther, see Martin Brecht's three-volume biography: *Martin Luther: His Road to Reformation, 1483–1521* (Minneapolis: Fortress, 1985); *Martin Luther: Shaping and Defining the Reformation, 1521–1532* (Minneapolis: Fortress, 1994); and *Martin Luther: The Preservation of the Church, 1532–1546* (Minneapolis: Fortress, 1999). Each volume was translated from the original German by James Schaff. An excellent summary of the life and writings of Martin Luther is Stephen Nichols, *Martin Luther: A Guided Tour of His Life and Thought* (Phillipsburg, NJ: P&R, 2002).

I, poor stinking bag of maggots that I am, come to the point where people call the children of Christ by my evil name?[7]

The story of his transformation from Catholic monk to Protestant Reformer began while he was a university student traveling home for vacation, and later took definitive shape when he was a professor preparing for his lectures. Like all German citizens of the time, Luther was raised as a Roman Catholic, but unlike the majority, he became more than just a nominal member when the fear of God struck his heart after a bolt of lightning nearly struck him dead. Prior to this incident he had been preparing for a career in law at the request of his father. But much to his father's chagrin Luther changed his vocation after appealing to a higher authority, the mother of Mary. During the storm he promised Saint Anne that if she spared his life, he would become a monk.[8]

Whereas most people reconsider such promises after the storm passes, Luther kept his word by entering an Augustinian monastery just two weeks later. Moreover, he took his vows so seriously that he surpassed even his fellow monks in their pursuit of holy living. "If any monk ever got to heaven by monkery, then I should have made it. All my monastery companions who knew me can testify to that."[9] Luther prayed more, fasted longer, slept less, and confessed every known sin, yet he was still dissatisfied with his performance. It was not that he wanted to show anyone up; rather, he wanted to show God he was serious about becoming holy. In essence, Luther's outstanding dedication was due to one underlying conviction—he feared that God hated him.

Historians have made much of Luther's *Anfechtungen*, or spiritual anxieties, but the reality is that medieval persons had reason to fear God. Emphasis on God's judgment overshadowed his mercy to such an extent that only the most pious could hope to be saved. Hence, Luther sought

---

[7]Martin Luther, *Luther's Works*, vol. 8, *Lectures on Genesis Chapters 45–50*, ed. Jaroslav Pelikan (Minneapolis: Concordia, 1965), 685; cited in Timothy George, *Theology of the Reformers* (Nashville: Broadman, 1988), 53.

[8]Luther's father, Hans, pressured him to leave the monastic life by asking if he could really obey the command to honor father and mother as a monk. The implication was that he could not, since he would not be able to provide for his parents in their old age or have children of his own to pass on the family heritage. In Roman Catholic theology, however, saints were people of exceptional merit whose intercession was often credited with answered prayer, and Luther sensed a higher obligation to keep his promise to Saint Anne.

[9]Cited in Nichols, *Martin Luther*, xx.

refuge in the monastic life as a possible deflection of God's wrath. But instead of finding security, he discovered insincerity, as corruptive elements were at work inside the Roman Catholic Church. Luther witnessed the darker side of organized religion when he traveled to Rome itself and saw the church bureaucracy in action. The viewing of relics and the sale of indulgences suggested that Roman Catholicism was more a racket than a religion. And the fact that many priests slept with prostitutes suggested that they were more like businessmen on vacation than men of God in vocation.

Luther's confessor, Johann von Staupitz, may have changed world history when he changed Luther's career. He sent him to study theology at the University of Wittenberg, a school that was still in its infancy but would soon become the prized possession of Germany, with Luther as its star professor. It was here that Luther discovered what he later called "the article upon which the church stands or falls"—the doctrine of justification by faith alone. As mentioned above, this discovery was partly professorial, but it was also intensely personal. His preparation for lectures on the Psalms helped him understand how Jesus's cry of dereliction on the cross opened the door of heaven for derelicts like himself. Luther had long felt forsaken by God because of his sins, but pondered why Jesus quoted from Psalm 22 on the cross. Since Jesus was without sin, his sense of abandonment came as he bore the sins of others. But Jesus did more than identify with sinners, on the cross—he died on their behalf, as their substitute. Luther's study of Romans further helped him understand how the righteousness that God requires is also a gift that God bestows, as those who live by faith in Christ are declared just. This was an astounding discovery since it cleared the way for Luther to serve God out of love rather than fear, and on the basis of grace rather than merit: "Here I felt that I was altogether born again and had entered paradise itself through open gates."[10]

As is the case with most university professors, Luther's grand discovery was little noticed by anyone but a few students. He was not a revolutionary of any kind at this point. In fact, neither the moral failures he witnessed nor the theological problems he discovered led immediately to his departure from the Roman Catholic Church. There were reform elements in the church that, given enough time, could work their way into

---

[10]Cited in ibid., 38.

the leadership. By all accounts, Luther's patience was not wearing thin. The turning point came, however, through events seemingly unrelated to Luther's studies. A building project for Saint Peter's Basilica in Rome was under way, and the person in charge of fund-raising, Johann Tetzel, went too far in claiming that those who gave contributions could get themselves and their loved ones out of purgatory.[11]

Luther still believed in purgatory, but he rejected the idea that one could avoid God's judgment simply in exchange for doing something good. In addition to his personal struggles and private studies, Luther opposed Tetzel because he was convinced that repentance, not penance, was what God required. Penance was promoted by the Roman Catholic Church as a means of enabling contrite sinners to make amends for their sins. Repentance was proclaimed by Christ himself as a way of calling sinners to stop sinning. As different ways of placating God, the former encouraged confession to a priest whereas the latter encouraged trust in the finished work of Christ.

Luther came to this conclusion after reading an annotated New Testament recently produced by Desiderius Erasmus. Though he lived and died a Roman Catholic, Erasmus inadvertently opened the door for the Reformation when his fresh Latin translation differed from the Vulgate on issues regarding the need for penance, the nature of grace, and the role of the sacraments. While the Catholic Church had centuries of tradition to back up its point of view, Erasmus had the best Greek manuscripts of his day to back up his conclusions. Luther began to realize that the church needed to recover the very gospel it had been entrusted to preserve. Thus, he wrote his Ninety-Five Theses as a summons to reform the church he was in, rather than to begin one anew. He actually thought he was doing the pope a favor by calling attention to these matters. Pope Leo X, who had sanctioned the sale of indulgences, was not amused.

Perhaps it is too easy at this point to put a white hat on Luther and a black hat on Leo in a good-priest-versus-bad-pope scenario. In reality, the possibility of heresy did not cease in the first century, and questionable interpretations of Scripture were regularly confronted by appeals

---

[11] The mere mention of purgatory is a reminder of one of the many differences that exist between Catholics and Protestants today. The idea that a person will suffer punishment for a period of time between the grave and the gates of heaven is a firmly entrenched doctrine among Catholics but regarded as pure fiction by Protestants.

to church tradition. With this in mind, Luther's concerns about the sale of indulgences and the role of penance crossed a line by raising questions about papal authority. Moreover, the fact that Luther's Ninety-Five Theses were translated and distributed among the German people added fuel to an already fiery sense of national identity. Ignoring Luther and his "novel" teachings would only further aggravate relations between the Germans and Italians. Luther was therefore summoned to appear before papal representatives on multiple occasions, culminating with his appearance at Worms, Germany, in 1521. When it became clear that he had to choose between fidelity to Scripture as he understood it and submission to the interpretation of Scripture as the papacy defined it, Luther declared that his conscience was captive to the Word of God.

His subsequent excommunication from the Roman Catholic Church drove him to question other practices taught by the church but not found in the Bible. By the time Luther died in 1546, his reforms offered thousands of Christians a new way of understanding the Christian life. He put the Bible in the hands of the people and told priests to take the hands of their brides, thereby introducing the priesthood of all believers and ending mandatory celibacy for church leaders. He encouraged pastors to preach, taught congregations to sing, wrote catechisms for children, and pronounced God's blessing on the most ordinary occupations in life. Anyone who has seen a pastor at church with his wife and children, heard a congregation sing hymns, received both elements of the Lord's Supper, or collaborated together as laypersons in a Bible study is indebted to Luther for making such practices normal in the Protestant tradition. Yet, it was necessary for him to break away from the Roman Catholic Church in order for such things to happen.

Presbyterian Beginnings

Presbyterians get their name from a form of church governance in which local congregations make decisions collectively. A local Presbyterian church, for example, is led by its pastor and a group of elders who are chosen by the church, but the process of ordination is a responsibility shared by other ministers and elders from surrounding congregations. In addition, Presbyterian churches are generally united by common confessions of faith, which may include the Belgic Confession (1561), the Heidelberg Catechism (1563), and the Westminster Confession (1646).[12]

This form of church government is an appropriate illustration of the early history of Presbyterianism, as it involves individuals from various areas who arrived at similar conclusions regarding the composition and leadership of the church. What began as a reform movement by Ulrich Zwingli in Switzerland was fine-tuned by John Calvin in Geneva and reached full fruition under John Knox in Scotland. The end result was one of the most sophisticated expressions of the Christian faith to emerge from the Protestant Reformation.

Ulrich Zwingli was born in Switzerland just six weeks after Martin Luther and began to embrace Reformation ideas one year before his German counterpart was excommunicated from the Catholic Church (1520). Like Luther, Zwingli came to his conclusions while serving as a Catholic priest and similarly credited his discovery of Reformation doctrines to his close reading of Scripture. In 1519, Zwingli's expository sermons through the Gospel of Matthew led him to reject the doctrine of purgatory, the call to monasticism, and the practice of praying to departed saints. And, like Luther, Zwingli found himself expelled by Catholic authorities but protected by the local magistrates.[13]

Zwingli and Luther had much in common, but their differences became so pronounced that the two Reformers were unable to unite their movements. Though they agreed that the Bible is the final authority for all Christians, one of their most foundational differences was how to implement matters not mentioned therein. This question needed to be answered as both men believed that the Roman Catholic Church had gone astray by incorporating human tradition in place of Holy Scripture. Interestingly, Luther took the more liberal view—whatever was not prohibited by the Bible could be implemented in the church. Zwingli was more stringent in his approach, believing that anything not mentioned in the Bible did not belong in the church. Practically speaking, the Reformed churches led by Zwingli dispensed with their organs and congregational singing, whereas Luther wrote "A Mighty Fortress Is Our God," a hymn

---

[12]These confessions of faith, along with many others, can be accessed at www.creeds.net.

[13]For more on the life of Zwingli, see G. R. Potter, *Zwingli* (Cambridge, UK: Cambridge University Press, 1976).

many Christians still sing and one that is especially effective with a pipe organ prelude.

Perhaps their most famous disagreement occurred in 1529 at the Marburg Colloquy. The meeting was designed to bring Luther's and Zwingli's movements together, but it turned out to be an ecumenist's worst nightmare as their disagreement on one of the fifteen points in discussion sent them on their separate ways. Ironically, the single obstacle to their joining ranks was their understanding of Holy Communion. Both men held that the Roman Catholic doctrine of transubstantiation is incorrect, but Zwingli's belief that the bread merely aids one's memory in reflecting on the body of Jesus went against Luther's understanding that the body of Jesus is somehow still present.[14] Though Zwingli is not as well known among Protestants as Luther, his work at establishing the Reformation in Switzerland, as later articulated by a brilliant young Frenchman, John Calvin, was destined to have a greater impact among Christians in Europe and North America.

Calvin is often referred to as a second-generation Reformer since he was barely ten years old when Luther and Zwingli began their reforms.[15] By the time Calvin joined the Reformation, Luther had translated the entire Bible, and Zwingli had taken his last breath. Calvin's late arrival notwithstanding, he made up for lost time by drafting some of the clearest yet most profound instructions on living the Christian life in light of Scripture and outside of the Roman Catholic Church. Calvin's *Institutes of the Christian Religion* (first published in 1536) underwent several revisions during his life, but the underlying themes remained unchanged. In every respect Calvin's *Institutes* reaffirmed the Reformation *solas*— salvation by grace alone through faith alone in Christ alone to the glory of God alone. The certainty with which he held these views was buttressed by his belief in Scripture alone as the church's final authority.

One of Calvin's most lasting contributions was his understanding of offices within the church. He divided ministerial responsibilities between the pastor, teachers, elders, and deacons. His identification of the pas-

---

[14]Zwingli later affirmed a spiritual presence of Christ during the Lord's Supper by the contemplation of faith. This position was still short of Luther's belief that Christ is present by, in, with, and through the elements. I am indebted to Doug Sweeney for this observation.

[15]The best recent biography of Calvin is Bruce Gordon, *Calvin* (New Haven, CT: Yale University Press, 2009).

tor as one of the elders in a local church effectively did away with the Episcopal form of church government practiced for centuries prior by virtually all Christian groups. Calvin argued that a plurality of elders form a common council within the church in which the pastor is a fellow member. In much the same way that Luther elevated the laity with his teaching on the priesthood of all believers, Calvin empowered congregations to have an informed choice about who would lead their local churches. And, contrary to the practice of the Roman Catholic Church, where one could literally purchase an office in the church, under Calvin one's calling to the pastorate was combined with moral integrity and the ability to teach, in conjunction with the stipulations of 1 Timothy 3:1–7.

Calvin did much more than simply write about what the church should be—he implemented these measures in Geneva, Switzerland, such that one Scottish refugee declared Calvin's Geneva to be the "most perfect school of Christ since the apostles." John Knox was the man behind these words, and his starry-eyed quote reveals that he was a man of keen observation and biblical resolve. His own journey to Geneva was necessitated by a sweeping persecution of Protestants throughout the British Isles, and his eventual return to Scotland resulted in a Reformation there equal to those in the countries of Luther, Zwingli, and Calvin. By 1560, just one year after Knox's return from exile, the Scottish Parliament abolished papal authority and adopted the Scots Confession of Faith, coauthored by Knox himself.[16]

Knox had abandoned transubstantiation, indulgences, purgatory, pilgrimages, and fast days as having no scriptural warrant. But perhaps even more than his Reformation predecessors, Knox gained a reputation for fearlessly confronting royal authorities. Becoming a Protestant cost two years of his life as a galley slave, and upon his release he continued to denounce Catholic doctrines before Catholic sovereigns. His preference for governing the church according to Presbyterian principles was drawn from the biblical text, but his focus on this style of church governance was also driven by the threats he saw to the church from people in high places. In fact, one of his primary examples of how kings and queens could steer the church in the wrong direction had occurred in the then recent history of the Church of England.

---

[16]For more on Knox's life, see Rosalind Marshall, *John Knox* (Edinburgh, UK: Birlinn, 2008).

Anglican Beginnings

Nearly a thousand years before the formation of the Church of England, missionaries from the Continent were sent to establish churches in England. Both events were set into motion by prominent leaders in the Roman Catholic Church, and both ostensibly arose out of a concern for children. In 597 an entourage, sent by Pope Gregory and led by Augustine (not to be confused with Augustine of Hippo), arrived in Kent for the purpose of establishing Christianity in the British Isles. The story is told that Gregory had developed an interest there after witnessing golden-hair boys for sale in a Roman slave market. Upon being told that they were "Angles," Gregory is said to have replied, "Not Angles, but angels. What a shame that God's grace does not dwell within those beautiful brows."[17]

Pope Gregory's missionary agenda made Catholicism the dominant religion in England for a millennium thereafter and was finally interrupted by the famed Henry VIII's desire to have a son. What may seem like a small reason to start a new church was actually a quite reasonable position for a sixteenth-century English monarch who constantly faced the threat of war and whose responsibility it was to protect the English people. The idea that only a male heir to the throne would ensure a secure future for England meant that Henry's duty and dynasty were intertwined. As he and his wife, Catherine, advanced in years with only a daughter, Mary Tudor, to succeed them, Henry concluded that God had withheld the blessing of a son because he and Catherine were unlawfully wed.

This thought had occurred to others many years earlier as Catherine had once been married to Henry's older brother, Arthur. Her previous marriage had been one of political convenience, assuring an alliance between England and Spain. The death of Arthur four months after the wedding did not end the treaty between the two countries, as Henry's father pledged him to Catherine. Her brief time with Arthur raised the possibility that the marriage had never been consummated, a condition that convinced the pope to grant a special dispensation for a widow to

---

[17] Jonathan Hill, *Zondervan Handbook to the History of Christianity* (Grand Rapids: Zondervan, 2006), 170. The story is told in various versions, making it almost certainly apocryphal, but Gregory's mission certainly marked the beginning of Roman Catholicism in England. For a helpful overview of the spread of Christianity throughout the British Isles, see Ivor Davidson, *A Public Faith: From Constantine to the Medieval World, A.D. 312–600* (Grand Rapids: Baker, 2005), 341–62.

marry her deceased husband's brother. For her part, Catherine insisted that she had never had sexual relations with Arthur.[18]

When a male heir was not forthcoming, Henry sought to have the marriage annulled, claiming that Catherine had lied and that he now wanted more than ever to please God. Ordinarily such arrangements could be made, but Henry's situation was complicated in that Catherine was the aunt of the Holy Roman Emperor, Charles V, a major political figure whom the pope could not afford to offend. Henry's advisors convinced him that as king his first loyalty was to the English people. In his quest for a son, he proceeded to marry Anne Boleyn and depose Catherine. The papal reaction was stern, eventuating in Henry's excommunication from the Roman Catholic Church. In turn, the king led Parliament to adopt the Act of Supremacy, which made him the head of the newly founded Church of England.

Though its beginnings seem to contain more political intrigue than divine design, the Church of England very quickly took on theological dimensions that would leave a rich historic legacy. Thomas Cranmer, appointed archbishop of Canterbury during Henry's reign, had Protestant sympathies that far exceeded those of his king (despite his falling out with the pope, Henry remained Catholic at heart). Consequently, Cranmer was cautious about making too many changes but was soon able to implement his Reformation ideas after Henry died and was succeeded by his only son from his third wife. Under Edward VI, Cranmer produced his most significant contributions to the Church of England—the Thirty-Nine Articles and the Book of Common Prayer.

Since their adoption in 1563, the Thirty-Nine Articles have defined the Church of England along Protestant lines. Specifically, the document affirms the doctrine of justification by faith alone, denies transubstantiation, advocates an Episcopal form of church government, and limits the books of the Bible to the sixty-six books of the Old and New Testaments. Cranmer's work in this regard has had a lasting impact as the Thirty-Nine Articles remain the doctrinal standard of the Church of England. Another influential work, the Book of Common Prayer, demonstrates how the Protestant movement involved both the head and the heart in worship. In addition to containing some of the most beautiful prayers outside

---

[18]An excellent biography of this queen who lived in the shadow of her husband and of history is Giles Tremlett, *Catherine of Aragon: The Spanish Queen of Henry VIII* (New York: Walker, 2010).

of the Psalms, the book also served the purpose of teaching ministers in the Church of England how to conduct worship services in keeping with Protestant principles. With a thousand years of Roman Catholicism behind them, priests serving in the Church of England found it difficult to reform overnight, even if they were sympathetic to Protestant ideas. By following the liturgy of the Book of Common Prayer, people were instructed how to pray to God, not the saints; to receive both elements of the Lord's Supper rather than just the bread; and to have their children baptized without assuming they were born again.

Cranmer's reforms have stood the test of time but were very nearly short-lived. He served at the king's pleasure, but when Edward died at the age of sixteen, Cranmer found himself on the receiving end of the new queen's displeasure. Mary, daughter of Catherine, came to the throne in 1554 with memories of her mother's embarrassing departure from the palace and with visions of her Catholic faith returning to England. Mary's efforts to stamp out Protestantism were so pronounced that even Cranmer himself, who had taught an entire nation to pray, became weak-kneed and recanted his Protestant beliefs. His effort to save his life in this regard failed, but his final actions in recanting his recantation succeeded in reassuring the faithful that he truly believed all that he had written.[19] The queen carried out her vengeance on the Protestant movement so swiftly that she earned the title "Bloody Mary." However, she was not successful in returning England to Rome, as she reigned only five years. Unlike her father, who had moved heaven and earth to have a son, Mary died without leaving an heir. Her half-sister Elizabeth was next in line and, politically speaking, became the son that Henry had always wanted.

England became a world power during Elizabeth's reign, defeating the Spanish Armada in 1588. More importantly for the history of the church, Elizabeth settled the vexed question of the Church of England's identity. Three previous rulers left three different possibilities. Henry had renounced the Roman Catholic Church but not the Catholic faith. Edward adopted the reforms of his Protestant advisors but died before they were fully implemented. Mary returned to the pope and his church but without her people or their blessing. Elizabeth chose a "middle way," preferring a church that was not Catholic but also not terribly offensive

---

[19]Cranmer was sentenced to burn at the stake by Mary, but in his final statement declared that his hand would be the first part of him to burn since it had signed the recantations.

to her Catholic subjects. She also wanted a Protestant church, but not one that could be branded along with other European alternatives such as the Germans (Lutheran) or the Swiss (Reformed) had embraced. With a few minor changes to the Book of Common Prayer and the Thirty-Nine Articles, she brought into being a distinctly Anglican church; with a subsequent reign of nearly half a century, she ensured that her middle way would become mainstream. Those who were still bent on reforming the English church soon found that their best option was to move to a different country.[20]

Baptist Beginnings

It has been said that where two or three Baptists are gathered, three or four opinions are in the midst of them. This observation is particularly true as it relates to the story of Baptist beginnings. A number of Baptists have argued (with straight faces) that their roots can be traced to John the Baptist himself, and that the church Jesus promised to build in Matthew 16 was in fact a Baptist church. When this view was challenged in 1896 by William Whitsitt, president of a Baptist seminary, he was forced to resign. Now, however, no serious Baptist historian argues for a succession of Baptist churches from the first century onward.

Another option has been to trace Baptist beginnings to the Anabaptists who emerged in 1525 from Zwingli's Reformed movement. Anabaptists were so named because they rejected their baptisms as infants and insisted that Christians are only truly baptized after a profession of faith. In the eyes of others they were "baptized again." Although Baptists and Anabaptists share a common view of baptism, there are significant differences between the two that point to separate identities altogether.[21] The most credible view of Baptists beginnings, then, is one that combines both historical and theological evidence connecting them to the modern Baptist movement. Their story thus begins in Holland with John Smyth, traverses through England with Thomas Helwys, and winds its way to America with Roger Williams.[22]

---

[20]For further reading on the history of the Church of England, see J. R. H. Moorman, *A History of the Church in England*, 3rd ed. (Harrisburg, PA: Morehouse, 1986).

[21]For example, the Anabaptists practiced communal living, refused to take oaths, were pacifists, and did not serve in government positions. Their closest spiritual kin are the Mennonites.

[22]For a thorough history of the Baptist movement, see H. Leon McBeth, *The Baptist Heritage: Four Centuries of Baptist Witness* (Nashville: B&H Academic, 1987). See also Michael Williams and

Smyth and Williams both had interesting denominational pedigrees that can be described as belonging, leaving, finding, and seeking. Smyth began his journey in the Church of England as a graduate of Cambridge and an ordained Anglican priest. Like many others, he was frustrated with the Elizabethan settlement, believing it stopped short of a full reformation. Smyth became part of a concerted effort to remove elements of Catholicism from the liturgy of the Anglican Church. This perspective earned him and others the pejorative title of "Puritan" since they all wanted to purify the church. He soon concluded that the hierarchical structure of the church was faulty because England's sovereign ultimately decided how priests and parishioners would practice their faith. While many Puritans remained in the Church of England, believing they could reform the church from within, Smyth and many others left in hopes of starting a different church altogether. Their departure earned them the title of "Separatists."

The accession of King James I was but a continuation of Elizabethan policies. King James viewed religious nonconformity as a threat to social order, so Smyth and his small congregation moved to the friendlier confines of Amsterdam, Holland. Their exodus from the only country they had ever known led to a more focused quest of what the Bible says about the composition of the church. Smyth concluded that the root of evil in the Church of England was its practice of receiving as members all who were baptized without much regard to beliefs or behavior. The solution, as he saw it, was to begin a new church where membership was reserved for believers only and management of the church belonged to the congregation alone. In short, he sought to establish a fully regenerate church.

Smyth convinced his congregation that baptism is for believers, not babies, and that each potential member of this new church needed to be baptized again. Incidentally, by repudiating his own infant baptism and declaring other churches to be false, Smyth veritably disqualified anyone from performing the rite on him or his congregation. Hence, he was in the unenviable position of having to baptize himself before proceeding to baptize members of his newly formed church! As awkward as this may seem, the baptismal service marked Smyth's belief that one could begin a genuine church by returning to the teachings of the apostles rather than belonging to a succession of the same.

Walter Shurden, eds., *Turning Points in Baptist History* (Macon, GA: Mercer University Press, 2008).

Smyth's congregation was satisfied that its constitution as a church through believer's baptism was valid, but the criticism he received for baptizing himself led Smyth to reconsider whether he had acted too hastily in forming a new congregation. His discussions with local Mennonites persuaded him to make yet another transition in his denominational pilgrimage. Smyth concluded that since the Mennonites' practice of believer's baptism preceded his own, he and his church should unite with the Mennonites for the sake of unity and good order. Though he had persuaded his congregation to leave their church and their country, Smyth was not able to persuade them to adopt his newfound position on church unity. He left the church he had founded but died before he could join another.

The continuation of the Baptist movement rested on the shoulders of Thomas Helwys, a layman who likely had financed the movement's relocation to Holland. After Smyth's departure, Helwys and the remaining members returned to England. In 1611 they planted the first Baptist church in England, located in Spitalfields. His confrontation with King James confirmed that he was more than a financier and tour guide, as he wrote a treatise on religious liberty arguing that no king has the right to determine the religion of his subjects. "The King is a mortal man and not God," Helwys wrote on the flyleaf of the king's copy, "therefore he hath no power over the immortal souls of his subjects."[23] King James may not have had power over Helwys's soul, but he did exercise power over his body as Helwys was imprisoned at Newgate, where he died the following year.

Queen Elizabeth's compromise on the church and King James's uncompromising stance toward dissenters led yet another Englishman into the Baptist fold, albeit through a circuitous route. Roger Williams left both the country and the Church of England in his attempt to remain true to his conscience as it related to worshiping God. His arrival in Boston, Massachusetts, in 1631 marked the beginning of more difficulties as he openly criticized the inhabitants of stealing land from the natives, and ministers of imposing their will on the people. Williams was shown the proverbial door, which at that time meant he was banished from the colony. When he found refuge in a land shown to him by the Narragansett Indians, Williams named it Providence in honor of God's gracious guidance. His

---

[23]McBeth, *The Baptist Heritage*, 103–4.

purchase of the land from the natives and his allowance of a multitude of religious perspectives in Rhode Island sealed his reputation as one who not only followed his conscience but allowed others to do the same.[24]

Williams's trip across the Atlantic Ocean and travels through the American frontier aptly symbolize his journey to find a denominational identity. Like John Smyth, he was an Anglican turned Puritan who became a Separatist and then a Baptist. Although he founded the first Baptist church in America in 1639, he, like Smyth again, left the Baptist movement in search of something better. But even though Williams died without finding what he was looking for, he left a legacy that Baptists have upheld ever since—God alone is Lord of conscience. Hence, the right to worship comes from God, not government. This perspective was not popular in Williams's day as most people believed that government had a role in promoting and even enforcing religion. Mandatory church attendance and taxes for church maintenance were the norm until the Bill of Rights was added to the Constitution. As the story goes, religious liberty was the work not only of famous founding fathers like Jefferson and Madison, but also of indefatigable Baptist leaders like Isaac Backus and John Leland.[25]

Yet the opportunity to worship according to one's conscience has, more than any other factor, led to the multiplicity of churches throughout America. Put simply, the Baptist insistence on religious liberty led to more than just the disestablishment of religion. It also meant that churches needed to enlist converts on a massive scale if they were to survive. And the one group in America that reaped the rewards of frontier evangelism more than the Baptists was yet another reform movement that emerged from the Church of England.[26]

Methodist Beginnings

Methodism derives its name from the methodical nature of the spiritual disciplines exhibited by its founder, John Wesley, and members of his

---

[24]A helpful treatment of how Roger Williams's interpretation of Scripture led him to advocate for religious liberty is found in James P. Byrd Jr., *The Challenges of Roger Williams: Religious Liberty, Violent Persecution, and the Bible* (Macon, GA: Mercer University Press, 2002).

[25]See J. Bradley Creed, "Baptist Freedom and the Turn toward Separation of Church and State: 1833," in Williams and Shurden, *Turning Points*, 153–66.

[26]For a fascinating examination of how various religious groups competed for their place in the American frontier, see Nathan Hatch, *The Democratization of American Christianity* (New Haven, CT: Yale University Press, 1991).

Oxford "Holy Club."[27] The term was initially hurled as a derogatory one, lampooning the concern they had over the salvation of their souls. Together they covenanted to be diligent in their devotions, studying the Bible and reading religious literature for hours each day, and to do works of charity on a regular basis, namely, visiting prisoners and contributing to the poor. Their dedication notwithstanding, at the time neither John nor his brother Charles fully grasped salvation by grace through faith alone. One might have thought that Luther's grand struggle and England's recent history would have made the way of salvation clear to all who were interested in such things, but the Wesleys were living at a time when rationalism had eclipsed revelation as the primary means of knowing God. Their Holy Club was essentially a righteous protest group designed to model the virtues of the Christian life to those who enjoyed critiquing the Bible rather than submitting to it.

Standing at five feet three and weighing roughly 130 pounds, John Wesley was not the most likely candidate to lead a revival that is still being studied over two hundred years later. Nor was he even remotely interested in breaking away from the Church of England to found one of the largest Protestant denominations of the nineteenth century. But his physical appearance belied his inner fortitude. His passion to make Christ known was such that he boarded a ship to Georgia in hopes of evangelizing Native Americans and later returned to England, traversing the countryside on horseback to evangelize poor cottagers. By the end of his life he had traveled more than a quarter million miles, preached over forty thousand times, and written over forty books. Yet it was not until he was in the process of taking the gospel to others that he learned to receive the gospel for himself. In this respect, Wesley's conversion bore a remarkable resemblance to Luther's, since both men were engaged in ministry before they understood the gospel.

The similarities continue. Like Luther, Wesley learned to fear God in a storm, and through Luther's writings Wesley learned to take comfort in the Savior. The storm occurred at sea, nearly sinking the ship that was carrying Wesley to America. He genuinely feared for his life, but he noticed a group of Moravian passengers who were visibly at peace

---

[27]Recent treatments on the life of John Wesley include Stephen Tomkins, *John Wesley: A Biography* (Grand Rapids: Eerdmans, 2003); and Iain Murray, *Wesley and Men Who Followed* (Edinburgh, UK: Banner of Truth, 2003).

the entire time. Wesley wondered what they had that he lacked, and it became clear that he did not have assurance of salvation, a most difficult position for a missionary. His visit to Aldersgate some two years later, where Luther's preface to Romans was being read aloud, put an end to his struggle for assurance as he felt his heart strangely warmed. This experience confirmed for him that he truly did trust in Christ alone. The result was a new beginning. Wesley was no longer hindered by doubts of his own salvation, nor did he hold people to his incredibly high standards before assuring them of their salvation. Consequently, he began proclaiming the gospel outdoors to all who would hear.

This transition was not easy for a person as methodical as Wesley. He cared about decency and good order to such an extent that he once thought it a sin to lead souls to Christ outside of a church building. He was forced to do just that when the Church of England tried to harness his efforts by refusing him pulpit time. The national church had drawn boundary lines, or parishes, for its preachers. Unless an invitation was forthcoming by a parish minister, one was in breach of order by crossing over. His choice between respecting these boundaries as decided by bishops and going into the highways and byways as commanded by Christ was decisively made when he declared that the world was his parish. The reception was nothing less than overwhelming as thousands of people who never darkened the door of an Anglican church went from darkness to light after hearing this Anglican preach.

Wesley and his converts were derided as "enthusiasts" for his preaching of the new birth and for their eager response to his message. Still, Wesley had no intention of breaking with the Anglican Church. He encouraged all who converted to Christ in his outdoor meetings to receive Communion inside the Church of England. Ultimately, the process of separation lay more in England's circumstance than in Wesley's design. The parish structure was ineffective to reach the masses, and Wesley's increasing number of converts required an increasing number of teachers. Wesley attempted to fix the supply side of this demand by appointing lay teachers over small groups. While this solution addressed the need for discipleship, it raised the question of whether lay preachers were qualified to take on other pastoral duties, like baptism and the Lord's Supper.

The Church of England had long prohibited lay persons from presiding over either, and this stance was reinforced during the Revolutionary War as the church refused to ordain bishops in colonial America. Wesley strongly opposed the war against England but felt even more strongly about the need for Christians to have access to the ordinances. He therefore ordained ministers without approval from English bishops and appointed Thomas Coke as their superintendent, effectively creating a new church structure independent of Anglicanism. Though Wesley never formally separated from the Church of England, the events he set in motion resulted in a wave of revivals on both sides of the Atlantic and a denomination whose membership surpassed all others in the newly formed United States of America. The world had indeed become Wesley's parish, but another movement with Methodist sympathies would soon prove that there was more territory to cover.[28]

Pentecostal Beginnings

Pentecostalism had beginnings similar to those of Methodism since each began with a prolonged revival. Pentecostals, however, can point to more extensive results as their movement became a worldwide phenomenon impacting continents that Wesley hardly knew about. The Pentecostals' emphasis on holiness provides another connection with Wesley in that both he and they understood the words of Jesus "be perfect, as your heavenly Father is perfect" to be achievable in this lifetime. Theirs was not a pharisaical attempt to restructure God's commands in order to say that they were compliant. Rather, they believed that the Holy Spirit enables the children of God to overcome their sinful desires and live according to their new natures.

In terms of founders, however, the two movements could not be farther apart. Contrary to the Oxford don renowned for organization, Pentecostals tell the story of a son of slaves, blind in one eye, who had to sit outside an all-white classroom when he wanted to learn about the Bible. And certainly no one ever accused William Seymour and his Azusa Street revival of excessive organization! Whereas Wesley was reluctant to preach outdoors, fearing the semblance of disorder, Seymour launched his ministry from a private home that became so crowded with worship-

---

[28]For a history of Methodism, including the social factors behind its rise and global spread, see David Hempton, *Methodism: Empire of the Spirit* (New Haven, CT: Yale University Press, 2005). See also John Wigger, *American Saint: Francis Asbury and the Methodists* (New York: Oxford University Press, 2009).

ers, the front porch collapsed. Hence, the name Pentecostal was for them a badge of honor as it pointed to another God-ordained revival where rules of decorum were replaced by the power of the Spirit.[29]

William Seymour was the leading figure in Pentecostal beginnings, but as with the denominational founders before him, there is also a backstory to tell. While Methodists agreed on the need for holiness, different groups within the movement interpreted the means to holiness differently. Charles Fox Parham made some of his Methodist brethren uneasy when he added divine healing to the quest for personal holiness. He left the Methodist movement to become an independent evangelist and later opened Beth-El Healing Home and Bethel Bible School in Topeka, Kansas. Parham believed that a worldwide revival similar to what occurred in Acts 2 was in store for the church and instructed his students to comb through the book of Acts in search of definitive evidence that the Spirit had been poured out on God's people. Together they concluded that speaking in tongues is the sign of God's work in the last days, as it miraculously enables people to speak in a foreign language when they take the gospel across the globe. The fact that a number of his students claimed to receive this gift confirmed to Parham that he had another angle on the Christian life. In addition to seeking a second blessing of holiness that would follow their conversion, he taught that Christians should also expect a third work, the gift of tongues.

In 1905, after traveling again as an itinerant evangelist, Parham opened another school, this time in Houston, Texas. Sitting outside an open door was William Seymour, who took in Parham's understanding of the last days and brought those teachings with him to Los Angeles. Seymour made his journey at the request of a black holiness congregation in need of a pastor, but his teaching that they were also in need of a third blessing was not well received. The church locked its doors on Seymour, but he soon found the windows of heaven open as he and several others began speaking in tongues on April 9, 1906. The date was significant as

---

[29]The story of the revival and Seymour's role in Pentecostal beginnings is told in Cecil M. Robeck Jr., *The Azusa Street Mission and Revival* (Nashville: Thomas Nelson, 2006). Recent scholarship has recognized that Pentecostalism was a multifaceted movement drawing from multiple global origins. The revival that began at Azusa Street was not the sole event but one very important component in the rise of this diverse movement. See Mark Noll, *The New Shape of World Christianity: How American Experience Reflects Global Faith* (Downers Grove, IL: InterVarsity, 2004), 109–26.

less than two weeks later the great San Francisco earthquake seemed to confirm that the last days had indeed finally arrived.

Of course the Lord did not return, but Seymour and his followers were prepared to embrace the revival as long as it would last. For the next three years he held revival services in an abandoned warehouse on Azusa Street, a ghetto neighborhood near Los Angeles. The location made little difference as Seymour regularly conducted three services a day. Indeed, the most remarkable trend alongside the constant attendance was the complexion of the attendees. Peoples of various races and cultural backgrounds worshiped together freely. In what seemed like fruits from the original Pentecost, where the barrier between Jew and Gentile began to fall, the Azusa Street revival broke down barriers of ethnicity and gender. Blacks and whites, women and men all shared significant roles at a time when separation of races and sexes was the norm.

Their attempts to be open to the Spirit in these and other ways quickly closed them off from other denominations. Pentecostals believed the Bible but relied extensively on their experience in support of their newfound emphases, such as speaking in tongues, prophetic utterances, and miraculous healing. It was not that people in other denominations believed God *could* not do such things, but rather that he no longer *normally* did what Pentecostals claimed. Nevertheless, it was this very angle—that God uses marginalized people to advance his kingdom—that enabled Pentecostalism to find a welcome home in many Third World countries.[30]

The worldwide spread of Pentecostalism was quite phenomenal even if the divisions that later occurred within the movement were somewhat predictable. People from around the world were drawn to Azusa Street and went out into the world to tell what they had seen. Three years after the revival began, Pentecostal churches could be found in places as far away as Australia, China, and South Africa. Unfortunately, as Pentecostalism began to expand, its adherents also began to divide. The most notable division came from Charles Parham himself, who deplored the intermingling of races at the revival meetings. Doctrinal divisions also occurred, as some Pentecostals debated among themselves the number of blessings to expect and the number of persons in the Godhead—some concluded that holiness is not a distinct work of the Spirit while others

---

[30]Alistair McGrath, *Christianity's Dangerous Idea* (New York: HarperOne, 2007), 427–32.

even argued that there are no distinct persons in the Trinity.[31] Thus, the movement that began by emphasizing the work of the Spirit in the last days seemed unable to unite Christians who still awaited the Lord's return.

Concluding Observations

Jesus's prayer that "they all may be one" (John 17:21) is often cited as a mandate for Christian unity, and rightly so. No Christian should take any words of the Bible lightly, but the fact that these words come from one of the final earthly prayers of Jesus gives them special importance. However, it is also notable that in the same breath Jesus prayed that his followers would be sanctified in the truth. He then declared, "Your word is truth" (v. 17). In answer to Jesus's prayer, then, unity in the Christian faith must be tempered by adherence to Christian truth. The common thread in each of the previous stories is that persons responsible for the formation of denominations were torn between visible unity and scriptural fidelity. When the former was no longer viable, they opted for what they understood to be scriptural.

Perhaps it can be said that denominations are intended to be a balance between cooperation and conviction. Christians of like mind gather together in order to display God's grace in Christ through the church. Baptists and Pentecostals will likely demonstrate this grace in a believer's church setting, whereas Anglicans and Lutherans will choose a church that baptizes the infants of believing parents. Each group's like-mindedness need not be seen as narrow-mindedness when it is understood that no single denomination is the sole expression of the family of God. Ideally, identification with a denomination—be it Methodist, Presbyterian, or another—should be seen as an act of unity in itself as one agrees to be part of a tradition that is larger than one's local church and life experience.

Admittedly, Christians who belong to nondenominational churches tend to give the appearance of caring more about unity since they are not labeled with traditional denominational names. Yet even their local churches are based on common agreements between pastor and parish-

---

[31] These differences are not on the same level in terms of ordinary divisions that occur among Christians. The question as to whether the baptism of the Spirit refers to speaking in tongues or an increased ability to serve the Lord can be tolerated, even if not agreed upon, among Pentecostals. However, the denial of the Trinity, as the United Pentecostal Church has done, falls completely outside of the bounds of orthodox Christianity. As such, it is rejected by the vast majority of Pentecostals.

ioners, which in effect give them an identity separate from that of other churches. Even if one substitutes the vogue word *networking* in place of the more nostalgic *cooperating*, a nondenominational church that links with other churches has formed, ironically, a nondenominational denomination. The nuts and bolts of a denomination are present even if a denominational name is absent.

On the other hand, refusal to network (or cooperate) is to be independent—the very antithesis of unity. Thus, belonging to a denomination actually opens avenues for cooperation while affirming the value of doctrinal conviction. Denominations enable local churches to identify themselves with a rich confessional tradition in which denominational distinctives are placed within the larger framework of historic Christian orthodoxy. And denominational entities enable local churches to train missionaries, educate pastors, and provide literature within those theological boundaries.

The negative side of denominations should also be recognized. They can be insular and divisive. Luther and Zwingli's failure to unite over one single point has been repeated innumerable times throughout the Protestant landscape. This is especially true in North America, where religious freedom and entrepreneurialism have joined together in such a way that anyone with a storefront lease or a cutting-edge blog can start his own church, claiming to possess the truth while being accountable to no one. Even the historic denominations need further qualifiers—PCA or PCUSA—to distinguish them from their former selves.

Denominations, along with their founders and followers, have plenty of faults. But one should not conclude that denominations are inherently divisive. This criticism has merit only if one holds to a nostalgic view of the church in which all Christians think alike on all issues, or all are willing to overlook important differences in order to provide a unified front. In reality, Christians do not think alike on all issues, and history reveals that when cooperation trumps conviction, the church loses its prophetic edge. Conversely, when narrow convictions prevent broad-based cooperation, the church misses the mark of love. A healthy dose of both cooperation and conviction enables Christians to avoid becoming either denominational diehards or empty-suit ecumenists. On this side of heaven, then, denominational identity and evangelical affinity can still be helpful for the people of God.

Why I Am an Evangelical and an Anglican

Gerald L. Bray

What Is an Anglican?

Few branches of the Christian church have as much difficulty defining themselves as the Anglican one has. Roman Catholics come in many different shapes and sizes, but they all acknowledge the bishop of Rome as the head of their church, membership in which is defined by being in communion with him. The Eastern Orthodox churches are more loosely structured, but they also have a strong sense of their corporate identity, which is represented in their liturgy and reinforced by a clearly defined hierarchy of bishops who recognize each other under the umbrella of the patriarch of Constantinople. Protestant churches define themselves in various ways, but most of them have a confession of faith to which their ministers must subscribe and which sets the tone for the members in general, or else distinctive practices that set them apart. A Lutheran will be expected to share the beliefs contained in the Formula of Concord, Presbyterians subscribe to the Westminster Confession of Faith or to one of its derivatives, Baptists reject infant baptism, and so on. Professional theologians in these denominations may lament the inadequate teaching that most of their laypeople receive, and deplore their flexibility about the extent to which they accept their church's official beliefs, but at least there is a recognized standard to which they fail to conform.

The Anglican Communion is different. Like the Roman Catholic and Eastern Orthodox churches, it has a hierarchy of bishops, but it is not defined by them. The archbishop of Canterbury has sometimes been regarded as a focal point for Anglican unity, but this is an unofficial designation and potentially misleading since he is not even the head of his own Church of England, whose supreme governor is the monarch. Most Anglican churches subscribe to the Thirty-Nine Articles of Religion, which were passed by the Church of England in 1563, but not all of them do, and there are many Anglicans for whom the articles are a dead letter. Similarly, most Anglicans have been shaped by the 1662 Book of Common Prayer, which is often said to have defined the traditional ethos of the church, but there are important exceptions to this (notably the American Episcopal Church, which has not used it since 1786), and modern liturgical revision has relegated the 1662 book to the sidelines in most places. Even the word *Anglican* is somewhat controversial and is not used by everyone. It was rarely heard before the mid-nineteenth century, when it was popularized by Anglo-Catholics, and even today there are Episcopalians in the United States who might not recognize the term, or think of it mainly as applying to those groups who have broken away from the Episcopal Church and laid claim to it as a badge of their identity. Even in England, many people describe themselves as "C of E" (Church of England) and might not know whether that makes them Anglican or not! So before explaining why I am still an Anglican, let me say what I think an Anglican is and where I would place myself on what is by any standard a remarkably broad spectrum.

To understand modern Anglicanism, one must grasp the distinction between the institutional church and the concept of a tradition that constitutes an ethos generally associated with it. All branches of Christianity have such a distinction, but in Anglicanism it is deeper and more significant than it is in most other churches. In institutional terms, the word *Anglican* refers in the first instance to the church(es) in the territories ruled by King Henry VIII that, at his insistence, broke communion with Rome in 1534. These include the Church of England, the Church in Wales (an integral part of the Church of England until 1920), and the Church of Ireland. The Church of Ireland never established itself as a truly national church; although it still exists, it has always been a minority denomination in its own country, so it cannot be considered typical. The Church in Wales has a more complicated relationship with the Welsh people, but as it did not acquire a distinctive identity until the twentieth century, it can also be disregarded for our present purposes.

That leaves the Church of England, by far the largest of the three and the one that set the tone for the other two and became and has remained the national church of the English people. Dissent from it was rare before the nineteenth century, and even today it still receives the passive allegiance of the majority of the population. Anyone who visits England or who spends time there, especially outside the main urban centers, will be left in no doubt about its position as a national institution. Other churches exist of course, and they are free to worship as they please, but they are alternatives patronized by a self-conscious minority. Roman Catholics are distinguished as a separate group, but other Protestants are all lumped together in the popular mind as "free churches," which may happen to be Methodist, Baptist, or Reformed, but that is essentially an afterthought. What strikes most people is that they are all "nonconformists," chapel goers instead of church people.

The Church of Scotland is an anomaly because it is both Presbyterian and a national church, making it difficult for English Anglicans to know what to make of it. Some accept it as a sister church because of its established status, while others reject it because it is not Episcopalian, preferring the tiny Episcopal Church of Scotland instead. Even at the highest level there is uncertainty here, because although the Church of England is in communion with the Scottish Episcopal Church (and not with the Church of Scotland), its supreme governor, the queen, is a member of the latter and not the former. In other words, the Church of England is the only church in the world whose titular head is also a member of another church with which it is not in communion—a good example of how hard it can be to decide what Anglicanism really is!

Things are very different outside the British Isles, where most Anglican churches are the result of overseas settlement by English people or of missionary activity conducted by them. The Church of England had a privileged position in most British colonies, and this has left its own legacy. This is true even in the United States, where the relatively tiny Episcopal Church retains an establishment aura, as can be seen from the so-called "national cathedral" in Washington, DC. No other American denomination would build such a thing or make a claim of that kind, but somehow it is expected of Episcopalians, who are disproportionately well-represented in the nation's governing classes. It is a pattern repeated in many former colonies, but however high their public profile may be, Anglican churches in other parts of the world have to coexist with other Christian bodies on equal terms, and this tends to make them more conscious of their own distinctiveness. In the United States especially, there has emerged a kind of "Anglicanism" that is oddly partial to the culture of Tudor England and regards Richard Hooker as its first and most typical theologian. It downplays the English Reformation and emphasizes the High Church anti-Puritanism that was characteristic of some prominent seventeenth-century divines but was unrepresentative of the church as a whole. English people, even those of a High Church disposition, tend to be surprised and somewhat disconcerted when they meet this kind of "Anglicanism" because, whatever its claims to be rooted in English tradition may be, it is somehow not a true reflection of the Church of England. In this case at least, a sense of Anglicanism as a particular theological tradition has parted company with the English mother church, making it difficult to say which of the two is more authentically "Anglican."

What is true of the United States is also true of other Anglican churches, though to a much lesser extent. One reason for this is that most of these churches were products of nineteenth-century British overseas expansion and have retained closer links with the Church of England. But it must also be said that many of them were founded (or quickly became dominated) by particular groups within the Church of England and are therefore much less diverse than the mother church is. In England evangelicals, Anglo-Catholics, and Broad Church people live side by side, but overseas they tend to be found clustered together in different dioceses or even in different churches. This is especially noticeable in Australia, where the diocese of Sydney is so different from those of Brisbane and Adelaide that they are barely in communion with each other, but it is also true elsewhere. In Africa for example, evangelical influence has been strong in Kenya, Uganda, and Tanzania, whereas Anglo-Catholicism is more prominent in South Africa. It is therefore not surprising that these two regional churches have seldom seen eye to eye, despite their common "Africanness."

Low, High, and Broad Church Anglicans

The different kinds of Anglicanism are designated by the term *churchmanship*, a concept unique to Anglicanism—so much so that it is untranslatable, and even incomprehensible, outside an Anglican context. Originally, churchmanship referred to one of three different ways of approaching the Church of England and its structures. Those who believe that the structures are a convenience—adopted for practical reasons but not imposed by divine authority, and therefore open to revision—have historically been known as Low Church. Those who take the opposite view are correspondingly referred to as High Church, while those in the middle are somewhat awkwardly classed as Broad. As may be imagined, the Broad Church is often the silent majority, but it cannot be defined with any precision and tends to side with the High or Low Church according to circumstances. To put it a different way, the Broad Church comprises the floating voters of the Anglican world whom the others must win over if they are to shape the policies of the church as a whole.

In the early days, churchmanship was largely a political phenomenon, only incidentally linked to doctrine or worship. Until well into the eighteenth century, all members of the Church of England subscribed to the same doctrinal formulations and worshiped according to the same Prayer Book, revealing their not inconsiderable differences mainly through the Whigs (Low Church) and the Tories (High Church) in Parliament. That way of thinking persisted into the modern era, but it gradually gave way to a different, and more theological, understanding of churchmanship differences.

The first move in that direction came with the emergence of evangelicalism in the mid-eighteenth century. John Wesley was a High Churchman, but other revivalists such as George Whitefield were not. Wesley's passionate desire to evangelize the masses led him to break with the Tories, who feared that his activities would lead to popular rebellion (as, in their eyes, it did in America). Although he was pushed in a Low Church direction, Wesley never fully embraced the Reformed theology that went with it. Despite his wishes, his followers eventually left the Church of England and established their own Methodist denomination(s). Those evangelicals who remained within the state church were more fully conscious of their Reformed and Puritan heritage, which they believed they were bringing back to life. Today, evangelicals tend to be the only Anglicans who still take the Reformation heritage of the church as the norm. Because of that, they regard themselves as the true Anglicans and think of others as having departed, to a greater or lesser degree, from what they ought to be. This attitude does not make them popular, of course, but it is hard to disagree with their analysis in terms of the church's official doctrinal standards.

In the early nineteenth century, evangelicalism seemed poised to take over the Church of England, but although its influence remained strong throughout the Victorian era, that did not happen. Instead, it was challenged by a revived Catholicism, based in Oxford and revolving around the charismatic personality of John Henry Newman. Newman became a Roman Catholic in 1845, but many of his followers remained in the Church of England and set out to remake it in their own image. It is to them that we owe the modern concept of Anglicanism, because they were determined to construct a distinctive theology and ecclesiology that could stand on a par with those of Rome and the Eastern churches as a third (and equal) branch of catholic Christianity. Theirs was a mammoth task that involved considerable massaging of the facts to make them fit their theory. The surprising thing, given the difficulties they faced, is that they were as successful as they were. Today, whether we like it or not, there is a significant body of Anglicans that scarcely acknowledges the church's Reformation heritage, that sees itself as a non-Roman form of Catholicism, and that sometimes promotes liturgical and devotional practices from which even many Roman Catholics recoil. Indeed, since the changes in the Roman Church brought about by Vatican II (1962–1965), some Anglo-Catholic churches claim to be the last bastions of traditional Catholicism—Latin mass and all!

By the end of the nineteenth century, Low and High Churchmanship had come to mean evangelicalism and Anglo-Catholicism respectively, and Broad Churchmanship was a compromise between the two. A Broad Church Anglican around 1900 would probably have accepted evangelical hymn singing and Sunday schools, but not revivalist preaching, and possibly also some moderately Anglo-Catholic vestments and rituals, but not the use of incense or the practice of private confession. By that time, however, a new and more powerful division was making its appearance. Nineteenth-century Anglican scholarship was generally conservative, but elsewhere that was far from the case. By 1900 the liberal theology then current in Germany was making inroads into the English-speaking world, and Anglicans were affected by this as much as other denominations, albeit somewhat more slowly.

By the 1920s both evangelicals and Anglo-Catholics were dividing into conservative and liberal subgroups, and the amorphous nature of the Broad Church made it a ready target for liberalism as well. Conservatives remained strong in many ways, but much of their energy was spent on foreign missions, which helps to explain why those mission churches are leading the conservative wing of the Anglican Communion today. But as the evidence of the official church documents of the period indicates, by about 1950 Anglicanism in the so-called First World was dominated by a benign liberalism that clung to the traditional forms of the church's ministry and worship but jettisoned its orthodox doctrine.

A generation later, the heirs of this liberal tendency were chafing at the retention of a superficial traditionalism, and they began to advocate a more consistently radical approach. From about 1960 onward, the worship of the church was transformed by so-called liturgical renewal, a curious blend of Patristic fundamentalism and modern radicalism, and traditional church discipline was progressively rejected. In the first stage, divorced people and women were accepted for ordination. Next, clergy who divorced after ordination were allowed to continue in office even if they subsequently remarried, and finally, practicing homosexuals were welcomed into the church and encouraged to promote their agenda. At that point, the conservatives, who had grumbled about earlier changes and done their best to resist or avoid them, finally realized that if they did not organize themselves and oppose these trends, they would be overwhelmed and the Anglican Communion would no longer be recognizable as a Christian body. Much to the consternation of the liberal establishment, they began to get together and to dissent collectively from the prevailing ethos among the governing bodies of the communion. Whether they will succeed in reversing the trends of the past generation remains to be seen, but this is where the church is now, and what the current struggle for the soul of "Anglicanism" is all about.

Given this situation, it is not possible for me or for anyone else to define the term *Anglican* in a way that would be accepted by everyone who claims that label. The most I can do is to explain what kind of Anglican I am—a conservative evangelical in the Church of England— why I think that my version of Anglicanism has a better right to the name than competing varieties, and why I believe that it is still worth defending when other Christian communions beckon and some openly tempt us away from our church with the claim that what they have to offer is an equally orthodox form of Christianity in a more dependable ecclesiastical framework.

Anglican Tradition and Authority

Every church defines itself by its doctrine, its discipline, and its devotional life, and although Anglican ones like to keep their options open, they are no exception to this. The Anglican Communion today is indebted to the English Reformation, which established a pattern for all three of these that is still recognizable today. Henry VIII's break with Rome in 1534 was the first step in this process, but it was not the start of the English Reformation in the theological sense. Henry lived and died a traditional Catholic, although his need for allies against the pope forced him to come to terms with the Lutherans, with the result that some changes were made in his lifetime—notably permission to print the Bible in English and the freedom to import Protestant literature. Gradually, and in spite of Henry, intellectual opinion was changing, and by the time Edward VI (1547–1553) succeeded to the throne, real reform was in the air. Edward was a minor, so church affairs were in the hands of the archbishop of Canterbury, Thomas Cranmer, and a few of his close associates. Between them, they produced two Prayer Books (the first being a dry run for the second, more clearly Protestant version), forty-two articles outlining their position on contested points of doctrine, a form for ordaining ministers (the *Ordinal*), and a scheme for church discipline that was never enacted. They also issued a book of sermons called the *Homilies*, which expounded the points of doctrine outlined in the articles in greater detail.

These documents were revised and reissued early in the reign of Elizabeth I (1558–1603), and they remain the charter documents of Anglicanism to this day. Over the years they have been roundly criticized, ignored, and derided by those who have found them too radical (or not radical enough), but they have survived and are now reemerging once more. The Articles of Religion (thirty-nine in their revised form) are a remarkably concise expression of Anglican doctrine. They are particularly impressive when we remember that at the time, they were the most systematic attempt to express Protestant teaching then available. They were never intended to be a comprehensive exposition of theology, but they point the way to the sources of Christian teaching in a clear and effective manner. For example, they list the canonical books of Scripture in a way that had not been done before, despite the Protestant insistence on *sola Scriptura*, and they lay down the important Anglican principle that whatever cannot be proved from the Bible must not be imposed on the church as its doctrine.

This way of dealing with the authority of Scripture was very wise because it allowed for the persistence of nonbiblical traditions that did not contradict the teaching of Scripture but were useful and even necessary for the order and good government of the church. Protestant bodies that tried to find scriptural proof for everything soon discovered that this was impossible, especially in the area of church government and worship. The New Testament does not tell us enough about how the first Christian communities functioned for us to be able to reconstruct them, and those who have tried to do so have inevitably fallen out with others who have started from the same premise but come to different conclusions. The truth is that there can be no going back to the first century, and traditional practices that have proved their value should not be abandoned merely because they are not mentioned in the Bible. Of course, if they are causing harm they have to be discarded, but that is a completely different thing. Roman Catholics claim that the so-called Petrine ministry of the pope, compulsory clerical celibacy, and the veneration of the saints are useful to the church, but Anglicans have examined the evidence and concluded that their disadvantages outweigh whatever benefits they may have. Such accretions have distracted believers from the centrality of the cross of Christ and done considerable harm to the preaching of the gospel, and so they must be rejected.

The Anglican approach to Scripture recognizes its supreme authority in the life of the church but is also sensible in the way in which that authority is applied, and much later division could have been avoided if that wisdom had received universal acceptance. It interprets the canonical text in the light of tradition and according to reason, or common sense. Some say that Anglicans accept Scripture, tradition, and reason as a threefold cord of authority, but that is misleading. Scripture comes first and is interpreted by the other two, which do not enjoy the same status. In particular, if a traditional belief or practice can be shown to be mistaken, it must be abandoned. Neither tradition nor reason can be adduced as an alternative to the Bible because each of them, in their different ways, acts only as a filter for interpretation, not as a controlling hermeneutic. Understood in this way, the Anglican approach to Scripture works very well, staying in touch with the Christian heritage but applying it in a sensible and relevant way.

The articles also underline the importance of the creeds of the early church, which contain its basic theology. The inheritance of Patristic thought is endorsed and accepted in principle, but without being canonized in the way that Scripture is. The ecumenical councils of the church can err, and have erred in the past, as have all the ancient churches, including Rome. In every case, their teaching must be evaluated and tested against the standard set by the Bible, and if that teaching can be shown to contradict the Scriptures, it must be abandoned. This of course, applies equally to the teaching and practice of the Church of England, for (unlike the other ancient churches of Christendom) it has never claimed to be infallible or in complete possession of the truth. Anglicans are, and always have been, open to receiving truth from wherever it may come, and because of this they have shown sympathy with a wider range of Christians than most other traditions have done. Even in the sixteenth century, the Church of England refused to call the pope the "Antichrist," however much it disagreed with him, nor was it prepared to excommunicate the Lutherans, despite its clear preference for a Reformed understanding of the sacraments. Very early on, it learned that some matters are best left to the judgment of the individual conscience because they are "things indifferent" (*adiaphora*) to the main issue of salvation.

These basic principles were first outlined in detail by Richard Hooker (1554–1600), whom some regard as the "founder" of Anglicanism. Hooker has often been given almost iconic status by High Churchmen, mainly because he opposed the Puritans, but their interpretation of his work is one-sided. Hooker was not a proto-Anglo-Catholic but a kind of Anglican fundamentalist, determined to uphold the doctrine and polity of the Church of England as Queen Elizabeth I had established it in 1559. Everything in that settlement, as it is usually called, he defended, whether it was really defensible or not! What Hooker wanted was not so much a state church as a church state, a society in which religious belief and practice would undergird the nation. That vision appealed to High Churchmen, especially after the Cromwellian period, but it was defeated in 1689 and had virtually disappeared from serious politics a generation later. Furthermore, Hooker was opposed to the Puritans on matters of ritual and polity, not on questions of doctrine. His argument was that since the points in dispute were *adiaphora*, the Puritans should accept the official line and stop trying to change everything. He was not trying to overthrow Reformed theology, and it is quite possible that had he been able to meet some of his later admirers, he would have recoiled from them in horror. Certainly he cannot be regarded as the founder or chief apologist of Anglicanism in any theological sense, and the status that he has been accorded by modern Anglo-Catholics in search of a pedigree is unwarranted. That he had a contribution to make toward our understanding of Anglicanism is certain, but that he created it is absurd, and his *Laws of Ecclesiastical Polity*, interesting as they are, cannot be accepted as the basis for Anglican thought and practice in the way that the articles, the *Homilies*, and the Prayer Book are.

Concentrating on the essentials, affirming what needs to be affirmed, denying what needs to be denied, and leaving the rest open to individual conviction has always been the hallmark of true Anglicanism, and when these principles have been observed, they have helped Anglicans maintain the preaching and teaching ministry that Christ gave to his disciples. This is not to deny that there have been lapses, and Anglicans must confess to their shame that at times their leaders have insisted (often for political reasons) that some things indifferent must be maintained. Inflexibility on this score undoubtedly contributed to the emergence of dissent after 1662, and it is only in recent years that a spirit of ecumenism has allowed such unnecessary divisions to be overcome to some degree. But having said that, we must insist that it is not the nature of Anglicanism, but the abuse of that nature, that caused these problems, and that it has been the rediscovery of first principles that has enabled the modern church to repair the damage caused by the excesses of earlier generations.

Anglican Ecclesiology

In matters of church discipline, the Anglican structure is basically a form of Congregationalism held together in an Episcopal framework. That will be disputed by ecclesiologists, but a glance at the reality will demonstrate just how true it is. Authority is dispersed in such a way that it is hard to say what the basic unit of the church is. Some claim that it is the parish; others say that it is the diocese, the national church, or even the Anglican Communion as a whole. A few would go even further and say that Anglicans have no right to alter traditional practices (like the ordination of men only) without the consensus of the entire Christian world. That such varied views on the locus of authority are possible shows how subtle the structures of Anglicanism are. A parish is free to order its pattern of worship in ways most suitable to it. It is expected to remain within the norms of Anglican liturgy, but that is by no means always the case nowadays, and for the most part wide latitude is permitted. The clergy are very diverse in theology and temperament, but this seldom causes much trouble because each parish operates as an autonomous unit. Outsiders think it contradictory that parish A has a woman minister who prays to a female God whereas parish B next door has a man openly opposed to women's ordination who regards praying to God as "she" as deeply heretical, and no doubt there is a sense in which they are right. It would obviously be better if they agreed, but what sort of agreement could they reach? Would one have to give way to the other, or would both be expected to accept a compromise solution that neither of them really liked?

The reality of life is that people will always find things to disagree about—the issues may vary at different times and in different places, but the urge to dissent stays the same. Given this situation, creating a structure in which both sides of an argument can find full and clear expression without being able to exclude the other has definite advantages. It permits a free flow of ideas and allows people to vote with their feet—after all, nobody is compelled to sit under the ministry of a preacher he or she does not like. Of course it is also true that this arrangement works to the benefit of both the wheat and the tares, which are allowed to grow together until the harvest. It is often deplored, and parish A may not be on speaking terms with parish B, but the system continues to function because everybody realizes that ultimately it works for them—my freedom to preach the gospel is protected by my willingness to allow others to say and do what they like, and as long as they remain within the guidelines set down by the church's official formularies, we can live with our differences. It is not an ideal situation, but the ideal is unattainable in a fallen world, and given the limitations of human nature, it may well be the best and most effective way of preserving both the unity and the diversity of the church.

Beyond the level of the parish, Anglican churches are held together by a network of bishops and synods that operate at different levels. A bishop is charged with the pastoral oversight of his diocese, but he cannot act alone. He has a synod to advise him and is unable to go against its wishes, although he can usually reject proposals from it that do not agree with wider Anglican practice (like allowing laypeople to celebrate Holy Communion). There have certainly been plenty of bad bishops, and many cases where bishops have tried to stack their dioceses with clergy amenable to them by excluding those of a different churchmanship. This is an abuse of Episcopal power, and in England it is minimized by a system in which many parochial appointments are out of the bishop's hands, but other parts of the Anglican Communion are less fortunate and often lack the safeguards they need in this respect. Tolerance for those of a different outlook is never easy, but it has always been one of the great strengths of Anglicanism, and bishops (in particular) need to be reminded of this when they seek to make their dioceses over in their own image.

Dioceses are grouped into provinces, which may form part of, or constitute, national churches. These national churches are fully autonomous, but they are expected to work in harmony with the other provinces of the Anglican Communion. It is the failure of the American Episcopal Church to do this that has led to the crisis that is causing the communion to reject it. The Americans have claimed that there is no limit to their autonomy, but if they wish to remain Anglicans in good standing, they must accept that in fact there is. It is a painful lesson to have to learn, but there is no alternative if the structures of the worldwide church are to mean anything. The future of American Anglicanism is impossible to predict, but it may be that the current problems will point the way to a restructuring that will create a genuinely Anglican church in the United States, one that will adhere to the communion's traditional faith and practice and accept that it cannot go its own way in the world.

Finally, the pattern of worship provided by the Book of Common Prayer is a model of balance in a field fraught with the dangers of succumbing to the excesses of personal taste. The Prayer Book provides daily services for morning and evening prayer, as well as a rite of Holy Communion explicitly designed to teach the doctrine of salvation by grace through faith alone. It is reverent without being superstitious and comprehensive without being exhaustive (or exhausting). Those who have had to sit through the seemingly endless prayers of pastors who say whatever comes into their heads and who end up repeating themselves over and over again have every reason to be grateful for Thomas Cranmer's remarkable economy of words and mastery of English style. There is nothing to compare with the elegant simplicity of classical Anglican worship.

Furthermore, virtually every word in the Prayer Book comes from the Bible; in a very real sense, it is the Scriptures turned into devotion. There are those who object to it on the ground that the words are fixed and do not allow for private expressions of prayer, but this is a misunderstanding. The Prayer Book is a guide to prayer, not a limitation placed on it. Nobody can be prevented from praying in his own words, and that was never the intention of Cranmer or of the others who subsequently revised and expanded his work. What they were concerned to do was to provide a model for people to absorb and to follow. The result is that it is possible to attend an Anglican service of worship and be spiritually edified by it, even if the leader is unskilled or indifferent and the preacher dreadful, because the words convey their own message. The value of the Prayer Book is nowhere more clearly seen than when it serves to remind the worshiper that God is present even in the direst circumstances, and that it is not the words of the minister but the ministry of the Word that characterizes the true church.

Relationships to (and with) Other Protestant Churches

No Christian church lives in a vacuum, and in the modern world what we think of other Christians has become a matter of immediate concern to everyone. The days when most people would seldom if ever meet a Christian whose views were very different from their own are over (if indeed they ever really existed), and the combined forces of globalization and secularization have made it necessary for us to develop a sense of solidarity with other Christian believers—an ecumenical movement at the practical level, which may or may not be related to the official dialogues that go under that name. Here Anglicans can fairly claim to have a good track record, even if it is far from flawless.

To understand Anglican attitudes toward ecumenical relations, we need to break them down into different categories. The first and most immediate of these concerns relations with churches that have broken away from the Church of England (or another member church of the Anglican Communion) and established separate denominations. The Methodists are the most obvious example of this, but we should probably include all the churches that have originated in the English-speaking world, like the Baptists, the Presbyterians, the Quakers, and so on. The second kind of relationship is the one between Anglicans and foreign Protestants, mainly Lutherans and Reformed churches with their roots in Northern Europe. Because most of these churches are national in character, relations with them have a political dimension that may outweigh other considerations, or a cultural one, especially in the United States, where churches of Dutch or Scandinavian origin can be somewhat difficult to relate to for that reason. Finally, there are relations with the ancient, pre-Reformation churches, mainly the Roman Catholic one of course, but also the Eastern Orthodox and the non-Chalcedonian churches of the East, which are unfamiliar to most of us but prominent in places like Ethiopia, Armenia, and India. Let us look at each of these in turn.

In the first case, the churches that emerged in England after the Reformation as dissenters from the national church are obviously problematic for Anglicans. Why did they leave us? Why do they stay separate now that the causes of the original schism have passed into history? Is there a problem with us, with them, or with both, and if so, how do we overcome it? Matters are not made any easier by the fact that dissenting groups are often much more aware of their origins than Anglicans are and are sometimes highly sensitive about them. For many people today denominational differences are mainly of historical interest and seldom affect relationships at a personal level. Members of dissenting churches are welcome at Anglican services and can participate fully in them, including Holy Communion. Such problems as there are usually affect only the clergy, who are more conscious of the reason for their separate existence than most laypeople are. But even here, it is the dissenting clergy who are more likely to be aware of the reasons for their existence than the Anglicans generally, who may have little knowledge of the history and feel no responsibility for what happened three hundred or more years ago. Anglicans tend to see these churches as bodies that started out enthusiastically but that over the years have mellowed, sometimes to the point where they are even deader than the church they originally left for that reason. Anglicans might worship in one of their congregations, especially if it happens to be a lively church in an area where the Anglican presence is weak or unsatisfactory, but few would be tempted to join one of them for purely theological reasons because it is hard to see that they have anything to offer that cannot be found somewhere within the Anglican fold. What do Methodists or Baptists have that Anglicans cannot find inside their own church? Not much is the answer, and so Anglicans see little reason to move in their direction. Even less would Anglicans be tempted to start their own independent churches, because the experience of those who did that in the past is a reminder of what is likely to happen again in the future.

As far as "foreign" Protestant churches are concerned, Anglican relations with them have usually been friendly but distant. In the past, that could be explained by political considerations. Englishmen seldom had much cause to go to Sweden or Switzerland, and those who did either fit in with what they found when they got there or else set up Anglican chaplaincies that served expatriate communities and ignored the locals. In Europe this is essentially the situation that still obtains, although there are intercommunion agreements with most of the Lutheran churches of Scandinavia and Germany. The fact of the matter is that barriers of language, culture, and political circumstance (many continental churches being much more closely tied to the state than the Church of England is) complicate matters to such an extent that there is little effort or desire to overcome them. On the other hand, Anglicans do not send missionaries to those countries, or if they do, the missionaries cooperate with the local churches and do not attempt to establish a separate Anglican denomination. The situation is different in settler countries like the United States, where people of many ethnic backgrounds live together, but there too, the problems created by a sense of "heritage" can be formidable. Anglicans usually have no problem worshiping in Lutheran or Reformed churches in America, and many do (and vice versa, of course), but the more they get involved with them, the more they realize that their background and traditions are different. In the end, it is usually easier to get along as good neighbors and cooperate wherever possible without trying to create a union that would achieve little and only upset those who are strongly attached to their own traditions and heritage.

Relations with Rome

Roman Catholics are in a different category altogether. In England they were not regarded as dissenters but as "recusants," that is, as people who refused to accept the Reformation, preferring to retain the old religion. In the sixteenth century a number of them went to the parish church and were known as "church papists," but after the defeat of the Spanish armada of 1588 that kind of compromise became harder to maintain, and church papistry died out. In Ireland there was a mass exodus from the state church and the establishment of a Roman Catholic alternative, but in England recusants dwindled in number and almost died out. When civil government broke down after 1640 and every kind of sect suddenly emerged, Catholics were not among them. The English civil war was fought between Episcopalians, Presbyterians, Baptists, and so on, but not Catholics, who were too few in number to matter. Roman Catholicism appeared to most English people as a foreign religion, which the pope, aided and abetted by the great powers of Spain, Austria, and France, was trying to reimpose on England. The fact that most Irish people remained Catholic did nothing to assuage these fears; on the contrary, the papacy was seen as trying to use Ireland as a dagger aimed at the Protestant heart of England.

In England today about 10 percent of the population is Roman Catholic, but most of these are of foreign or Irish origin and are felt to be somewhat exotic. A number of prominent Anglo-Catholics have embraced Roman Catholicism over the years, having persuaded themselves that the Anglican Church is not Catholic after all, but many of these people are eccentric and often highly critical of the church they have left. They are seldom a good advertisement for the Roman Church, which often discourages such conversions for that reason.

In other parts of the world, things can be very different, of course. In Latin America, for example, the flourishing Anglican churches in several countries are made up largely of ex-Catholics and their children, won to the Reformed faith by the preaching of the gospel. Anglicans in those countries are not particularly anti-Catholic, but they recognize that the Roman Church has been part of a corrupt establishment for centuries and has largely failed in its duty of reaching the masses for Christ. As is also the case in Ireland, Catholicism has been so mixed with folk religion and even with outright paganism that primary evangelism to nominal

Catholics is fully justified. One of the attractions of Anglicanism in such conditions is that it is sufficiently like the Roman Church in its outward forms as to make the transition from one to the other psychologically easier for many. It can also be said that Anglicans generally dislike the sort of bitter anti-Catholicism that is often found in Protestant converts and do their best to discourage it. We do not want to fill our pews with people who are there mainly because they are dissatisfied with some other church!

Does Roman Catholicism hold any attraction for Anglicans? For Anglo-Catholics it clearly does, but this is because they have been taught to be unhappy with their own church and cannot be regarded as typical. For others, the situation is more complex. On the one hand, Anglicans often appreciate good Roman Catholic theology and are affected by the art, music, and literature that comes from that church as much as anyone else. They may be moved by Catholic devotional writing and happily attend Catholic services, especially in European countries where a Protestant alternative is not readily available. On the other hand, they are usually repelled by the veneration of saints and their relics, and by the cult of the Virgin Mary, which strikes them as alien and unbiblical.

At the more sophisticated theological level, the great weakness of Roman Catholicism is that its claims are not sufficiently grounded in Scripture. There is no evidence that the apostle Peter was the first bishop of Rome or that Jesus ever intended him to be the leader of the church. Yet everything the Roman Catholic Church claims for itself is predicated on those assumptions! We have no hesitation in saying that papal infallibility is a false doctrine, forced down the throats of the bishops assembled in Rome in 1870, at the very moment when the papacy had to shore up its spiritual authority to counter its loss of secular power. The record of the Roman Church as the oppressor of its own people, especially in Ireland, is too well known for anyone to accept that Catholicism is a superior form of Christianity, and its clericalization and internal censorship contrast badly with the active lay involvement and intellectual openness found among Anglicans. The classic argument that the Roman Catholic Church goes back to the New Testament whereas Protestantism dates from only the sixteenth century does not wash with Anglicans, because Anglicans claim the heritage of the pre-Reformation church, especially in the British Isles. It may be stretching things somewhat to claim Patrick for the Anglican Church (though some have done so), but with the Venerable Bede there is no doubt in the minds of most Anglicans that he was a proper Englishman, in communion with Rome to be sure, but not subject to its authority in the way that modern Roman Catholics are. To the Anglican mind, the study of the church fathers supports their view of the church, not that of Rome, which they believe has changed beyond all recognition since the days of Ambrose or Augustine. Modern Roman Catholicism is at least as different from the ancient and medieval church as Anglicanism is, and so Roman claims to historical continuity fall flat on Anglican ears.

Relations with the East

This attitude is fortified by the existence of the Eastern Orthodox churches and the rather warm relations that Anglicans have traditionally had with them. To some extent, Anglican-Orthodox understanding has been based on the existence of Rome as the common enemy, but that is not the whole story. Orthodoxy's preference for national churches in close relationship to the state strikes a chord with Anglicans, who have often perceived the Church of England in much the same way. The decentralized nature of authority in the Orthodox world, the relative freedom to discuss ideas, and the prominence of laypeople in theological faculties also appeal to Anglicans, who are suspicious of overclericalization. In recent times, the persecution many Orthodox believers have suffered at the hands of the Turks or the communists has also created a bond of sympathy for them that should not be underestimated. Having said that, however, we must recognize that there are also big problems with the Orthodox churches from the Anglican point of view, and these must be weighed very carefully.

First of all, there is a wide gap between what the Orthodox church claims for itself and the reality on the ground. Orthodoxy claims to be the one true, universal church, yet it is more closely tied to certain national groups than any other Christian body. Anglicanism may be the national church of England, but there is no fusion between it and "Englishness" comparable to what one finds in Greece or Russia, and Anglicans would be appalled if there were. As much as Englishmen like their country, they would never dream of suggesting that theirs is the only true church! Orthodoxy also claims to be a spiritual communion free of the juridical bondage to legalism so prominent and so divisive in the

Western churches. Begone endless disputes about election, justification, and the validity of orders, all of which the Orthodox attribute to just that kind of mentality. Yet they seem not to notice that the Orthodox world itself is riven by disputes that are not merely legalistic, but petty to boot. Westerners may be wrong to argue about the finer points of justification, but at least it is the salvation of mankind that is at stake. Can this be said for the interminable Orthodox arguments about whether to use the Gregorian or the Julian calendar? What about the schism of the Old Believers in Russia, in which thousands of innocent people were put to death merely because their ritual practices failed to keep up with the times? How is it that such a supposedly warm brotherhood of churches is forever falling out over jurisdictional quarrels, like the status of the churches of Macedonia and Estonia, which have broken away from Serbia and Russia (respectively) but have been recognized only by some and not by all the other Orthodox churches, almost entirely for political reasons? (The situation in Ukraine is even more appalling in this regard.)

Orthodox theologians boast of their church's willingness to bend the rules when necessary, a practice they refer to as "economy," and contrast favorably with what they perceive as Western rigidity. One of their favorite illustrations of this is the way they accept divorce—an Orthodox person can marry and divorce three times before it is forbidden! This sounds compassionate when compared to the Western unwillingness to accept divorce at all, but it has to be balanced against the fact that a married Orthodox priest who loses his wife, even in childbirth, is not allowed to remarry. Economy clearly has its limits! How is it possible for a church as important as this one to be so blind to its own behavior?

Then too, there are important differences of doctrine that are all too easy to overlook or regard as of secondary importance. One of them concerns the procession of the Holy Spirit, which the Western churches agree is from the Father and the Son, a view rejected by the Eastern Orthodox for a variety of reasons, some of which are better than others. Without going into this in detail, we have to say that the procession of the Holy Spirit from the Son as well as from the Father is an important ingredient in Western spirituality because it ties the work of the Son into the experience of the Spirit, who comes to dwell in our hearts by faith. It is one thing for the Orthodox to object that the Western church added the phrase to the Nicene Creed without consulting them, but the vehemence with which the Orthodox have consistently denied the substance of the doctrine is disconcerting, especially as it can be defended by a careful exegesis of the relevant New Testament texts. It is hard not to think that the Orthodox have allowed tradition to close their minds to the truth, and that the need to defend the former will forever prevent them from accepting the latter.

There is also a problem with the place of icons in the life and worship of the church. This is defended on the ground that Jesus was visible in the flesh, and so it must be possible to make pictures of him. To deny that is to deny the reality of the incarnation. Anglicans and other Western Christians certainly agree with the Orthodox about that, but they also note that there is no description of Jesus in the New Testament, so that any portrait of him must be conjectural. To make one and then venerate it as a true representation of the Son of God is going too far, and of course the phenomenon of wonder-working icons and the like is totally without biblical support. As with the veneration of relics, that of icons is little more than a reintroduction of paganism into the church by the back door. Some Western Christians, including evangelicals, have been attracted to Eastern Orthodoxy because it offers liturgical pomp and mystical experience of a kind not readily available in evangelical churches, but Anglicans have (or can have) both of these if they want to, so the attraction of Orthodoxy is only the appeal of the exotic—hardly a sufficient basis for conversion.

Having said all this, I should emphasize that Anglicans do not dismiss Roman Catholics or Eastern Orthodox as non-Christians or regard their churches as somehow inferior to our own. We do not plant Anglican churches in Italy or Greece, other than chaplaincies that minister to expatriate congregations of English-speaking people. The Anglican churches that exist in Spain and Portugal are exceptions, but they have emerged from local breakaways from the Catholic Church and are not the result of Anglican proselytizing. It is true that we often cooperate with minority Protestant churches in those countries and defend their right to evangelize without interference, but we are also keen to see the Catholic and Orthodox churches reformed according to the Word of God, in the way we believe happened to us in the sixteenth century.

The Enduring Legacy

So why am I still an Anglican? It is not because I have considered the alternatives, decided that each of them has its problems, and concluded that I might as well stay where I am. I am neither a dyed-in-the-wool Anglican, incapable of going elsewhere, nor a particularly strong critic of other churches. At various times I have worshiped with Presbyterians, Baptists, Plymouth Brethren, Lutherans, Roman Catholics, and Eastern Orthodox, among others. I do not agree with everything those churches say and do—it would be impossible to agree with them all—but I have grown to respect them and to learn from them. Nor can I honestly say that I am equally at home with every different kind of Anglican—that too would be impossible, or at least implausible! Even within my own conservative evangelical subset of Anglicanism, I find some things more congenial than others and would be reluctant to give a blanket endorsement to everything that goes under that name. Here too, I have learned to appreciate different approaches without feeling obliged to agree with them. Some of them indeed I would actively oppose because (to my mind at least) they go beyond what is acceptably Anglican, or even Christian. If it is the lot of the saints to have their patience tried to the limit, then the Anglican Communion must be God's chosen vessel for the purpose! But having said that, I remain an Anglican for a number of positive reasons that I would outline, by way of conclusion to this essay, as follows.

First, Anglicanism's glory is that it strives to be "basic" or "mere" Christianity. It is no accident that two of the best-selling popular Christian books of the last century have borne precisely those titles, nor that both have been written by Anglicans—John Stott's *Basic Christianity* and C. S. Lewis's *Mere Christianity*. Stott spent almost all his active ministerial life attached to the church of All Souls, Langham Place (London), but he rapidly became known around the world as a gifted speaker and evangelist. After becoming rector emeritus of the church in 1975, he spent the remaining years of his ministry traveling the globe, and as time went on became better known in parts of Asia and Africa than he was at home. His Anglicanism was sincere and ably defended, but it was never a barrier to others, and his message was universally well received by those who love the gospel, regardless of their own church or national background. The opposition that he faced came mostly from other Anglicans, for whom basic Christianity was just too much to swallow.

C. S. Lewis had in some respects an even more remarkable career. After having been a young atheist, he was converted to Christianity at Oxford and became one of the best popular apologists for the Christian faith until his death in 1963. Lewis was a Broad Churchman who avoided party labels and stayed out of the controversies that defined them, but the fact that he is claimed by evangelicals and Catholics alike, including Roman Catholics, testifies to his ability to hold the middle ground in a positive and winsome way. He also became a widely read children's author, even though he was a bachelor almost all his life and never had children of his own. In their different ways, these two men typify something essential about Anglicanism. It is concerned not with itself or its own identity, but with the truth of the gospel, with basic, mere Christianity—the faith that can undergird a wide range of individual beliefs and practices because it concentrates on what is fundamental.

Interestingly enough, neither Lewis nor Stott has been branded as a "fundamentalist," though both were uncompromisingly orthodox in their theology and recognized the liberalism of their time as the greatest enemy they had to face. Somehow, the way they engaged in controversy and defended their faith made it difficult to pin the fundamentalist label on them. They were too reasonable, too willing to take their opponents seriously, too gracious in replying to them, for such a negative description to stick. They were, in a word, too Anglican—too open to other ideas and influences, too willing to compromise on nonessentials, too interested in life beyond the narrow confines of theological controversy. Like all men, they had their limitations and their blind spots, but their legacy has defied their critics, and there is no doubt that they will both be widely read long after the latter have passed into oblivion (as many of them have already done).

To the legacy of these two men can be added an impressive list of creative writers, stretching right back to the Reformation. It is obvious that the canon of English literature is heavily populated by Anglicans, but this tradition has continued to the present day. The novelist P. D. James, for example, manages to be a top-notch crime writer and a devout Anglican, and both Susan Howatch and Jan Karon write from the perspective of a deep Anglican faith. The world of music and of the visual arts has a similar roll call of prominent Anglican names, and Anglicans can be found at the forefront of many social and political enterprises designed to promote and apply the Christian gospel in different walks of life. Anglicanism is not just mere Christianity, it is *applied* Christianity, a faith that leads to action. Furthermore, it is important to note that many of those who are most active in these areas are not ordained clergy, but laypeople. Unlike Roman Catholicism, Anglicanism is not clergy dominated, and media focus on the utterances of bishops and archbishops gives a misleading impression. Anglicans certainly have their share of official church spokesmen and bodies set up to deal with a vast array of issues great and small, but it is not there that the church makes its greatest impact. Rather, it is in the dedication of particular individuals who draw strength from their heritage and who put their faith into practice that the true influence of Anglicanism is brought to bear on the world.

As the Book of Common Prayer was designed to do, Anglicanism has created a participatory church. The laity are not passive recipients of whatever the clergy throw at them, but active participants in both worship and church government. It has even been claimed that the English Reformation was the victory of the laity over the clergy, because ultimate authority for the church's life and doctrine was vested in the king and Parliament, not in the bishops. Whether that is really true or not, today's Anglicanism combines a traditional clerical hierarchy with a democratic church government in a way that is unique in the Christian world. Order is preserved, but everyone has a voice, and the flexibility of the structures makes it possible for a vast range of competing and sometimes mutually incompatible views to coexist under a single ecclesiastical umbrella.

This is not to say that this coexistence is always easy, and it must be admitted that many subsets of Anglicans are barely on speaking terms with one another. It is also sadly true that the Anglican Communion harbors openly heretical elements that are difficult to expunge, precisely because of this extraordinary tolerance. But people like David Jenkins (the former bishop of Durham who denied the bodily resurrection of Christ) and John Shelby Spong (the retired bishop of Newark, New Jersey, who has denied almost everything) come and go, rattling a few cages during their brief time in the spotlight and then disappearing into eternal darkness. The church will survive them as it has survived countless others in the past who have done similar things. The best-selling religious book of 1963 was John Robinson's *Honest to God*, in which the then bishop of Woolwich tried to debunk much of traditional Christian orthodoxy. But Robinson's fame was ephemeral, as many predicted it would be. He died in 1983 and is no longer read by anyone—remembered only by the dwindling company of those who knew him.

It can be hard to let such people have their say and to refrain from prosecuting them for their clear and unambiguous deviations from the faith, but leaving them alone robs them of the glory of martyrdom and ensures that they will soon be forgotten. Many people still read Jim Packer's little book *Fundamentalism and the Word of God*, but how many remember that it was written in response to Gabriel Hebert's attack on Billy Graham in a book entitled *Fundamentalism and the Church of God*? No one reads Hebert now, or has ever heard of him, and it is safe to say that future generations will learn of him only by reading Dr. Packer's reply—rather in the way that we now know about second-century Gnostics only because of the rebuttals produced by their orthodox opponents.

Anglicanism's patience and willingness to tolerate a wide range of ideas means that it is also a church in which the freedom of the Spirit is more than just an intellectual expression. Anglicans are free to start spiritual initiatives, and many of them do. In recent years, churches all over the world and of every denomination have done the Alpha Course, but how many people realize that this was conceived and developed at Holy Trinity, Brompton (London), and remains fundamentally Anglican in expression and outlook? Alpha has many critics, and there is much in it to criticize, but the fact remains that it has been picked up, often in a modified form, and used around the world by thousands of churches that are in no way "Anglican." Can any other branch of Christendom produce something comparable? One of the great blessings of this Anglican sense of freedom is that Anglican initiatives are always open and readily available to Christians of every denomination. Just as everyone is welcome to take Communion in an Anglican church without being quizzed on his or her theological soundness, so all are welcome to take what the Anglican Church has to offer and use it as they wish. Would Catholics touch Alpha if it were Baptist, or Baptists if it were Catholic in origin? Probably not, but as it is Anglican, both can and do use it without hesitation. At the same time, other Anglicans are free not to use it, and even to develop alternatives that their creators regard as superior, because at the end of the day, Alpha is a private initiative, not an official church product, and carries neither copyright nor imprimatur from any church authority.

Anglicans give a great deal to world Christianity, but the reverse is also true. They are happy to pick up things from any church and use them to the glory of God, without asking where they came from. It is by no means uncommon to find Anglicans using material derived from Roman Catholic and evangelical sources side by side, the only criterion for acceptance being the glory of God. There is no tendency to hero-worship anyone or to canonize anything—Henri Nouwen or John Piper will be read and enjoyed by different kinds of people, but neither will be regarded as a being above criticism, and neither will appeal equally to every Anglican. All that can be said for sure is that in neither case does the denominational label they wear matter in the slightest; they are judged and appreciated (or not) on their merits, not on their backgrounds.

Freedom of this kind is a very precious thing, and while it does not prevent the indiscriminate use of unsuitable material, it does help train people to try and examine things for themselves, to see whether they are of God or not. Anglicans respond badly to being told what to do, but they are not fools, and usually they can discern the good from the unacceptable and choose accordingly. The fact that they are free to do so is a reminder that Anglicanism is a faith designed for mature, responsible adults, a breed that is in constant danger of imminent extinction in a world where fashion and prejudice so often tend to rule all.

Finally, and perhaps most important, Anglicanism is outward looking. It is not possible to be a national church and claim responsibility for what is now a worldwide cultural community without recognizing that not everyone who comes under that umbrella has a living faith in the God of the Bible. There will always be a large number of people in every walk of life who do not believe in that God, or who have serious doubts about a faith they would like to have but find difficult. Many churches ignore such people or accommodate them in inadequate ways. The stricter Protestant bodies would most likely put up barriers and exclude them, whereas the Roman Catholic Church would demand minimal compliance but not expect anything more—weekly mass attendance perhaps, with no questions asked or answered about what they think, say, or do the rest of the time. Anglicanism is not like that. Anglicans tackle society head on, sometimes with unexpected and unfortunate results, but never without courage and determination.

This is obvious in the present crisis over homosexual practice. The Anglican Communion is the only major Christian church dealing with this as an internal matter, although it is obvious that social attitudes are changing fast and traditional Christian values are being questioned all over the place. The Roman Catholic Church, which harbors a wide assortment of pedophiles in its midst, keeps its head down and says little about the subject. Many other churches do the same, or content themselves with blanket condemnations, but Anglicans engage the issues, with partisans on all sides of the debate. It is often a messy business, but it is fair to say that nowhere outside the Anglican Communion is such a debate going on. Most secular authorities have caved in to the homosexual lobby, and liberal Anglicans who take their cue from them would like to follow suit. But their attempts to impose their views on the wider church have failed, and they have stirred up widespread opposition instead.

Moreover, that opposition is far from being mindless or knee-jerk in its reaction. On the contrary, it has taken the whole thing very seriously and explored the questions raised by the homosexual lobby, sometimes in great detail. That this opposition has dared to challenge such a powerful vested interest is very much to its credit, and the American Episcopal Church, which has bowed to the homosexual lobby on the pretext that acquiescence is required by the church's mission to the world, may find that it is excluded from the Anglican Communion precisely because it has failed to take that mission seriously enough. For an open-minded approach to such matters is not to be confused with an uncritical acceptance of them. Anglicans can be polite and thoughtful in their assessment of new ideas without being persuaded by the arguments put to them, and the true genius of their tradition is that they can defend orthodoxy with grace and conviction in a way that discredits the opposition and brings glory to the gospel of Christ. We are no more afraid of sex than we are of science—both are necessary ingredients of human life, but neither defines the purpose of human living, and those who think they do must be strenuously resisted.

That is why I am an Anglican and glad to remain one. I do not want to be on the sidelines in the battle for the soul of the world, but to be engaged in the thick of the fight, clothed with the whole armor of God and fighting every inch of the way against the wiles of the Devil. That is what Jesus did during his sojourn on earth, and that is what we who are called to follow him are also expected to do. May God grant us the grace to fulfill our mission, so that at the end of the day we may stand before his throne and hear him say to us, as he will say to all those who have faithfully given their lives for his sake, "Well done, good and faithful servant; enter into the joy of your Lord."

Why I Am an Evangelical and a Baptist

Timothy F. George

I am writing this essay to explain, for those who may be interested to know, why I am an evangelical and a Baptist. Such a project seems justified in that there are certainly many evangelicals who are not Baptists, and some Baptists who would not call themselves evangelicals. There are still others who are both evangelical and Baptist but who do not bring to this dual commitment all the excess "baggage" that I seem to have accrued during my life of more than six decades. For example, I have been called, with varying degrees of plausibility, a fundamentalist, an inerrantist, a premillennialist, an ecumenist, a liturgist, a Calvinist, and a Barthian, among other appellations best left unremembered. One can certainly be an evangelical and a Baptist without embracing all of that!

For a conference on ecclesiology, I once prepared a talk called "The Confessions of a Catholic-Friendly Reformed Baptist with a Hankering after Lutheranism and a Strong Affinity for the Book of Common Prayer." That talk and this essay are perforce more autobiographical than might be expected of one who has read in the New Testament that "what we preach is not ourselves, but Jesus Christ as Lord" (2 Cor. 4:5).[1] But we are also admonished to be ready ever to give an *apologia*, a reasoned defense, to anyone who asks for an account of the faith and hope we have in Jesus Christ (1 Pet. 3:15). To refuse to do so would be an act of supreme ingratitude, as Saint Augustine realized in writing his own *Confessions*. In his struggles against the Pelagians, Augustine often quoted Paul's three questions: "For who makes you different from

---

[1] Unless otherwise indicated, Scripture quotations in this chapter are from the New International Version, 2011 edition.

anyone else? What do you have that you did not receive? And if you did receive it, why do you boast as though you did not?" (1 Cor. 4:7). Those questions have resonated deeply in my own life ever since Augustine made me aware of them.

For all that, I still have a lingering reservation about the theme of this essay. Several years ago I participated in a symposium sponsored by *Touchstone*, a magazine that calls itself "A Journal of Mere Christianity." The conference, which included speakers from various traditions— Orthodox, Catholic, Lutheran, Methodist, and Baptist—was dubbed "Christian Unity and the Divisions We Must Sustain." The conference framers might well have called our gathering "Christians Divided and the Unity We Seek." But their emphasis, I think, was rightly put on the fundamental unity we shared as believers in Jesus Christ, not on the differences that in conscience we all agreed we had to maintain.

Another way to express this point is to refer to the Roman Catholic notion of the "hierarchy of the truths of faith." This concept is based on the belief that in the economy of divine revelation, greater priority, more theological weight, as it were, is given to those teachings that relate directly to the foundational truths of the Christian faith, such as the doctrine of the Holy Trinity, than to other teachings of the church, such as the requirement of clerical celibacy. In this vein, I would like to propose a "hierarchy of ecclesial identity." What do I mean by this? While I recognize myself as a Protestant, an evangelical, and a Baptist, none of those labels defines my spiritual and ecclesial identity at the most basic core level. Being an evangelical Protestant, a Baptist, indeed a Southern Baptist, are all important markers of my place within the community of faith, but there is a more primary identity I must confess: I am a Trinitarian Christian who by the grace of God belongs to the whole company of the redeemed through the ages, those who are "very members incorporate in the mystical body" of Christ (Book of Common Prayer).

Far from being a new construal, this way of putting things goes to the very heart of what it means to be a genuine Protestant, a true evangelical, and an authentic Baptist. Central to each of these commitments is a desire to be faithful to the Scripture-based apostolic witness of the early church. When Polycarp of Smyrna, a disciple of the apostle John, was brought before the Roman tribunal before being cast into the arena with wild beasts, he confessed publicly the faith that he knew would lead to his certain martyrdom. In that critical moment, Polycarp did not say, "I am a Paulinist. I am a Petrist. I am an Ignatian" (after his great contemporary Ignatius of Antioch). Nor did he say, "I am an Irenaean" (after his famous disciple, Irenaeus of Lyon). Rather he confessed, "*Christianus sum*" ("I am a Christian"). While Polycarp is not a name every Baptist would know, the Bedford tinker, John Bunyan, was one of us. Bunyan was a Protestant greatly influenced by Luther; a Puritan, as evangelicals in seventeenth-century England were called; and a Baptist, of the open-membership Calvinistic variety. But when asked by which party label he desired to be called, Bunyan replied:

> Since you would know by what name I would be distinguished from others, I tell you I would be and hope I am a Christian; and choose, if God should count me worthy, to be called a Christian, a believer, or other such name as should be approved by the Holy Ghost. And as for those factious titles of Ana-Baptist, Presbyterian, Independent, or the like, I conclude that they come neither from Antioch nor from Jerusalem, but from hell and Babylon, for they tend to division. You know them by their fruits.[2]

As John Bunyan knew well, labels can be libels. Labels are supposed to be accurate descriptors, but they often distort as much as they reveal. Nonetheless, the desire for a generic Christianity shorn of all particularity carries its own risks. The Corinthian church of the New Testament had its own "factious titles": the Paul party, the Peter sect, the Apollos coterie. Frustrated with such fractiousness, another group in the church at Corinth arose claiming to have no human leader at all: "We belong to Christ," they said. But, in fact, the Christ party at Corinth was soon beset by the same spirit of arrogance and divisiveness that had marked all

---

[2]John Bunyan, *Peaceable Principles and True* (1674), 2:648. Bunyan's single-minded commitment to stay close to the heart of the gospel makes him an attractive model for Baptist evangelicals of all generations. In his spiritual autobiography, *Grace Abounding to the Chief of Sinners*, Bunyan described his own strategy for engaging in theological polemics: "I never cared to meddle with things that were controverted, and in dispute among the saints, especially things of the lowest nature; yet it pleased me much to contend with great earnestness for the word of faith; and the remission of sins by the death and sufferings of Jesus; but I say, as to other things, I should let them alone, because I saw they engendered strife, and because I saw that they neither in doing nor in leaving undone, did commend us to God to be his; besides, I saw my work before me did run in another channel even to carry an awakening word; to that therefore did I stick and adhere." Bunyan, *Grace Abounding to the Chief of Sinners* (New York: Penguin, 1987), 284.

the other partisan groups in the congregation. This is a recurring theme throughout the history of the church. In nineteenth-century America, Alexander Campbell, a sometime Baptist, wanted to eliminate denominational labels and "restore" the one true "Christian" church. In the end, of course, he succeeded in further fracturing the body of Christ by founding yet another sect, a new denomination that, within one generation, had itself further subdivided into three distinct and often mutually hostile church bodies. This will sound like déjà vu to anyone familiar with the history of Presbyterians in Scotland, Lutherans in Scandinavia, Reformed churches in the Netherlands, Anglicans in Africa, and Baptists almost anywhere. With these caveats in mind, it remains for me to say why I am an evangelical and a Baptist.

Evangelical Renewal

Once I wrote a brief article for *Christianity Today* titled "If I'm an Evangelical, What Am I?" I pointed out that it is relatively easy to say who a Roman Catholic is: a Roman Catholic is a person who belongs to a church whose bishop is in communion with the bishop of Rome. Likewise, Orthodox believers can be fairly easily recognized by certain creedal commitments and liturgical practices, as well as by national and ethnic loyalties. But evangelicalism is a movement of bewildering diversity, made up of congregations, denominations, and parachurch movements whose shared identity is not tied to a particular view of church polity or ministerial orders. Evangelicalism has been fed by many diverse rivulets and tributaries, including Puritanism, Pietism, and most vigorously in the last hundred years, Pentecostalism.

Historian David Bebbington's famous quadrilateral identifies four distinguishing markers of this heterogeneous family. Evangelicals, Bebbington declares, are a worldwide fellowship of Bible-believing Christians characterized by four primary traits: (1) the authority and sufficiency of Holy Scripture, the only normative rule of faith and practice for all true believers; (2) the uniqueness of redemption through the death of Christ upon the cross (what Bebbington calls *crucicentrism*); (3) the necessity of personal conversion wrought by the Holy Spirit through personal repentance and faith, the experience of being "born again" that issues in a life of obedience and growth in Christ; and (4) the priority and urgency of evangelism and missions in fulfillment of the Great Commission of

Christ himself. These traits are often blended into a kind of intense activism that prompted theologian Wolfhart Pannenberg to recognize evangelicals, along with Roman Catholic and Orthodox believers, as one of three ascendant, resilient forces within world Christianity at the dawn of the third millennium.

This is a helpful way of describing the global evangelical family, but I have proposed a more diachronic definition: Evangelicalism is a renewal movement within historic Christian orthodoxy, a movement that has been shaped in various ways by three historical complexes or "moments." Each of these continues to affect evangelical theology and identity today.

The Trinitarian and Christological Consensus of the Early Church

Evangelicals accept without hesitation what Anglican theologians used to refer to (perhaps some still do) as the *consensus quinquesaecularis*, the theological consensus of the first five centuries as represented by the historic creeds of the early church. That is to say, evangelicals worship and adore the one and only and true and living God, who has forever known himself as the Father, the Son, and the Holy Spirit. They further believe that this triune God of love and holiness became incarnate in Jesus of Nazareth, the Son of Man of the four canonical Gospels. Evangelicals, no less than Roman Catholics and Orthodox believers, thus stand in fundamental continuity with the Trinitarian and christological consensus of the early church, including the affirmation of Mary as *theotokos* (the term but not the doctrine has been questioned by some), the condemnation of Pelagianism (Reformed and Wesleyan Christians agree on this), and the Definition of Chalcedon: Jesus Christ fully God and true man.

From time to time evangelicals have explicitly stated their agreement with the historic creeds of the church. For example, an English Baptist confession, known as "The Orthodox Creed," published in 1679, reproduced the Apostles', Nicene, and Athanasian Creeds in toto and commended all three as worthy to be received and believed, as their teaching was deemed consonant with Holy Scripture. More recently, at the opening meeting of the Baptist World Alliance of 1905 in London, Alexander Maclaren asked the entire assembly to rise and confess in unison the Apostles' Creed as a way of expressing Baptist solidarity with the orthodox Christian faith. This same act was repeated one hundred years later at the centennial celebration of the BWA at Birmingham, England, in 2005.

In the year 2000, some twelve thousand evangelical Christians from 210 countries around the world, more than the number belonging to the United Nations at the time, gathered in Amsterdam at the invitation of Billy Graham to pray, reflect, and renew their commitment to world evangelization. Out of this assembly emerged the "Amsterdam Declaration," which again echoed the language of the Trinitarian christological faith of the church:

> God in his own being is a community of three co-equal and co-eternal persons, who are revealed to us in the Bible as the Father, the Son, and the Holy Spirit. Together they are involved in an unvarying cooperative pattern in all God's relationships to and within this world. God is the Lord of history, where he blesses his own people, overcomes and judges human and angelic rebels against his rule, and will finally renew the whole created order.

The Protestant Reformation

Evangelicals are reformational Christians in that they embrace both the formal and material principles of the Protestant Reformers. The formal principle declares that the Bible, God's Word written, is the supreme standard, the *norma normans*, by which all other teachings and traditions are to be judged. Holy Scripture is the sure rule of all Christian doctrine and conduct. The material principle of the Reformation centers on the doctrine of justification by faith alone. This was not a new doctrine discovered for the first time in the sixteenth century but, as the Reformers all believed, the logical and necessary consequence of the ecumenical orthodoxy affirmed by Catholics and Protestants alike. Jaroslav Pelikan has summarized well the essence of their argument:

> If the Holy Trinity was as holy as the trinitarian dogma taught; if original sin was as virulent as the Augustinian tradition said it was; and if Christ was as necessary as the christological dogma implied—then the only way to treat justification in a manner faithful to the Catholic tradition was to teach justification by faith.[3]

---

[3] Jaroslav Pelikan, *Obedient Rebels: Catholic Substance and Protestant Principle in Luther's Reformation* (New York: Harper and Row, 1964), 50–51.

John Calvin spoke for all of the mainline Reformers when, in his debate with Cardinal Jacopo Sadoleto, he argued that Protestant believers represented true Catholicism while the Church of Rome had become a sect.[4]

Awakenings

At this point, some readers may well think, "Thus far you haven't told us anything that is unique to evangelicals! All of this material is common to Protestants and Christians in general." And, of course, *this is precisely the point*! Theological innovation is not a hallmark of the evangelical faith. Evangelicals aim to be mere Christians, not *mere* in the weak, attenuated sense of the word, in the sense of "only this," "nothing more than," "such and no more," "barely," "hardly." In its full, undiluted sense, the word *mere* means "truly," "indeed," "absolute." This is what C. S. Lewis meant by the term "mere Christianity," and it is the sense in which evangelicals belong to what has been called the Great Tradition of Christian faith and doctrine.

Evangelicals gladly identify with the early church and the Protestant Reformation, but they also take their bearings from the spiritual awakenings of the eighteenth and nineteenth centuries, which produced many of the forms and modalities of evangelicalism recognized today. The awakenings were international, transatlantic movements of ecclesial and spiritual renewal embracing Pietism in Germany, Methodism in Great Britain, and revivalism in the American colonies. Only in the light of these various awakenings can we understand what historian Timothy L. Smith has called "the kaleidoscopic diversity of our histories, our organizational structures, and our doctrinal emphases."[5] The awakenings spawned a host of interdenominational ministries, including orphanages, Bible societies, publication boards, colleges and academies, and above all, an evangelical missionary movement of global proportions.

The world Protestant missionary movement began humbly enough when an English Baptist shoemaker named William Carey encouraged his fellow Calvinistic Baptists to establish a society for "the propagation of the Gospel among the heathens." By 1793, Carey had arrived in

---

[4]John Calvin and Jacopo Sadoleto, *A Reformation Debate*, ed. John C. Olin (New York: Harper and Row, 1966).

[5]Timothy L. Smith, "The Evangelical Kaleidoscope and the Call to Christian Unity," *Christian Scholar's Review* 15 (1986): 125.

India to begin his remarkable career of more than forty years. Carey's work included the planting of churches, the building of schools, the organization of an agricultural society, the establishment of India's first newspaper, and the translation of the Scriptures into some forty languages and dialects. Carey was a Baptist, indeed a rather strict one, but from the beginning of his mission to India, he saw the importance of working closely with non-Baptist evangelicals, including the Anglican missionary Henry Martyn. The school he established at Serampore was interdenominational, although all professors were required to embrace the essential evangelical doctrines, such as the deity of Christ and his substitutionary atonement. Carey also called for a gathering of Christians of all denominations, which he hoped would meet in 1810 to coordinate a strategy for world evangelization. Precisely one century after the year Carey had proposed for such a gathering, the first international mission conference convened in Edinburgh in 1910. Whatever may be said about the course of recent modern ecumenical endeavors, the modern movement for Christian unity was born on the mission field, and its midwife was an evangelical Baptist. The awakenings also gave rise to numerous evangelical movements for social reform including, in England, a call for the end of the slave trade and, in North America, the abolition of slavery itself.

Growing up as a Baptist in the South, I was an evangelical without being aware of it. As a teenage youth evangelist, I greatly admired Billy Graham—a Southern Baptist who helped to define post–World War II global evangelicalism—and also had personal contact with figures such as Stuart Briscoe, Major Ian Thomas, and Robert G. Lee, a Baptist icon known for his pulpit oratory who had also been present at the founding meeting of the National Association of Evangelicals. But it was Francis Schaeffer who really introduced me to the broader evangelical family outside my own Baptist briar patch. As a student in college, I devoured Schaeffer's early books on apologetics. Even then I knew enough philosophy and history not to accept uncritically everything Schaeffer wrote, but he showed me how the Christian faith could engage with art, music, competing worldviews, and diverse religious thought.

All of this was preparation for the seven years (1972–1979) I spent in New England as a student at Harvard Divinity School. My own sense of evangelical identity was solidified during those turbulent years from two separate but interrelated trajectories. First, I was forced by my studies to dig deep into the primary sources of Christian theology. I was especially interested in the development of Christian doctrine and became well acquainted with the classic studies of John Henry Newman, Adolf von Harnack, and Jaroslav Pelikan. I also read extensively in the church fathers, the medieval schoolmen, and the Reformers of the sixteenth century. I came to appreciate what the great Orthodox theologian Georges Florovsky once called the "ecumenism of time" as well as of space. And though I had doubts along the way, I also learned how to doubt my doubts. I learned how to think critically, constructively, and dialogically. I learned how to "think with the church," with the body of Christ extended throughout time as well as space. Through such testing, I found the fibers of the evangelical faith to be resilient and sustaining. During those years of critical reading and rigorous study, I discovered no argument against the historic evangelical faith that had not already been considered and refuted by many others who had come before me. This gave me the confidence to face new challenges in the future with humility and equanimity.

During the years I spent in Boston, my theological education was done in stereo. On the one hand, I was immersed in books, ideas, discussion, and debate—the kinds of things that go with the intellectual ferment of serious academic work. At the same time I also served as a pastor, first of a small Baptist church in the inner city, and then of a largely student congregation near the Harvard campus. That pastoral experience saved me from the kind of academic gnosticism and abstractionist theology to which many seminary students fall prey. During the day I was confronted with new ideas and mind-stretching seminars, lectures, and research, but each evening I came home to the messy life-and-death issues confronted in the crucible of ministry. This experience helped me to see that true theology, a theology for the people of God, had to be lived out in the midst of suffering and pain, and on the boundary as it were. Genuine theology, the kind embodied by evangelicals and Baptists at their best, had to be contextual and covenantal.

In the course of my student pastoral work, I became involved with many other evangelical ministries in New England. I also became acquainted with a number of evangelical leaders whose work I had long admired. Some of these became friends and mentors, notably Harold John Ockenga, pastor of Boston's Park Street Church, a leading evangelical congregation in the region; Roger Nicole, a Baptist theologian and Reformed thinker at Gordon Conwell Theological Seminary; John Stott, whom I first met on one of his student missions to Harvard; and J. I. Packer, an irenic champion of unitive evangelicalism, whose studies of Puritan thought influenced my own scholarly work. Later, Carl F. H. Henry, another Baptist evangelical, became a close friend. When I was invited to become the founding dean of Beeson Divinity School, Carl Henry spoke at my installation. More important than any of these individuals was the vision of the founders of Harvard College, who came to the New World on "an errand into the wilderness." That errand involved a *translatio studii*, the forging of a new model of life and learning that brought together the two ideals of classical education and biblical faith: the Republic of Letters and the School of the Prophets.

Baptist Reform

If evangelicalism at its best is a renewal movement within the one holy, catholic, and apostolic church, then the Baptist tradition represents a renewal within the renewal. But where do Baptists come from? Throughout the history of the church there have been various dissenting and nonconformist groups that have embodied some of the elements found among Baptists today. In the stream of Baptist historiography known as Landmarkism, some Baptist thinkers have tried to parlay such affinities into a full-blown theory of Baptist succession, a so-called trail of blood that includes an odd assortment of marginalized, schismatic, and heretical movements such as the Monatists, the Donatists, the Petrobrusiani, the Cathari, the Waldensians, the Lollards, and many others.

Recognizing even stronger points of similarity between sixteenth-century continental Anabaptists and the later Baptist movement, other historians have pointed to the Radical Reformation as the seedbed of Baptist origins. While some possible connections cannot be denied, the best response to this theory is the Scottish verdict of "not proved."

In fact, it is difficult to place Baptists into any set typology of religious groupings, as Ernst Troeltsch discovered when he tried to fit them into his church-type/sect-type schema. While he too found some strong affinities with a continental Anabaptist tradition, including believer's baptism, voluntary church membership, and the requirements of moral discipline, he concluded that "on account of their historic origin and their permanent environment, the Baptists became strongly impregnated with the spirit of Calvinism."[6] Indeed, the Baptist tradition as we know it today emerged in early seventeenth-century England out of the ferment for reform agitated for by those "precise" believers, the "hotter sort of Protestants," as radical Puritans and separatists were dubbed at the time. Like Robert Browne, who publicly burned his license to preach and who left the Church of England because of its "false" polity, liturgy, and ministry, the early Baptists were determined to effect what Browne called a "Reformation without tarrying for any."[7]

We can identify two separable beginnings of the English Baptist movement: the General Baptists, who evolved out of the church planted by Thomas Helwys at Spitalfields near London in 1612, which was an offshoot of the rebaptized exiled congregation of John Smyth; and the Particular Baptists, who arose among the underground London congregations of the 1630s. The General Baptists stressed the universal scope of the atonement, holding with the Dutch theologian Jacobus Arminius that Christ died for all persons. The Particular Baptists, on the other hand, were Calvinistic in their soteriology, agreeing with the five heads of doctrine propounded by the Synod of Dort (1618–19). Recent scholarship has suggested some back-and-forth between these two groups, and there were later efforts to bring them together. It is significant that John Bunyan's more charitable views on church membership and open Communion were published following his long imprisonment in Bedford jail. Just so, the experience of persecution, and the social ostracism experienced by Baptists in England even after the Act of Toleration in 1689, helped to forge common links that eventually led to the formation of the Baptist Union in the nineteenth century.

---

[6]Ernst Troeltsch, *The Social Teachings of the Christian Churches*, vol. 2 (Chicago: University of Chicago Press, 1976; originally published in German in 1911), 707.

[7]Though Browne later returned to the Church of England, his separatist ecclesiology anticipated important elements in the later Baptist understanding of the church. Chief among these was his effort to define the church in the context of a covenant relationship. The church, Browne declared, was "a company or number of believers which by a willing covenant made with their God are under the government of God and Christ and keep his laws in one Holy Communion." For so-called Brownists, as for later Baptists, the basic ecclesiastical unit was not the parish but the congregation—a congregation that elected its own officers, disciplined its own members, and administered the sacraments to its committed initiates. See Timothy George, *John Robinson and the English Separatist Tradition* (Macon: Mercer University Press, 1982), 33–44.

The eighteenth century was a watershed in Baptist history, with consequences that continue to shape Baptist identity, theology, and mission today. The impact of the Enlightenment, especially in its English manifestations of deism and latitudinarianism, affected the two major wings of the Baptist movement in disparate ways. A large part of the General or Arminian Baptist movement was swept up in the rising tide of rationalist theology and largely absorbed into English Unitarianism. This development represented the single largest departure from historic Christian orthodoxy in Baptist history. The acceptance of patterns of "enlightened" thought led many Baptists to abandon not only the Patristic doctrine of the Trinity but also *pari passu* the christology of Nicaea and Chalcedon, the doctrine of Christ's substitutionary atonement, and the teaching of justification by faith alone.

This devolution of theological commitment went hand in hand with a rejection of confessional subscription. Many Baptists feared that the embrace of any confessional standard would result in an abridgment of Christian liberty. But there was a dark side to such Baptist libertarianism. Historian Raymond Brown has aptly described the upshot of this development: "Resistance to subscription became the prelude to heterodoxy. People who refused to sign the articles came eventually to deny them and those General Baptists who were theologically uncertain ultimately became committed Unitarians."[8] Early on the General Baptists, represented by figures such as Henry Denne and Thomas Grantham, had been aggressively evangelistic in winning many to faith in Christ and planting churches throughout England. However, by the mid-eighteenth century they had ceased to be a vital force within evangelical Christianity.

Particular Baptists, on the other hand, resisted such liberalizing tendencies and affirmed strongly the orthodox Calvinist theology set forth in their First (1644) and Second London Confessions (1677, 1689). To be sure, the Particulars experienced numerous controversies of their own—over whether the Lord's Supper should be open to all Christians or restricted only to believers properly baptized, over whether baptism should be accompanied by the laying on of hands, over whether hymn singing was appropriate for public worship, among many others. But more serious than any of these disputes was the development among

---

[8]Raymond Brown, *The English Baptists of the Eighteenth Century* (London: Baptist Historical Society, 1986), 23.

eighteenth-century Particular Baptists of what Andrew Fuller called "false Calvinism."

What later scholars would call hyper-Calvinism was really an import from a Congregationalist minister named Joseph Hussy, who in 1707 published a book titled *God's Operations of Grace but No Offers of His Grace*. Hussy declared that anyone who claimed to believe in God's election and yet offered Christ to all was only a "half-hearted Calvinist." Eventually a large number of Particular Baptist pastors came to embrace a complex of ideas related to this emphasis. These included the backloading of justification into the eternal decrees of God, a theological move that minimized the importance of repentance and faith; the denial of free moral agency and the responsibility of sinners to repent and believe; the restriction of the gospel invitation to the elect only; the teaching that sinners have no warrant to believe in Christ until they feel the evidence of the Spirit's moving in their hearts; and the denial of the universal love of God. These views gained currency among Particular Baptists in the mid-eighteenth century with a consequence that many such churches were "chilled to the very soul," as Spurgeon put it later.

Both of these developments—the liberalizing evacuation of orthodox theology among General Baptists and the hardened Calvinism of Particular Baptists—were transformed by what I have called above the third major "moment" in the development of the evangelical tradition, the Awakenings. The revival movement led by George Whitefield, John and Charles Wesley, Howell Harris, and others infused new life into both Particular and General Baptist churches. In 1770 Dan Taylor, a former Methodist lay preacher, organized the New Connection of General Baptists, rejecting the doctrinal laxity that had led to the near ruin of the movement while embracing the open evangelism and missionary spirit of the Wesleyan revival.

Among the Particulars, the evangelical awakening took deep root in the emergence of a new theology of missions that was given classic expression by Andrew Fuller in his *Gospel Worthy of All Acceptation* (1785). This book, and Fuller himself, played a major role in the missionary call of William Carey, the Baptist shoemaker-pastor who challenged his fellow believers to "expect great things from God; attempt great things for God." Out of this ferment, what Baptist historian Kenneth Scott Latourette called "the great century" of missionary advance was launched, with Carey's remarkable work in India as a harbinger of the harvest to follow.

The evangelical awakening was an intensely ecumenical affair and posed with new urgency the question of denominational identity in an age of interdenominational activity. Baptists were caught up, along with other evangelicals, in a whole range of extra-ecclesial or parachurch ministries, including foreign missions, ministerial training, the Sunday school movement, orphanages, campaigns for literacy, prison reform, the abolition of the slave trade, and much more. In the early nineteenth century, *The Evangelical Magazine*, imbued with a vision of eschatological optimism, anticipated that great heavenly assembly where all of God's people would blend their voices in one united anthem:

> A great variety of denominations dwell together and worship before the throne of God and the Lamb, without one jarring note. . . . There Whitefield and Erskine, Toplady and Wesley, Romaine and Gill, Jonathan Edwards and Latrobe, can all unite in one song of praise to that true God to whose sovereign grace and almighty influence they cheerfully own themselves indebted for their complete salvation.[9]

Baptist particularity and evangelical identity are not mutually exclusive. Throughout history, the Christian church has always been pulled toward one of two poles: *identity* or *adaptability*. This tension arises from the most central theological affirmation of the New Testament itself: the Word became flesh (John 1:14). The need to communicate the gospel in such a way that it speaks to the total context of the people to whom it is addressed courses through every age of church history and shapes the various disputes and controversies that have marked the development of Christian doctrine and spirituality: rigorism and laxism, orthodoxy and heresy, ecumenism and schism, and reformation and retrenchment, to name only a few.

When seen in the wider perspective of Christian history, evangelicalism, as I have claimed, is best understood as a renewal movement within historic Christian orthodoxy. At its heart it is the theological core shaped by the Trinitarian and christological consensus of the early church, the

---

[9]Quoted by W. R. Ward, "The Baptists and the Transformation of the Church, 1780–1830," *Baptist Quarterly* 25 (1973): 181.

formal and material principles of the Reformation, the missionary movement that grew out of the Great Awakening, and the new movements
of the Spirit that indicate that "surprising works of God" are still happening in the world today. This understanding has led me to stress the
fundamental continuity that the evangelical faith shares with the Great
Tradition of Christian belief, confession, worship, and action through
the centuries, while not discounting the many local histories that must
be written to explain this phenomenon in any given era.

The Baptist tradition finds a place within this narrative as a distinctive reform movement within the wider evangelical renewal. Baptists are
indeed heirs of the Reformation, but they are not, nor have they ever
been, mere clones of Luther, Calvin, Zwingli, the Anabaptists, or anyone
else. For Baptists, the great doctrines of the Reformation were refracted
through the prism of the persecution and dissent that informed their
intense advocacy of religious liberty and, especially in the American setting, the separation of church and state. With all true Christians, Baptists
are loyal to Jesus Christ the Lord, the eternal Son of the heavenly Father,
who "for us and our salvation" became man. He died for our sins on
a cross, rose triumphantly over death, ascended to the Father, and one
day will come again in power and glory. In the meantime, he still reigns,
rules, and redeems through the Holy Spirit.

The church is the body of Christ extended throughout time as well
as space. It encompasses all of the redeemed of all of the ages. This is a
reality already glimpsed in the New Testament by the writer of Hebrews,
who admonished the believers in his day:

> You've come to Mount Zion, the city where the living God resides.
> The invisible Jerusalem is populated by throngs of festive angels and
> Christian citizens. It is the city where God is Judge, with judgments
> that make us just. You've come to Jesus, who presents us with a new
> covenant, a fresh charter from God. He is the Mediator of this covenant.
> . . . Do you see what we've got? An unshakable kingdom! And do you
> see how thankful we must be? Not only thankful, but brimming with
> worship, deeply reverent before God. (Heb. 12:22–23, 28, MESSAGE)

This dramatic vision of the universal church in no way minimizes
or mitigates the importance of the local congregation, the covenanted
community of God's pilgrim people that regularly gathers to worship,

praise, sing, pray, proclaim, discipline, love, serve, and send. Significantly, the same passage in Hebrews that describes so vividly the reality of the heavenly church gathered in eschatological assembly with the angels and believers of all time also provides the strongest proof text in the Bible for regular church attendance: "Let us consider how we may spur one another on toward love and good deeds, not give up meeting together" (Heb. 10:24–25). It is not a mark of sound Baptist churchmanship to play the universal church against the local church, or vice versa. As the Amsterdam Declaration of 2000 puts it:

> The church is the people of God, the body and the bride of Christ, and the temple of the Holy Spirit. The one, universal church is a trans-national, transcultural, transdenominational and multi-ethnic family of the household of faith. In the widest sense, the church includes all the redeemed of all the ages, being the one body of Christ extended throughout time as well as space. Here in the world, the church becomes visible in all local congregations that meet to do together the things that according to Scripture the church does. Christ is the head of the church. Everyone who is personally united to Christ by faith belongs to his body and by the Spirit is united with every other true believer in Jesus.[10]

So why am I a Baptist? I am a Baptist because it was through the witness of a small Baptist church that I first heard the gospel of Jesus Christ. Many of the things I still believe in I first learned in that modest Baptist community of faith: that Jesus loves me and died on the cross for my sins; that the Bible is the totally true and trustworthy Word of God; that all human beings are made in the image of God and are infinitely precious in his sight. Through the loving nurture I received from that congregation, I confessed my personal faith in Jesus as Savior and Lord of my life. I was then baptized in the name of the Father, the Son, and the Holy Spirit. When I was called to preach the gospel, it was in a Baptist church that I was set apart and ordained as a minister of the divine Word.

It is important to say that all of this came to me as a gift from beyond myself. It is not as though I had studied carefully and weighed objec-tively every religious possibility before committing myself to the Baptist cause. My experience was rather of a person who finds himself standing,

---

[10]The Amsterdam Declaration, *Christianity Today*, available online at http://www.christianitytoday.com/ct/2000/augustweb-only/13.0html.

wading, and eventually swimming in a flowing mountain stream. The Baptist formation I received as a young Christian was a gift, unbidden and undeserved, for which I can claim no credit. Later, as I studied the Bible more deeply and became aware of many other church traditions, doctrines, and denominations, my Baptist convictions grew stronger. I gradually came to understand the meaning of what I believed: *fides quaerens intellectum.* What at first I had intuitively grasped or only dimly glimpsed, I came to own with greater clarity and confidence. I came to see that being a Baptist was for me the most faithful way of being an evangelical, a Protestant, and a Christian.

Being a Baptist is a blessing but also sometimes a burden. From time to time I have considered the possibility of becoming something else. There are aspects of each of the traditions represented in this book, among others, that have enriched my life and calling to serve the body of Christ. Each brings distinctive treasures to our labors together—*pro Christo et ecclesia.* Being a Baptist gives me all the freedom I need to appropriate as fully as I can the gifts that they offer without abandoning the Baptist principles and ways that I cherish.

Several years ago, I published an essay titled "Is Jesus a Baptist?" This was originally a talk given at a conference on Baptist identity, and I recommended three strategies for Baptists to consider in our strategic mission of fulfilling the Great Commission: retrieval for the sake of renewal, humility in the presence of the holy, and particularity in the service of unity. On that last point, I made these comments, which still remain valid today:

> Particularity in the service of unity? Yes, by all means, let us maintain, undergird, and strengthen our precious Baptist distinctives: our commitment to a regenerate church membership, believer's baptism by immersion in the name of the triune God, our stand for unfettered religious liberty, and all the rest—but let us do this not so that people will say how great the Baptists are but rather what a great Savior the Baptists have, what a great God they serve. May they be able to say, "Just look at those Baptist Christians, see how they love one another. See how they work together with other believers. See how they put others ahead of themselves. You know, I think I'll give a listen to what they are saying about all of this Jesus Christ stuff."[11]

---

[11]Timothy George, "Is Jesus a Baptist," *Southern Baptist Identity: An Evangelical Denomination Faces the Future,* ed. David S. Dockery (Wheaton, IL: Crossway, 2009), 101.

Why I Am an Evangelical
and a Lutheran

Douglas A. Sweeney

I have not always been a Lutheran. I was raised, in fact, as a Baptist. Both of my grandfathers were Baptist pastors trained for pastoral ministry at Moody Bible Institute in Chicago. My parents met at Moody. Most of their siblings went to Moody. My father and four uncles have been licensed and/or ordained for Christian ministry by Baptists. One of my aunts has served for decades as a Baptist missionary. I grew up in a Baptist church and serve today at a divinity school that is owned by a denomination that used to define itself in *opposition* to state-church Lutheranism in Scandinavia. Large numbers of my students, as well as others in the Evangelical Free Church of America (the church that owns my school), testify to having been raised in spiritually dead Lutheran churches, hearing the gospel clearly only after leaving said churches, and then migrating to mainstream evangelical congregations, usually credo-baptist ones (that is, believer's-baptist ones), in which they have grown in grace steadily ever since.[1] Given my family's spiritual history, the history of my school, and the fact that my testimony differs so remarkably from the common plot of evangelical spiritual autobiographies, I should probably do some explaining.

---

[1] For a short version of the history of the Evangelical Free Church, see my article, "Evangelical Free Church of America," in vol. 2 of *Religion in Geschichte und Gegenwart*, 4th ed. (Tübingen: Mohr Siebeck, 1998–2000). For a longer version, see Calvin B. Hanson, *What It Means to Be Free* (Minneapolis: Free Church, 1990). For a wonderful explanation of the theology of the Free Church, see *Evangelical Convictions: A Theological Exposition of the Statement of Faith of the Evangelical Free Church of America* (Minneapolis: Free Church, 2011).

An Unusual Spiritual Narrative

I was raised in a Christian home. I was a "child of the covenant" in a context in which that phrase was hardly ever used. I was surrounded by Christians who loved me. My Grandma Sweeney, the godliest person I have ever known in my life, prayed for me every day until she died in 1997. Our home was full of lively theological conversation. My family went to church at least three times a week, twice on Sunday (back in the day when churches met on Sunday evenings) and once on Wednesday night for spiritual testimonies and prayer. After Sunday evening services we often got together with Christian friends for food and fellowship. Most of them were leaders of our church and other ministries. I had faithful Sunday school teachers. I matured in a town known as a hub for evangelical agencies. I attended its historic evangelical Christian high school (today's Wheaton Academy, formerly Wheaton Christian High School). I was an evangelical thoroughbred—as to the law, a Pharisee; as to zeal . . . you get the picture. I have a lot for which to be thankful. I was bathed (immersed!) as a boy in what the Puritans liked to call the special means of saving grace: Scripture, sacraments (or ordinances, as I usually called them then),[2] prayer, and genuine Christian fellowship.

During my earliest years of life, my father worked as a youth pastor, finished a master's degree at Wheaton College, taught in a Christian college in Oregon, and moved us back to Illinois so he could work at Moody. He served at WMBI, as an assistant to the president (the Rev. George Sweeting), and in Moody's correspondence school before he found his niche as the director of Moody's publishing enterprises (Moody Press, *Moody* magazine, and Moody Literature Ministries). As a licensed gospel minister, he was often asked to preach at area churches needing pastors. I would sometimes travel with him to these foreign congregations. I have always enjoyed learning about the Christian lives of others. I would relish the attention I received as the preacher's son. It was also fun to hear my dad expound the Word of God. To this day, I remember some of his homiletical themes. My favorite sermon of his explained the second half of James 1. He stressed the importance of being quick to hear, slow to speak and get angry (v. 19). He told the story of a wise man who said

---

[2] Almost all Christians recognize that Jesus *ordained* baptism as well as the Lord's Supper for regular use within the church, and thus refer to them as ordinances. Some Christians believe that they are special means of grace, and thus refer to them as sacraments as well.

that God has made us with two ears and one mouth for a very important reason: he intends for us to listen to others twice as much as we speak. Then Dad drove the sermon home by exhorting all who heard him to be "doers of the word, and not merely hearers" (vv. 22–25).[3]

Late in the summer of 1971, when I was six years old, I accompanied my father on a Sunday morning assignment on the west side of Chicago (my mother and brother stayed behind, attending our own congregation). In the car on the way to the church, we spoke of personal faith in Christ. Dad asked me if I understood the seriousness of sin and my need for saving grace. Of course, I did. I had been thinking about these things for quite a while. Dad asked me if I wanted to pray with him—then and there—to invite Jesus Christ to be my Savior and my Lord. Again, I did. So in the parking lot of the church where he was to preach, I prayed a simple sinner's prayer, turning my life over to God. When we got home that afternoon, there was rejoicing all around. I told my mother and my brother what had happened to me that morning. I called my grandparents in Oregon, repeating the story for them. They were thrilled, as you can imagine. I continued to grow in grace under the ministry of the Word at First Baptist Church in Wheaton. Three years later, I was baptized by our pastor, Edward Hales.

I had been spiritually regenerated before I prayed that prayer. This sounds strange to some readers. It would have sounded strange to me and to my relatives and friends if I had said as much back then. We were encouraged to associate our spiritual rebirth with a self-conscious choice to trust in Christ for our salvation. Getting saved was something to do. It happened when, and only when, we responded to the gospel with a personal act of faith—a sinner's prayer, a raised hand, a trip to the altar in response to a preacher's invitation. It required that we understand and claim the gospel message—and decide, voluntarily, to give our lives to God. I still believe that personal faith, confessed and practiced in the world, is essential to salvation. Nevertheless, I also think that God was working in my heart and mind, indwelling me by his Spirit, long before I prayed the sinner's prayer with Dad that Sunday morning. I had been

---

[3]Scripture quotations in this chapter are taken from the New American Standard Bible, 1977 edition, an autographed copy of which was given to me by a family friend, Charles C. Ryrie (inscribed with a reference to Matt. 6:33), and studied throughout my childhood. I continue to use and treasure this old and well-worn heavenly gift.

savingly converted as a very young boy. God had renovated my soul, reoriented my affections, and attracted me to himself before I was old enough to perceive what was really going on. I had been raised upon the Word and can't recall a time in my life *before* I trusted in the gospel and desired to follow Jesus.

Back then, though, I didn't understand that this was possible. I thought that one was saved by subjectively appropriating the gospel for himself, making it real in his own life by means of study, earnest devotion, and bold personal testimony. I would never say today that these things are unimportant. On the contrary, personal discipleship is crucial. Today, however, I understand devotion and discipleship, subjective appropriation of the faith and public testimony, as ways in which God calls us to respond to *his* leading, to his saving, supernatural initiative in our lives. We are saved by grace through faith, not by earnest personal effort. And the grace by which we are saved often begins its work in our lives before we recognize that God has made us his. Romans 5 does not speak about this order of things directly, but it does establish a theological pattern that applies: "while we were still *helpless*," the apostle Paul explains by inspiration of the Spirit, "Christ died for the ungodly." Indeed, "while we were yet sinners," even "while we were [his] enemies, we were reconciled to God through the death of His Son" (vv. 6–10). We don't reconcile ourselves to God, grant him permission to save us, or determine the timetable for his saving work in our lives. We simply cling to his gift of grace, respond in gratitude and praise, and then submit our lives to him, trying to walk in step with his Spirit.

I must have prayed to receive Christ, raised my hand at invitations, and gone forward at public meetings about a dozen more times after I prayed that prayer with Dad. I found it difficult to be sure that I had understood things well enough, or meant what I prayed strongly enough, to meet with God's approval. I wanted desperately to be saved and go to heaven when I died. But I really didn't understand the gospel very clearly. I was a soldier in the Boy's Brigade, a card-carrying member of the Scripture Memory Fellowship (the Bible Memory Association, as we knew it in the 1970s). I had probably committed Romans 3:28 to memory. But somehow I failed to hear its liberating news: we are "justified by faith," it says, "apart from works of the Law." God declares us just in Christ before we understand things well enough or mean what we pray strongly enough.

God saves in spite of our sin—by a free, unmerited gift of mercy, grace, forgiveness, and love.

The Baptist church in which I was raised provided a wonderful environment for people who converted as adults from lives of sin—I mean really blatant sin, of course, the kind that made for heartrending personal testimonies. It was also a fine place for people raised in mainline churches who for one reason or other never heard the gospel clearly, or were never goaded on to lives of personal discipleship. Such people had dramatic, adult conversion stories to tell. They sought to set themselves apart from the worldliness in their past. Our congregation was a warm, friendly, nurturing environment in which to change their lives. And baptism, for them (rebaptism for some), offered a means by which to mark this change publicly (though there were other such means as well). It gave them something they could *do* to symbolize their death to sin and their determination henceforth to live their lives for God.

But for people like me, people raised upon the gospel who had always trusted Christ and tried our best to follow him, such a context could perplex. Of course, people like me are just as guilty as the rest, just as much in need of a Savior. We "have sinned and fall short of the glory of God," to be sure (Rom. 3:23). But we do not have radical conversion stories to tell. We never lived in unbelief, or walked away from the love of God, or even sowed wild oats. Our sins are far more subtle, conceited, sinister than that. The standard spiritual rites of passage in the churches I knew best rarely matched with my experience as a child of the covenant. The notion that my sinner's prayer and baptismal testimony marked a major change in my relationship with God probably caused more harm, indeed consternation, than good. And the sectarian urge to define ourselves in opposition to older, more traditional sorts of Christians, while helpful to those who needed a push to "come out from their midst and be separate" from the world (2 Cor. 6:17), proved a recipe for ignorance, arrogance, and worse in the lives of kids like me.[4]

---

[4]That is, ignorance of the traditions we had separated from, arrogance in acting like our modern ways were better, and even heresy, consequently, in opposing central tenets of Christian orthodoxy. *Heresy* is a strong word. I use it here cautiously—not to suggest that our elders ever engendered such departures from historic Christianity, or that children like me ever intended such departures, but only that ignorance and arrogance in children like me yielded attitudes and statements that were seriously at odds with most traditional definitions of Christian orthodoxy (regarding the

Another thing that did some harm to me at First Baptist Church was the effort of our pastor during my teenage years (not beloved Pastor Hales) to turn our Sunday morning worship into a media event. I won't go into details, for it would not do any good. I mention it briefly only to say that while I wound up in the Lutheran church for theological reasons, I confess that I was prepared psychologically for this by the liturgical devastation wrought by the effort of this pastor to expand his church's influence. Our church never made it onto local television, but we did join the ranks of those who made it on the radio. Lengthy corporate prayers, confession of sin, Scripture reading, and detailed exegesis rarely fare well on the air—so our worship changed for the worse. I was a smart, sensitive kid. I appreciated the need for God's people to reach out beyond the borders of their churches. But I also knew the difference between the public worship of God according to biblical priorities and a spiritual pep rally.

I entered college as a Baptist who was heading for corporate law. However, a couple of things happened there that would change my life forever. I got serious with a girl I had met in Christian high school. Wilhelmina Hamster was the daughter of Dutch immigrants who attended Wheaton's only Christian Reformed congregation. I won't bore you with the details of our courtship during college. Suffice it to say that Wilma's church was right next to Wheaton College (an easy walk from my dorm), that her mother would invite me over for dinner after services, that her pastor preached the Scriptures very well on Sunday mornings and the Heidelberg Catechism well on Sunday nights, and that my time at Wilma's church contributed mightily not only to my relationship with her, but to my growing appreciation for traditional and confessional Protestant worship.

During my sophomore year in college, I also took an elective history course that changed my sense of direction. It was taught by Mark Noll, the man who soon became my mentor and continues to this day to play an important role in my life. It was on the Reformation. Nearly one third of the course, in fact, was on the life of Luther. I had never before thought so long and hard about my place within the history of the church. I had learned the Bible well, but not the reasons why my people

---

gospel message itself, not to mention other doctrines pertaining to God, the end times, the nature and ministries of the church, etc.).

read the Bible as they did, taught the doctrines that distinguished them from other kinds of Christians, worshiped as they did, engaged culture as they did. I found these subjects fascinating. My reflection on them deepened my faith like never before in my life, inspired a new love for Scripture and the doctrines it proclaims, took me further into the world of classical Protestant Christianity, and led to a change of majors. I had no idea, then, that I would become a church historian. I only knew that God was using history to draw me near, that I yearned for this to continue, and that my reasons for wanting to be a corporate lawyer had not been good. I soon became a history major. I took every course I could on the history of the church. And as I continued to read and write about historic Christianity, I gravitated closer to liturgical worship practices, classical Protestant doctrines, and confessional Protestant churches.

Many of my friends at Wheaton joined the Anglican Church. Robert Webber taught there then, encouraging students and other followers to revise their worship practices and embrace what he later called an "ancient-future faith."[5] He had become Episcopalian, and the faith that he commended sunk its roots in ancient worship more than in Protestant theology. I admired Dr. Webber and enrolled in one of his classes. But on balance, my spiritual journey had more to do with doctrinal history than liturgical renewal. I did enjoy the Anglican liturgy. It brimmed with Christian doctrine. In the main, however, I found nonliturgical and non-ecclesiological[6] Anglican thought to be anemic and excessively enamored of secular trends. To state the matter bluntly—with apologies and all due respect to Anglican friends whose spiritual journeys have proceeded from different places and been mapped with somewhat different needs in mind—I was being transformed by an existential struggle with the history of our faith, not the allure of smells, bells, and high ecclesiastical culture.

I was also being changed by my encounter with Martin Luther. Though our lives were separated by 482 years, nearly four thousand miles, and many layers of cultural difference, I could identify with Luther's evangelical conversion. I thrilled at the clear profundity of his pastoral

---

[5]For an introduction to this teaching, see Robert Webber, *Evangelicals on the Canterbury Trail: Why Evangelicals Are Attracted to the Liturgical Church* (Waco, TX: Word, 1985); and Robert Webber, *Ancient-Future Faith: Rethinking Evangelicalism for a Postmodern World* (Grand Rapids: Baker, 1999).

[6]Ecclesiology is the study of the church, so ecclesiological thought is thought related to the doctrine of the church.

theology, especially his theology of the cross (more below). Luther helped me understand the gospel message in its purity. He showed me that God granted saving faith because of Christ, not for (sinful) spiritual earnestness. I only had to receive this precious gift and thank the Lord. I gained assurance of my faith, stopped my spiritual navel gazing, and began to get over myself. I discerned that Luther was right for being an evangelical catholic, risking his life on the Scripture principle[7] while keeping all he could of the great tradition(s) of Christianity. My immersion in his corpus and the history of Protestant thought put me in touch with the "one holy catholic and apostolic Church."[8] It enriched my spiritual life. It helped me read the Bible better. I was not yet a Lutheran, but I left Wheaton College dead set on moving into a more traditional, Reformational, confessional, catholic church.[9]

A Home in the Lutheran Church

I went to Trinity Evangelical Divinity School shortly after graduating from college—as a young and restless newlywed—not because I sensed that God was calling me to the pastorate, but rather because the Lord was doing a number on my life, and we needed more time to figure out where this was leading. Wilma and I joined a local Presbyterian church, primarily because its youth pastor asked us for our help. I studied the history of Christian thought in order to carry on my journey. As I read, talked, and prayed about the history of theology, I moved further and further into Lutheranism.

I prefer to avoid harping on the differences between historic evangelical Protestants. We hold more in common than what divides us from each other. What we share, furthermore, is more important than our differences. I get along well with other orthodox believers. I am pleased

---

[7]The Scripture principle is the doctrine that Scripture alone (*sola Scriptura*) is the ultimate source of authority and theological standard for the church. It is the "norm that norms" all others (or, in Latin, the *norma normans*), so when popes, councils, or any other humans contradict it, they stand in need of correction and reform. Luther risked his life on this doctrine at the famous Diet of Worms (1521), where he stood against the emperor on the basis of the Word. It is a principle that animated his Ninety-Five Theses (1517) and gave birth to the Protestant Reformation.

[8]This quotation is taken, of course, from the Nicene Creed.

[9]Our English word *catholic* comes from the Greek word *katholikos* and Latin word *catholicus*, meaning "general," "universal," even "orthodox." My point here is not that *Roman* Catholicism is right. Rather, Luther was right to resist giving the Roman Catholic Church exclusive rights to the small-*c* catholic faith.

to worship with them, work with them in gospel ministry, and teach with them in ecumenical, interconfessional schools. My assignment in this chapter is to explain "why I am an evangelical Christian and a Lutheran," though, so let me offer a word about the things that first attracted me to Lutheran theology.[10]

The *main* attraction for me has always been the Lutheran stress upon God's real, objective, reliable, durable presence in the world—and availability to us—most importantly in the person of Christ, the Bible, and the sacraments. That sentence may not mean much yet to nontheologians. I hope that it will be clarified for you as you read on, because this emphasis upon the *objectivity* of the Lord's work in the world, and in our lives, really is the most compelling thing to know about Lutheranism—especially for sensitive, introspective evangelicals.

As one who had often assumed that saving faith was mainly subjective, that saving grace was available only insofar as I asked for it with motives strong and pure, and that my piety was genuine only when my heart was stirred, I found this classical Lutheran emphasis a key to the gospel itself. It freed me from the fear that I had not done what I had to do to seal the deal with God. It released me from the urge to custom build my own faith, work it up within my soul by means of strenuous mental effort. It helped me see that God had come to me for real, from without, *giving* me faith as well as the longing I had felt to live for him. He did so long before I knew it. He had been present all the time, extending grace to me objectively in Word and sacrament. That grace was powerful and effective, independent of my effort to make it *feel* more real inside. God wanted me to appropriate the faith in a personal way, but this is not what made it saving—or even secured it—in the first place.

This emphasis on the real, objective presence of God in the world—and saving grace in Scripture and sacrament—is rooted in Luther's unusually "high" christology.[11] Christology is difficult. It deals with how Jesus could have been both God and man—not an easy thing to consider. But

---

[10]For more Lutheran doctrine, see the definitive doctrinal standards in *The Book of Concord: The Confessions of the Evangelical Lutheran Church*, ed. Robert Kolb and Timothy J. Wengert (Minneapolis: Fortress, 2000); the summary of early Lutheran thought in Heinrich Schmid, *The Doctrinal Theology of the Evangelical Lutheran Church*, 3rd ed., trans. Charles A. Hay and Henry E. Jacobs (Minneapolis: Augsburg, 1899); and, of course, the works of Luther.

[11]Christology is the study of the person of Jesus Christ. It usually involves profound discussion of the relationship between the divine and human natures of Christ. For better and for worse, "high"

give me a paragraph to present the part of Luther's own christology that renders God and his grace more reliable and real (at least to people like me).

According to Luther, God is present and available in Christ in a remarkably powerful way. Indeed, the divine nature of Christ is so bound up with his humanity that Jesus's flesh and blood put us in touch with God himself. As Luther put this (rather starkly) in a sermon on John 4, Christ's divine and human natures "are so united" in his person that Mary "suckle[d] God with her breasts, bathe[d] God, rock[ed] Him, and carrie[d] Him; furthermore, that Pilate and Herod crucified and killed God." Luther said this kind of thing in several other places too. In one of his most famous treatises, *On the Councils and the Church*, he claimed that "if it cannot be said that God died for us, but only a man, we are lost; but if God's death and a dead God lie in the balance, his side goes down and ours goes up like a light and empty scale." Further, God

> could not sit on the scale unless he had become a man like us, so that it could be called God's dying, God's martyrdom, God's blood, and God's death. For God in his own nature cannot die; but now that God and man are united in one person, it is called God's death when the man dies who is one substance or one person with God.

Some Christians grow queasy when they hear this kind of talk. They argue that "finite things cannot receive or bear God" (*finitum non capax infiniti*, a common refrain among the Reformed). They find it more important to emphasize the "otherness of God" (that is, his infinite transcendence) and the humanity of Jesus (considered by itself) than to accentuate the nearness of God in Christ. Nevertheless, most Lutherans affirm a full "communication" (sharing) of the "properties" of Christ's divine nature with his humanity. We confess that he is a man in and through whom God *himself* really suffered, really died, and really offers himself today through finite, earthly, physical forms such as the Bible and the sacraments.[12]

---

christologies are those that pay the most attention to Christ's divine nature (and sometimes give short shrift to key features of the human nature of Jesus).

[12]Martin Luther, *Sermons on the Gospel of St. John: Chapters 1–4*, in *Luther's Works* (hereafter *LW*), vol. 22, ed. Jaroslav Pelikan (Saint Louis: Concordia, 1957), 491–93; and Martin Luther, *On*

The Bible, for Luther, is the most important form of God's presence in the world. It is the very Word of God to us, divine speech in writing. Many modern theologians (liberal Lutherans included) teach that Scripture can *become* the Word of God to God's people, on occasion, when the Holy Spirit chooses—but that Scripture is not always and in every case from God. In the manner of the Swiss Reformed pastor Karl Barth, they warn that Scripture cannot "contain" or "bind" God within its pages (as if anyone said it could). And they blame traditional Protestants for old-fashioned views of the Bible's inspiration and a reverence for its contents often labeled "bibliolatry."[13] These moderns tend to leave us with a weak, subjective view of Scripture's doctrinal significance and practical authority. Often in their churches, God speaks to us in Scripture only when, or as, we feel the Spirit moving in our midst, or when its verses can be said to confirm our own cultural prejudices. For Luther, on the other hand, the Bible simply *is* the Word of God to God's people—objectively and constantly. Sinners can rely on it to bear his truth to them, convey the gospel to them surely, without committing the sin of idolatry or lapsing

the Councils and the Church, in *LW*, vol. 41, ed. Eric W. Gritsch (Philadelphia: Fortress, 1966), 103–4. For the original German, see *D. Martin Luthers Werke: Kritische Gesamtausgabe*, 69 vols. (bound as 88) (Weimar: Hermann Böhlaus Nachfolger, 1883–2002; hereafter *WA*), 47:199–200, and 50:589–90. Just to be clear, Luther did *not* teach that God the Father suffered and died for us (that is the Patripassian heresy), but that God the Son did. For more on his christology, see Ian D. Kingston Siggins, *Martin Luther's Doctrine of Christ*, Yale Publications in Religion (New Haven, CT: Yale University Press, 1970); Marc Lienhard, *Luther, Witness to Jesus Christ: Stages and Themes of the Reformer's Christology*, trans. Edwin H. Robertson (1973; repr., Minneapolis: Augsburg, 1982); Franz Posset, *Luther's Catholic Christology: According to His Johannine Lectures of 1527* (Milwaukee: Northwestern, 1988); Oswald Bayer and Benjamin Gleede, eds., *Creator est Creatura: Luthers Christologie als Lehre von der Idiomenkommunikation*, Theologische Bibliothek Töpelmann (Berlin: De Gruyter, 2007); and the following work by Dennis Ngien, who tends to radicalize Luther's sometimes inconsistent statements about the communication of divine and human properties in Christ, thereby rendering Luther (falsely) as a source of the late-modern affirmation of divine passibility (that is, the late-modern notion that God suffers even apart from Jesus Christ): Dennis Ngien, *The Suffering of God According to Martin Luther's 'Theologia Crucis,'* American University Studies (New York: Peter Lang, 1995); Ngien, "Chalcedonian Christology and Beyond: Luther's Understanding of the *Communicatio Idiomatum*," *Heythrop Journal* 45 (2004): 54–68; and Ngien, "Ultimate Reality and Meaning in Luther's Theology of the Cross: No Other God but the Incarnate God," *Andrews University Seminary Studies* 42 (2004): 383–405.

[13]For an introduction to Barth's doctrine of Scripture, see Karl Barth, *The Word of God and the Word of Man*, trans. Douglas Horton (Boston: Pilgrim, 1928), originally published in German as *Das Wort Gottes und die Theologie* (Munich: Kaiser, 1924).

into magic. We can stake our lives on its promises and base our faith on its teachings. It is not a mere projection of our own wishful thinking, but an injection—revelation—from the very God who made us for communion with himself.[14]

The sacraments, for Luther, when they are based upon the Word, also bear the presence of God to us, sustaining us with grace. Indeed, the sacraments, for Luther, are *nothing other than* the Word wrapped in sacramental signs ordained by Jesus for our benefit (water, bread, and wine). The signs themselves convey the biblical truths that God has made them symbolize, aiding comprehension of those truths in Christian worship. They render the Word tangible and keep us from excessively subjective, strictly mental, hyperspiritual relationships with God.[15]

Baptism, for instance, is described by Luther himself as "water enclosed in God's command and connected with God's Word."[16] It is not something Christians do to signify their own decision to love and obey God (at least not primarily). It is a rite that God has given us to signify *his* promise to regenerate and clothe those adopted into his family with the righteousness of *Christ* (a promise specified in Scripture).

Luther taught that water is associated in Scripture with the renewing and regenerating work of the Holy Spirit. It symbolizes the drowning of our sin by God's help and the cleansing and rebirth that God effects in us as well. Much as Israel was "saved" by its passage through the Red Sea (Ex. 14:30) and Noah and his family found salvation in the flood, so "baptism now" signifies our own salvation from the ravages of sin, death, and the Devil (1 Pet. 3:18–22). It is a symbol of our "washing" and "renewing" by the Spirit (Titus 3:4–7). Its water offers "cleans[ing]" and spiritual rebirth (John 3:3–5; Eph. 5:26). It is "the

---

[14]Although Luther preached and taught about the Bible every week for nearly forty years of his life, he did not publish a book on the doctrine of Scripture. For a brief introduction to his view of this doctrine, see Mickey L. Mattox, "Martin Luther," in *Christian Theologies of Scripture: A Comparative Introduction*, ed. Justin S. Holcomb (New York: New York University Press, 2006), 94–113. For a longer presentation, see Mark D. Thompson, *A Sure Ground on Which to Stand: The Relation of Authority and Interpretive Method in Luther's Approach to Scripture* (Carlisle, UK: Paternoster, 2004).

[15]The best place to go for an authoritative Lutheran understanding of the sacraments is the Lutheran Book of Concord. For a basic introduction, see Luther's Large Catechism, in Kolb and Wengert, *The Book of Concord*, 456–75.

[16]Luther's Small Catechism, in *The Book of Concord*, 359.

circumcision of Christ," which depicts for us "the removal of the body of the flesh" (Col. 2:9–14).[17]

Despite what many people say (including many Lutheran pastors), Luther himself did *not* affirm what most people think of as "baptismal regeneration." He did not believe that water itself—or baptism by itself—ever saves anyone. He knew that many are saved (that is, converted or regenerated) long before they are baptized. He also knew (and lamented the fact) that many who are baptized later fall away, even run away from God and his regenerating grace. Still, he thought that Scripture presents the rite of baptism to sinners as a sure, reliable sign of genuine, spiritual rebirth. The major difference between Lutherans and other evangelicals is not that Lutherans rest upon a magical or Roman Catholic notion of the nature and significance of baptism.[18] It is that Lutherans believe that God's sacramental signs point reliably and truly to the realities they signify. God does not mislead. God's promises are sure. Indeed, when based upon and accompanied by the relevant Scripture promises, baptism assures us that the Lord is at work in the baptizand (the one being baptized) in just the way that he says—even if that person is too young to understand what is really going on.[19]

---

[17]For more on this biblical language and its broader associations, see Everett Ferguson, *Baptism in the Early Church: History, Theology, and Liturgy in the First Five Centuries* (Grand Rapids: Eerdmans, 2009), 25–198. Though Ferguson himself maintains a minority view of baptism (found almost exclusively in the Restorationist churches), his work is nonetheless both up-do-date and comprehensive.

[18]We reject the Catholic doctrine that God's grace comes by virtue of the sacramental rite (*ex opere operato*), contending rather that his grace comes by virtue of the Word, which is signified and proclaimed in a special way by the rite.

[19]It will help to remember here that, while many evangelicals hold to what some call the "once saved always saved" teaching, Lutherans believe that many regenerated people later walk away from God, rejecting his work of grace in their lives. Indeed, Luther believed that this is taught in several parts of Scripture, such as much of the book of Galatians (written to people who had received the gospel in faith but fallen away and been bewitched by false teachers who persuaded them to earn their justification by works of the law); 1 Tim. 1:18–20; and much of the book of Hebrews (esp. 3:12–4:16; 6:1–8). Several others in this volume serve in pedobaptist churches, so this is probably not the place for a long defense of infant baptism. Suffice it to say for now that, like the Anglican, Presbyterian, and Methodist contributors, I find support for this traditional Christian practice in the baptism of households found in the New Testament (the households of Lydia and the Philippian jailer in Acts 16; the household of Stephanus in 1 Corinthians 1); the fact that Jesus invited children to himself demonstratively, insisting that the kingdom of heaven belongs to such as these (Matt. 19:14; Mark 10:13–16); the widespread biblical practice of addressing God's promises to believers and their children; and the fact that most of the heroes of the evangelical faith affirmed and practiced pedobaptism (Augustine, Hus, Luther, Zwingli, Calvin, Wesley, Edwards, Whitefield, Wilberforce, et al.).

Relatedly, baptism signifies our union with the Lord in both his death and resurrection. As Paul says in Romans 6, "All of us who have been baptized into Christ Jesus have been baptized into His death. . . . We have been buried with Him through baptism into death, in order that as Christ was raised from the dead through the glory of the Father, so we too might walk in newness of life" (vv. 3–4).[20] Paul adds in Galatians 3 that those "baptized into Christ have [thus] clothed [them]selves with Christ." Because of what Jesus did on Calvary and the Spirit does in joining us to Christ in regeneration, we enjoy the wonderful blessing of wearing his righteousness as a robe (v. 27).[21] God declares us just in Christ because we really are in him. When he looks at us he sees not our sin, which he overcomes by killing it with Christ, but Jesus's righteousness, imputed at the cost of his own blood (Acts 20:28). This is obviously a far greater privilege and position than we can attain by mere resolve, which is why Luther always insisted that the sacrament of baptism signifies mainly not our own decision for Christ, but God's determination to make us one with Christ supernaturally: "Everything depends upon the Word and commandment of God," he said, for "baptism is simply water and God's Word in and with each other; that is, when the Word accompanies the water, baptism is valid, even though faith is lacking. For my faith does not make baptism; rather, it receives baptism."[22]

The same biblical theology applies to Luther's doctrine of the sacrament of Communion. When accompanied by the faithful proclamation of the Word, he taught, the Lord's Supper offers us the body and blood of Christ. "This is My body," say the words of institution. "This is My blood" (Matt. 26:26–28; cf. Luke 22:19–20 and 1 Cor. 11:24–25). "Is not the cup of blessing which we bless a sharing in the blood of Christ?" Paul warned while teaching against participation in idol feasts. "Is not the bread which we break a sharing in the body of Christ?" (1 Cor. 10:16). Luther *opposed* the Roman Catholic understanding of the Eucharist with

---

[20]Paul presents this teaching in other New Testament letters as well, such as 1 Cor. 12:13 and especially Colossians 2.

[21]This is why Lutherans often wear white gowns at baptism.

[22]Luther's Large Catechism, in *The Book of Concord*, 463. For more on Luther's doctrine of baptism, see Jonathan D. Trigg, *Baptism in the Theology of Martin Luther*, Studies in the History of Christian Thought (Leiden: Brill, 1994).

clarity and force.[23] He denied that the bread and wine themselves *are* Christ. But he argued that they bear the presence of Christ to us objectively. As he phrased this in his catechisms, the Lord's Supper conveys to us

> the true body and blood of the Lord Christ, in and under the bread and wine, which we Christians are commanded by Christ's word to eat and drink. And just as we said of baptism that it is not mere water, so we say here, too, that the sacrament is bread and wine, but not mere bread and wine such as is served at the table. Rather, it is bread and wine set within God's Word and bound to it.[24]

Luther's unusually high christology meant that Christ is not divided. Nor does his presence in the Supper depend on our own mental effort. Other Protestants would teach that he is present to us "spiritually" by "the contemplation of faith." But for Luther, Christ's presence is an all-or-nothing affair. In an effort to resist the ancient heresy of Nestorius (who maintained that Christ's divinity works *apart* from his humanity), Luther held that Christ is *wholly* present in the Supper, even bodily present in, with, and under the bread and wine.[25] Those who receive the

---

[23]He opposed the Catholic doctrine known as transubstantiation. (When a priest consecrates the bread and wine during the Mass, it taught, their substance is transformed into the substance of the body and blood of Christ. Their accidents—or qualities that we take in with our senses—remain as they were before. So the bread and wine still look, smell, and taste like bread and wine. But their substance—that which stands under the accidental qualities, forming them, or making them into what they truly are—is now the body and blood of Christ.) He opposed the Catholic doctrine of the immolation of Christ, or the re-presentation of the sacrifice of Christ during the Mass on behalf of the sins of the people (especially on the basis on Heb. 10:1–18). And he opposed the Catholic doctrine that grace is given in the sacrament by virtue of the performance of the rite in a proper manner (*ex opere operato*).

[24]Luther's Large Catechism, in *The Book of Concord*, 467.

[25]This teaching is difficult for many to understand. We live in a time when few believe that *anything* supernatural occurs during Communion. Further, Scripture says that Christ is at the right hand of the Father (Acts 2:33; Col. 3:1; etc.). Some people take this literally (as if God the Father really has a physical right hand) and have a hard time seeing that he could now be anywhere else. However, Luther believed the Bible taught that God has the power to make a thing present ubiquitously (in many places at once). Out of respect for God's omnipotence and faithfulness to his promises, and in order to teach that Christ is *really* present in the Supper, he affirmed that the sacramental signs (bread and wine) point objectively and truly to the reality they signify (the presence of the body and blood of Christ). Luther did not teach that Christ is now present in his *resurrected body* just as he was before his death. Rather, he employed scholastic language (when pressed to this by critics—his preference was to stick to Jesus's words of institution, leaving the mode of Christ's presence in Communion to the Lord) to specify the way in which the Savior must be present as we

Lord in faith receive forgiveness of their sins and spiritual nourishment for living. But even people lacking faith, those who eat in what the Bible calls "an unworthy manner," receive the body and blood of Christ—bringing judgment on themselves (1 Cor. 11:27–29). His availability to us is not contingent on our faith, thoughts, prayers, or anything else. Our faith is not what makes him present; God's Word makes him present. So we should examine ourselves and "judge the body rightly" (1 Cor. 11:28–29). For as Luther liked to say, this sacrament "was not dreamed up or invented by some mere human being but was instituted by Christ without anyone's counsel." Further,

> just as the Ten Commandments, the Lord's Prayer, and the Creed retain their nature and value even if you never keep, pray, or believe them, so also does this blessed sacrament remain unimpaired and inviolate even if we use and handle it unworthily. . . . This must always be emphasized, for thus we can thoroughly refute all the babbling of [those] who, contrary to the Word of God, regard the sacraments as something that we do. . . . The Word must make the element a sacrament; otherwise, it remains an ordinary element. Now, this is not the word and ordinance of a prince or emperor, but of the divine Majesty at whose feet all creatures should kneel and confess that it is as he says, and they should accept it with all reverence, fear, and humility.[26]

This historic Lutheran emphasis on the real, objective presence of God in Christ, Scripture, and sacrament has led to other distinctives I appreciate as well. It has led, for example, to what some call today an "incarnational" approach to Christian living. Now that Jesus has ascended and has sent to us the Spirit of God to help us live for him

---

celebrate Communion. He denied that Christ is "locatively" or "circumscriptively" present in the eucharistic elements (circumscribed or contained by the elements themselves—in the way that beer is present in a bottle). He denied that Christ is "repletively" present during the Lord's Supper (without any spatial limit—in the way that God is with us in his utter omnipresence). But he affirmed that Christ is present in a real, "definitive" way (delimited geographically but not circumscriptively—in an intermediate way, such as the way in which the human soul is present in the body, or in which angels, or resurrected/glorified bodies, are really present in a place but not restricted by the physics of the mundane, fallen world). See Martin Luther, *Confession Concerning Christ's Supper*, in *LW* 37:151–372 (*WA* 26:261–509). For more on Luther's doctrine of the presence of Christ in the Supper, see Hermann Sasse, *This Is My Body: Luther's Contention for the Real Presence in the Sacrament of the Altar* (Minneapolis: Augsburg, 1959).

[26]Luther's Large Catechism, in *The Book of Concord*, 467–68.

(John 14; 16; Acts 2), now that our bodies and "the body of Christ," the church, have together become the temple of the Spirit, bearing the presence of God in the world (1 Cor. 3:16–17; 6:19–20; 2 Cor. 6:16; Eph. 2:19–22; 1 Pet. 2:4–8), God expects us to incarnate, or put flesh upon, his goodness, truth, and beauty in the lives of those around us. As his incarnation testifies, our faith was never intended to be a disembodied, strictly spiritual, mental exercise. Rather, God reaches out to us in real and tangible ways, even through the work of the church. Many other Christian groups have come to emphasize this theme. But it is rooted in the rich soil of Lutheran theology.[27]

This incarnational emphasis has fueled a Lutheran penchant for the arts in Christian worship. Inasmuch as God has come to us in earthy, finite forms, Christians need not fear the use of forms, Lutherans suggest, as we offer back to him the work of our hands, lips, and limbs. Other Protestants, especially—such as Zwingli, Calvin, the Puritans, and the Restorationist churches—have forbidden the arts in worship (though mostly in the past), excluding the use of visual art and musical instruments in church. Concerned to counter the Roman Catholic use of art in church settings, and confused about the command that prohibits making likenesses "of what is in heaven above or on the earth beneath or in the water under the earth" (Ex. 20:4, a rule against idolatry), they instituted what they called the "regulative principle," which stipulated that anything not taught or found in Scripture should be banned from Christian worship. Luther took a different tack in purifying the church. Rather than banning all that is not found explicitly in Scripture, he banned only things that clearly contradicted Scripture. This is why our services and many of our sanctuaries appear to be more "Catholic" than most other churches. Luther loved to sing. He played the lute as

---

[27]For further Lutheran reflection on this incarnational theme, read the poignant words of the famous pastor and martyr Dietrich Bonhoeffer, *The Cost of Discipleship*, trans. R. H. Fuller, with some revision by Irmgard Booth (1937; repr., London: SCM, 1959), 223–344. For contemporary Reformed opposition to this view of God's presence in the world (or at least to a few of its potential implications), see especially John Webster, "The Church and the Perfection of God," in *The Community of the Word: Toward an Evangelical Ecclesiology*, ed. Mark Husbands and Daniel J. Treier (Downers Grove, IL: InterVarsity, 2005), 93–95; John Webster, "'The Visible Attests the Invisible,'" in Husbands and Treier, *The Community of the Word*, 96–113; and Webster, *Perfection and Presence: God with Us, According to the Christian Confession*, Kantzer Lectures in Revealed Theology (Grand Rapids: Eerdmans, forthcoming).

well as the flute. He reformed the Catholic liturgy and wrote three dozen hymns as an amateur musician, saying "next to the Word of God, music deserves the highest praise. . . . Let this noble, wholesome, and cheerful creation of God be commended."[28] Some of his friends were famous painters. Further, many other Lutherans have engaged the arts as well. We do not believe that the best ways of leading people to God are always cognitive, spiritual, and otherwise immaterial. We celebrate the tactile condescension of the Lord, employing palpable and audible materials and forms as we share his goodness, truth, and beauty with others.[29]

These emphases are summarized best by Luther himself in his theology of the cross. "The cross alone is our theology," he once declared defiantly, insisting that believers kneel humbly at the condescension of God in Jesus Christ (as well as the earthly means of his presence that remain with us today). Some are tempted to make an end run around the cross of Christ, seeking "higher," more ethereal, less carnal and ignoble routes to "genuine spirituality" (theologies of glory, as Luther usually dubbed them). Many look for God in largely self-invented ways, avoiding embarrassment by association with messy, mundane faith.[30] But as Paul wrote in the second half of 1 Corinthians 1, there simply is no other route to God than Jesus and his cross. "The word of the cross," he confessed,

---

[28]Martin Luther, "Preface to Georg Rhau's *Symphoniae iucundae*," a collection of fifty-two motets (or "Delightful Symphonies") published in 1538 by a musician friend and follower, in *LW* 53:323–24 (*WA* 50:368–74). On Luther's musical efforts, see especially Martin Luther, *Liturgy and Hymns*, ed. Ulrich S. Leupold (Philadelphia: Fortress, 1965), whose contents are found in numerous volumes of the *WA*; Robin A. Leaver, *Luther's Liturgical Music: Principles and Implications*, Lutheran Quarterly Books (Grand Rapids: Eerdmans, 2007); and listen to the boxed set of four compact disks, *Martin Luther: Hymns, Ballads, Chants, Truth* (Saint Louis: Concordia, 2004), the most comprehensive recording to date of genuine Luther songs.

[29]For more on early Lutherans and the arts, see John Dillenberger, *Images and Relics: Theological Perceptions and Visual Images in Sixteenth-Century Europe*, Oxford Studies in Historical Theology (New York: Oxford University Press, 1999); Christopher Boyd Brown, *Singing the Gospel: Lutheran Hymns and the Success of the Reformation*, Harvard Historical Studies (Cambridge, MA: Harvard University Press, 2005); Carlos M. N. Eire, *War against the Idols: The Reformation of Worship from Erasmus to Calvin* (Cambridge: Cambridge University Press, 1986); Peter Matheson, *The Imaginative World of the Reformation* (2000; repr., Minneapolis: Fortress, 2001); and Joseph Leo Koerner, *The Reformation of the Image* (Chicago: University of Chicago Press, 2004).

[30]The classic example of this quest in recent American cultural history is the religion of "Sheilaism," constructed by a young American nurse, Sheila Larson, and described by Robert N. Bellah et al., *Habits of the Heart: Individualism and Commitment in American Life*, rev. ed. (Berkeley: University of California Press, 1996), 221, 226, 235.

is to those who are perishing foolishness, but to us who are being saved it is the power of God. For it is written,

> "I will destroy the wisdom of the wise,
> And the cleverness of the clever I will set aside."

Where is the wise man? Where is the scribe? Where is the debater of this age? Has not God made foolish the wisdom of the world? For since in the wisdom of God the world through its wisdom did not come to know God, God was well-pleased through the foolishness of the message preached to save those who believe. For indeed Jews ask for signs, and Greeks search for wisdom; but we preach Christ crucified, to Jews a stumbling block, and to Gentiles foolishness, but to those who are the called, both Jews and Greeks, Christ the power of God and the wisdom of God. Because the foolishness of God is wiser than men, and the weakness of God is stronger than men. For consider your calling, brethren, that there were not many wise according to the flesh, not many mighty, not many noble; but God has chosen the foolish things of the world to shame the wise, and God has chosen the weak things of the world to shame the things which are strong, and the base things of the world and the despised, God has chosen, the things that are not, that He might nullify the things that are, that no man should boast before God. But by His doing you are in Christ Jesus, who became to us wisdom from God, and righteousness and sanctification, and redemption, that, just as it is written, "Let him who boasts, boast in the Lord." (vv. 18–31)

This is the part of the gospel Luther helped me see most clearly. God has come to me in Christ. This is truly *good news*, a clear message from the Lord about what he has done to rescue me from sin and self-absorption. It is the power of God to save me. I do not have to find another, nobler way to God, raise my hand at further meetings, or think better, purer thoughts in my approach to the throne of grace. The way of the cross will lead me home. It is the only way to God. Though I will always fail to be as good as God rightly expects, the Lord Jesus has become my goodness, wisdom, and redemption. My assignment is to humble myself and kneel at the foot of the cross, grabbing hold of the incarnate Savior crucified for me—and, then, to walk the way of the cross myself, dirtying my hands within the real world around me as I live for God and neighbor sacrificially (Matt. 10:38; 16:24; Mark 8:34; Luke 9:23; 14:27).[31]

My wife and I first joined a Lutheran church late in 1989 after moving south to Nashville for doctoral work at Vanderbilt. Nashville is not exactly Lutheranism's Mecca. (In North America, that title goes to Saint Paul, Minnesota.) Local residents refer to it as the buckle of the Bible belt. Christian churches abound, but most are Baptist, independent, Restorationist (Disciples of Christ and Churches of Christ, mainly), Presbyterian, and Methodist. There were several different Lutheran congregations then in town, though, and we took several weeks to find the one that we would join.

Over the course of American history, there were scores of different Lutheran denominations following Jesus. But by 1989, there were but three of any size: the Evangelical Lutheran Church in America (ELCA, which was the largest of the three with over 5.2 million members in the late 1980s), the Lutheran Church–Missouri Synod (LCMS, over 2.6 million members), and the Wisconsin Evangelical Lutheran Synod (WELS, over four hundred thousand members).[32] They shared the same confessional standards (or at least they did in theory, as they all held to the standards in the Lutheran Book of Concord). They employed the same polity (Congregational with bishops overseeing synod offices, the bishops being called "presidents" by the anti-Catholic LCMS and WELS). But in practice, they were different. Indeed, they *felt* exceedingly different. The ELCA was quickly moving toward the other mainline churches (ecumenically and socially), while the LCMS and WELS were more traditional

---

[31]For the source of Luther's saying, "the cross alone is our theology" (*crux sola est nostra theologia*), see his comment on Ps. 5:11, WA 5:176, 32. (For an English translation, see *Luther's Commentary on the First Twenty-Two Psalms*, in *The Precious and Sacred Writings of Martin Luther*, ed. John Nicholas Lenker, 31 vols. [Sunbury, PA: Lutherans in All Lands, 1903–1910], 1:289.) For his theology of the cross more generally, start with Luther's *Heidelberg Disputation* (LW 31:39–58; WA 1:353–74), especially theses 19–20. And interpret these texts with the help of Robert Kolb, "Luther on the Theology of the Cross," *Lutheran Quarterly* 16 (Winter 2002): 443–66; and Gerhard O. Forde, *On Being a Theologian of the Cross: Reflections on Luther's Heidelberg Disputation, 1518* (Grand Rapids: Eerdmans, 1997).

[32]For membership statistics, see the *Yearbook of American and Canadian Churches: 1989*, ed. Constant H. Jacquet Jr. (Nashville: Abingdon, 1989), 61, 77, 121, for which the ELCA reported 5,288,230 members, the LCMS 2,614,375, and the WELS 418,791.

and German (many within their ranks had descended from German immigrants).[33]

We tried the LCMS first, for it was the church best committed to confessional Lutheranism. But we found it too ingrown, too distrustful of other Christians. And we balked at "closed Communion," which in most Missouri Synod churches means the exclusion from Communion of anyone not fully committed to a Lutheran understanding of the presence of Christ in the Supper.[34] WELS churches proved to be the most parochial of them all. So when a friend of ours at Vanderbilt invited us to help him at the church where he was serving, we accepted and attended First Lutheran Church of Nashville, plugged in right away, and spent the next twenty years in ELCA congregations. Our current church left the ELCA in 2010 over concerns about its drift away from orthodoxy. But Wilma and I remain joyful Lutheran evangelicals, grateful for our Reformation heritage.

Being Lutheran Is Not Enough, but Neither Is Being an Evangelical

But being Lutheran is not enough. My Baptist friends are right. There are all too many Lutheran congregations that are sick. There are all too many Lutherans who have left their first love (Rev. 2:4) and forgotten what it means to have a right relation to God. Many Lutheran churches harbor halfhearted, nominal Christians. Few Lutheran churches feature meaty exegetical preaching. (Perhaps these problems are related?) What is more, God has called us not to Lutheranism anyway, but to the way of Jesus. Luther himself never intended to found a new denomination, but to reform the Catholic Church. He sought to return the church to Scripture, to renew the church's piety. And today, the people doing this the best are evangelical.

But being an evangelical, by itself, is not enough, either. Evangelicals do not have a theology of their own. They depend on older churches for

---

[33]For an overview of American Lutheran history, see especially L. DeAne Lagerquist, *The Lutherans*, Denominations in America (Westport, CT: Greenwood, 1999); and E. Clifford Nelson, ed., *The Lutherans in North America*, rev. ed. (Philadelphia: Fortress, 1980).

[34]We favor the practice of including all who believe—in whatever way—that Christ is really present in the sacrament. We hold a Lutheran view of Communion, but do not believe that Christ ordained the Supper only for Lutherans, or ordained that we unite around a uniquely Lutheran view of Jesus's presence in the Supper as we share the meal together.

their theological substance. They handle the Bible well but overwork the Scripture principle, distorting it with (modern) claims to "the right of private judgment." Whether they recognize it or not, they encourage one another to invent their own faith—without much guidance from the past or even from experts in the present. Thus, their faith is too subjective—fueled by uninformed feelings, idiosyncrasies of leaders with little theological training, and a postfundamentalist inferiority complex. All too many of their best and brightest leave, in time, in search of substance, assuming that the grass is greener somewhere else. And their leaders lack the means within the evangelical bubble to address this phenomenon convincingly.

Let me finish with some counsel for my fellow evangelicals. We need both objective *and* subjective Christian faith. As the theologians say, we need the faith that is believed by true Christians everywhere (*fides quae creditur*) and the kind of faith that clings in a personal way to what is held by Christians everywhere (*fides qua creditur*). You do not have to join me in the Lutheran church for this. The Lord knows that the Lutheran church is not right for everyone. He never meant it to be a final destination for *anyone* (especially not for Lutherans). No, this world is not our home. Like the patriarchs and matriarchs who fill the leaves of Scripture, we are "strangers and exiles" here within our earthly institutions, even our Christian institutions. We desire "a better country," a heavenly destination (Heb. 11:13–16). And the best way to run the race that God has set before us (Heb. 12:1) is to trust in the real presence of Christ in Scripture and the sacraments, cling to him and the faith that God has given us by grace, *and* make good on that gift of grace in true devotion and discipleship.

May God bless you as you seek to keep both head and heart together, and may he enable you to embody his truth and beauty in the world.

Why I Am an Evangelical and a Methodist

Timothy C. Tennent

I have always appreciated the wonderful way in which historic Christianity is able to simultaneously embrace universality and particularity. On the one hand, the great truths of the faith are embraced and proclaimed by all major Christian bodies. The *kerygma* can be heard and recognized in movements as varied as house-church movements in China, African Independent Churches, and Roman Catholic, Protestant, and Pentecostal churches. This is known as the great *semper ubique ab omnibus*—the faith that is confessed and proclaimed "always, everywhere, by everyone." On the other hand, the Christian church is marked by amazing particularity. There are beliefs, practices, and emphases that are peculiar to Quakers or Presbyterians or Roman Catholics and so forth. We tend to emphasize our differences more than our catholicity. There are quite a few unresolved tensions in the faith that tend to be reflected in various ways by Christian movements, but this should not obscure the great unanimity of Christian proclamation. The fact that all branches of the church have embraced the Nicene Creed, for example, reflects a deep and abiding *sensus communis* of the church that must be acknowledged before we discuss the particularities of being a Methodist, Lutheran, or Baptist.

It is this deep unity which is reflected in my use of the word *evangelical*. Today, the term has been adorned with a wide array of associations, caricatures, and political overtones. However, in my use of the word, it primarily refers to a deep commitment to historic orthodoxy. It is this desire to rediscover that great common resonance throughout the history of the church that has always affirmed the centrality of Christ, the authority of Scripture, and the great saving power of the Christian gospel.

This chapter therefore, is not focused on what makes me a Christian, or even a historic, evangelical Christian, since that is the common ground upon which all the contributors to this book stand. Rather, this chapter seeks to set forth why I am a *Methodist* Christian. On a personal note, although I am a direct descendent of William Tennent, who is famous in Presbyterian circles for his founding of the Log College, I was born and raised in a United Methodist church in Atlanta, Georgia, known for its biblical preaching and solid evangelical message. I have studied at many of the great institutions that, broadly speaking, stand in the Reformed tradition, including Gordon-Conwell Theological Seminary, Princeton Theological Seminary, and the University of Edinburgh in Scotland. I later taught missions at Gordon-Conwell for eleven years. Throughout my entire spiritual journey I grew to appreciate many of the great emphases in Reformed theology. However, I was always drawn to the deep roots of my Methodist upbringing. Today, I serve as the president of Asbury Theological Seminary, the largest seminary in the world within the Methodist/Wesleyan tradition. My sojourn for so many years with brothers and sisters from different traditions helped me to appreciate simultaneously the deep richness and texture of the Christian faith and what is distinctive in the Methodist tradition. For me, Methodism did not lose any of the great themes of Reformed theology, but it seemed to bring to the table so much that has often been neglected in the church.

In this chapter, I will explore nine reasons why I am a Methodist.

Prevenient Grace

First, I am a Methodist because I believe in *prevenient grace*. For Wesley, the spiritual life has no hope of a beginning without God's prior action on behalf of the sinner. Prevenient grace is a collective term for all the ways in which God's grace comes into our lives *prior* to conversion. Prevenient grace literally means "the grace that comes before" and captures well what the early church called the *preparatio evangelica*, the preparation for the good news.

One of the ways in which the Methodist/Wesleyan tradition is sometimes misunderstood by those in other traditions is in regard to our doctrine of sin. It may come as a surprise to some of our Reformed readers that the doctrine of total depravity (the famous *T* in the Calvinistic TULIP) is held by Wesleyans and Methodists just as ardently as by

Calvinists. Methodists, like our Reformed brothers and sisters, believe that salvation is impossible without a free and prior act of God on behalf of the sinner. Total depravity means that we are dead in our sins and therefore cannot help or assist ourselves. Sin is not merely a "ball and chain" that impedes our progress. We are *dead* in our trespasses and sins (Eph. 2:5). Methodists affirm this truth.

However, Methodists take very seriously the theological tension that exists between, on the one hand, the clear teaching of Scripture that we are dead in our sins and totally void of any ability to save ourselves (Luke 15:24; Eph. 2:1; Col. 1:21; 2:13), and the universal call to the gospel, which requires us to "come" (Matt. 11:28), "repent" (Acts 2:38), "believe" (Acts 16:31), and a whole array of other commands, all of which call us to specific acts of faith and obedience. Since spiritually dead people have no capacity to respond, it is clear that God is bestowing grace in countless ways into our lives prior to our regeneration or conversion. Prevenient grace provides the link between human depravity and universal call.

The important difference between Methodists and Reformed Christians is not on the fact of depravity, but on whether God's prior action is limited to the elect (limited atonement—the *L* in the TULIP) or is universal. Despite the enormous respect we have for John Calvin, Methodists do not believe that the Calvinistic doctrine of limited atonement fits the biblical data as well as the doctrine of prevenient grace. Methodists believe that God has universally acted on behalf of Adam's fallen, depraved race. We believe that Christ, as the second Adam, rescued the human race with an act of grace that grants it the capacity to accept or reject the good news of the gospel when it is proclaimed. Wesleyans believe that if the doctrine of human depravity is not linked to God's action in prevenient grace, then it creates an untenable theological conflict that, at least potentially, makes God either unjust or the author of evil, neither of which fits with a biblical view of God. For if a spiritually dead person is incapable of responding to God's call, then upon what basis is he or she held accountable for sin? Prevenient grace demonstrates how we can be totally depraved yet be given grace to respond and, if we do not respond, be held fully accountable for our disbelief.

For Methodists, prevenient grace is the bridge between human depravity and the free exercise of human will. Prevenient grace lifts the human race out of its depravity and grants us the capacity to respond further to God's grace. Jesus declared that "no one can come to me unless the Father who sent me draws him" (John 6:44). Methodists understand this text as referring to a divine drawing rooted in the triune God that *precedes* our justification. It is God's act of unmerited favor. It is God's light "that gives light to every man" (John 1:9), lifting us up and giving the human race the capacity to exercise our will and respond to the grace of Christ. Thomas Oden puts it well when he says that "the divine will always 'goes before' or 'prevenes' (leads the way) for the human will, so that the human will may choose freely in accord with the divine will."[1]

Wesleyan thought affirms that God has taken the initiative to create a universal capacity for the human race to receive his grace. Many, of course, still resist his will and persist in rebellion against God. Wesleyan thought is actually a middle position between a Pelagian view (which makes every person an Adam and admits no sin nature or bondage due to Adam's nature) and the Reformed view (which affirms limited atonement). What Wesleyans mean by free will is actually "freed will," a will in bondage that has been set free by a free act of God's grace. It is, of course, not free in every possible respect, since we are all influenced by the effects of the fall in many ways, but we now have a restored capacity that enables our hearts, minds, and wills to respond to God's grace. I love the fact that Methodists believe that even if you go to the ends of the earth with the gospel, you will always find that God precedes you and, in effect, "beats you there"! Perhaps prevenient grace is summed up best by the famous interruption of a missionary who was lecturing in Africa about how the missionaries brought the gospel to Africa. The African believer interrupted and said, "The missionaries did not bring the gospel to Africa; God brought the missionaries to Africa." This insightful comment shifts the emphasis to God's prior agency and the great *missio Dei* (mission of God) whereby God is always the first actor in the great drama of redemption. Wesleyans fully embrace the importance of human decision and the exercise of the will. However, this is not possible without God's prior action.

---

[1] Thomas Oden, *Systematic Theology*, vol. 2, *The Word of Life* (Peabody, MA: Hendrickson, 2001), 189. Unless otherwise noted, Scripture quotations in this chapter are from the New International Version, 1984 edition.

Means of Grace

Second, I am a Methodist because I believe in the "means of grace." John Wesley lived two centuries after the start of the Reformation. This gave him a unique perspective on the strengths and the weaknesses of the Reformation. On the positive side, Wesley was a strong supporter of the major emphases of the magisterial Reformers. Wesley could affirm all the great *solas* of the Reformation: *sola Scriptura*, *sola fide*, *sola gratia*, *solus Christus*, and *soli Deo gloria*: Scripture alone, faith alone, grace alone, Christ alone, all to the glory of God alone. However, Wesley also understood that the restoration of the doctrine of justification by faith alone and the emphasis on the sole sufficiency of the work of Christ in our salvation could, tragically, lead some in the church to adopt a more antinomian view regarding the life of holiness and the call to continue growing in Christ.

Wesley saw that in the years since the invigorating message of the Reformation, the churches were doctrinally and theologically sound, but the lived experience of Christians was still at a very low ebb. He responded by developing a more robust understanding of how God's grace works throughout the life of a believer. He was a keen listener to the nonmagisterial Reformers such as the Pietists, as well as the earlier Patristic Christians (Eastern and Western) who could assist him in this reflection. It is here that Wesley developed his views regarding the means of grace. He defined the means of grace as "outward signs, words, or actions, ordained of God, and appointed for this end, to be the ordinary channels whereby he might convey to men, preventing, justifying, or sanctifying grace."[2] Wesley went on to identify three primary means of grace that God has given to us: prayer (private or public), Scripture (reading or listening), and the Lord's Supper.

Now, quite a wide array of Christian groups accept the general idea that prayer, Scripture, and the Lord's Supper are means of grace. They are widely understood as the general means by which Christians grow stronger in their faith and grow in the grace of Christ. In other words, they are God's instruments to *sanctify* us. However, Wesley had a much broader understanding of the means of grace. What makes Wesleyan thought distinctive is that he saw these means of grace as a channel to

---

[2]*The Works of John Wesley*, vol. 5, *First Series of Sermons (1–39)* (1872; repr., Grand Rapids: Baker, 2007), 187 ("Means of Grace," 2.1).

convey not just sanctifying grace, but also preventing (prevenient) and justifying grace. In other words, Wesley understood that prayer, Scripture reading, and even the Lord's Supper can be used by God to convert someone to the faith. Wesley understood this because the means of grace have no power in themselves to save anyone. Rather, they have the power to convey all forms of grace precisely because Christ himself is present in prayer, in the reading of Scripture, and in the Lord's Supper. So, for Wesley, there is no such thing as an autonomous person reading Scripture or praying or taking the Lord's Supper. These are all done in the presence of the risen Christ. Remember, Christ is the only true means of grace. The customary means of grace are given to the church as channels to Christ himself. So we should exercise our freed wills and avail ourselves of the full range of the means of grace. Wesley encouraged people to wait *in* the means of grace, not *outside* them. He wrote, "All who desire the grace of God are to wait for it *in the means* which he hath ordained; in using, not in laying them aside."[3]

Wesley conveys a deep reliance upon Christ not only in his coming to faith, but also in his remaining in the faith. In his journal Wesley records a time in his life when he felt a complete lack of faith. He writes about it on March 4, 1738 (remember, Wesley's heartwarming experience at Aldersgate does not occur until May 24, 1738). Wesley decided to quit preaching because, he reasoned, "how can you preach to others when you have no faith yourself?" When he asked his good friend Peter Böhler whether he should give up preaching, Böhler famously replied, "Preach faith till you have it; and then because you have it, you will preach faith."[4] This captures well the importance of waiting *in* the means of grace, not outside the means of grace.

Conversion through Faith in Jesus Christ

Third, Methodists affirm (along with *most* evangelical movements) the importance of conversion. On May 24 of each year Methodism around the world celebrates one of the most famous conversions since Saint Paul on the road to Damascus. It was on May 24 that Wesley went "unwillingly" down to a Christian society meeting and there encountered a reading of

---

[3]Ibid., 190 ("Means of Grace," 3.1).
[4]*The Works of John Wesley*, vol. 1, *Journals from October 14, 1735, to November 29, 1745* (1872; repr., Grand Rapids: Baker, 2007), 86 (journal entry, Saturday, March 4, 1738).

Martin Luther's preface to Paul's epistle to the Romans. It was during this reading that John Wesley had a profound conversion. Listen to his own words recorded in his diary:

> About a quarter before nine, while the reader was describing the change which God works in the heart through faith in Christ, I felt my heart strangely warmed. I felt I did trust in Christ alone for salvation; and an assurance was given me that He had taken away my sins, even mine, and saved me from the law of sin and death.[5]

Scholars and historians still debate about what precisely happened to Wesley that night. What is clear is that, at some deep level, Wesley really *heard* the central truth of the Reformation, namely, that we are justified through the completed work of Jesus Christ on the cross of Calvary. We cannot add to that work. It is no mistake that this transformation came as someone was reading Martin Luther's preface to the book of Romans. Martin Luther had experienced a similar conversion in his so-called "tower experience" in the Augustinian Black Cloister in Wittenberg. As Luther was reading Paul's words in Romans 1:17 on how the righteousness of God is revealed through faith, he recalled, "I felt myself to be born anew and to enter through open gates into paradise itself!"

This emphasis on conversion was rediscovered in the Reformation and, by Wesley's day, was a vital feature of the Pietistic movement. Finally, it became fully embedded in Methodism because of Wesley's own experience and, later, through the strong emphasis on revival preaching and conversion in the camp meetings and frontier church planting work of American Methodism.

Sanctifying Reorientation of the Heart

Fourth, I am a Methodist because of Wesley's strong emphasis on the importance of holiness in the life of the believer and the necessity of Christian sanctification. On New Year's Eve 1738, Wesley went to another society meeting. It was an all-night prayer vigil to bring in the year 1739. In the early hours of the new year, something dramatic happened to Wesley. He received a sanctifying experience whereby God reoriented his heart and life. Wesley explains:

---

[5]Ibid., 103 (journal entry, May 14, 1738).

On Monday morning, January 1, 1739, Mr. Hall and my brother Charles were present in Fetters Lane, with about sixty of our brethren. At about three in the morning, as we were continuing instant in prayer, the power of God came mightily upon us insomuch that many cried out for exceeding joy and many fell down to the ground. As soon as we were recovered a little from that awe and amazement at the presence of His majesty, we broke out with one voice, "We praise Thee, O God, we acknowledge Thee to be the Lord."[6]

This experience helped Wesley understand God's ongoing work in the life of the believer. We have already seen the role of prevenient grace prior to our conversion. Then, we examined the role of justifying grace at the point of conversion. Now, Wesley understands that God's work continues in the life of the believer through sanctifying grace. Methodists have a view of God's grace working before, at, and after conversion. This helps to build on the Reformation, which focused on *becoming* a Christian, with a broader and equally biblical emphasis on what it means to *be* a Christian.

The doctrine of entire sanctification is one of the most misunderstood of all Methodist doctrines. When most of us hear the word *sanctification*, we think of it as a forensic term—meaning that you are divinely certified before God's court of justice as someone without any sin in your life and, once sanctified, you will never sin again. That is not what Wesley taught or meant by sanctification. For Wesley sanctification is not primarily a forensic term. You could be justified alone on a deserted island, but sanctification, in contrast, is inherently relational since it involves the whole of our daily interactions.

For Wesley, sanctification is what happens when we are brought fully into relationship with the triune God. Sin and God's righteous judgment can never be reduced to only breaking God's law, that is, forensic guilt. Our sins are, of course, never *less* than that. But they are also deeply relational. When we sin we are not only breaking God's law (1 John 3:4), but also breaching a *relationship*. When we sin we are, at that moment, electing the absence of God in our lives. Sin separates us from God himself, not just from the right side of God's law.

---

[6]Ibid., 170 (journal entry, January 1, 1739).

Methodists build on the Reformers' understanding of "alien righteousness" by emphasizing that we must not only be declared righteous, but also increasingly live righteously. Luther famously said that Christians are "dung hills covered in snow." Wesley would not disagree, but would point out that salvation is about more than justification. Righteousness for Wesley is about more than God's looking at us through a different set of glasses—that is, we are filthy rags, but God sees us through the blood of Christ and thereby sees the alien righteousness of Christ imputed to us. Wesley stressed that alien, imputed righteousness must increasingly become native, actualized righteousness, wrought in us not by our own strength but through the power of the living God. We are marked, oriented, and reoriented by love.

We are justified by faith in Jesus Christ, but we are sanctified by faith as we come into full relationship with the triune God. Wesley taught that we are justified by faith and we are sanctified by faith. As a relational term, entire sanctification means that your whole life, your body, and your spirit have been reoriented. Entire sanctification means that your entire heart has been reoriented toward the joyful company of the triune God. You are in a new colloquy. It was, for Wesley, not the end of some long drudge out of the life of sin, but joining the joyful assembly of those who have truly found joy. For Wesley, holiness is the crown of true happiness.

To be sanctified is to receive a gift from God that changes our hearts and reorients our relationship with the triune God and with others, giving us the capacity to love God and neighbor in new and profound ways. The language of "entire sanctification" in Methodism uses the word *entire* in reference to Greek, not Latin. In Greek, that which is *entire* or *complete* can still be improved upon. It is a new orientation that no longer looks back on the old life of sin but is always looking forward to the new creation. It is a life that has been engulfed by new realities, eschatological realities, not the realities of what is passing away.

Wesley also understood that holiness is not merely a negative term. It is not just about sins we avoid. Methodists believe that even if you were to eradicate every sin in your life, you would only be halfway there. Because, for Wesley, holiness is never just about sins we avoid; it's about fruit we produce! In Wesley, faith and fruit meet and are joyfully wed. We no longer have a view of holiness that is legalistic, private, negative, and static. It is not merely legal, but relational; not merely private, but embedded in community; not negative, but a true vision of the in-breaking of God's rule and reign! The witness of the Spirit that confirms faith becomes in Wesley the power of the Spirit to produce fruit and to transform the world—to spread scriptural holiness throughout the world!

Discipleship: Catechesis in Community

The fifth reason I am a Methodist is the strong emphasis on discipleship in our tradition. Eighteenth-century Oxford, where Wesley was a student, was a place filled with spiritual apathy, deism, practical atheism, and low-christology Arianism. In short, it was a world quite a bit like North America and Europe today. John and his brother Charles decided to gather a few students together to "observe the method of study prescribed by the statutes of the university." The statutes (long ignored) required that students engage in the "frequent and careful reading of the Scripture." The Wesley brothers decided to promote this by forming a small group for studying the Greek New Testament. It became known as the Holy Club. They were so methodical in their practice that the people in the Holy Club were given the nickname "methodist." So the very origin of the word *Methodist* is rooted in a small-group-formation approach to catechesis.

Catechesis is, of course, a very important feature of the Reformed tradition. In my own experience, the Reformed emphasis on catechesis has been very effective in teaching the great doctrines of the faith. What is distinctive about the Methodist emphasis is how it seeks to go beyond simply giving correct answers to doctrinal questions. For Wesley, catechesis was learning to echo the entire rhythms of the Christian life (the word *catechesis* comes from a root word meaning "to echo"). This is a natural extension of the Methodist theme to focus not only on *becoming* a Christian, but also on what it means to *be* a Christian. Wesley learned this from the Patristic mystagogy model of discipleship.

Normally, new believers were put through an initial instruction period prior to their baptism. This was an introduction to the Christian faith and culminated on Easter Sunday when the new believers were baptized. However, after baptism, the new Christian was put through a second phase, known as mystagogy, which brought the believer into the mystery of what it meant to be a member of the church. This was a period of instruction *after* baptism, between Easter and Pentecost. Wesley took this idea and united it with the community model of the early Celtic Christians. This developed an entire system of putting new believers in small groups or classes and various discipleship bands. The leader would report to the pastor on the spiritual state of those under his or her care. These small groups would meet and give an account of their week, sustain each other in prayer, and transparently confess their sins. Members in sin would be disciplined. The new Christians would also be instructed in some aspect of the apostolic faith. They would worship together by singing a song. The meeting would be over in about an hour, and everyone would participate. It is still an excellent model.

Missional Movement, Social Consciousness

The sixth reason I am a Methodist is that Methodism has managed to retain its DNA as a missional movement. Historically, Methodism was born as a renewal movement within the Anglican Church. Wesley carried this missional, renewal emphasis right out into the streets. He brought the gospel to broken, hurting people who had been marginalized and forgotten by the church of his day. Wesley famously declared, "The world is my parish."[7]

Throughout the history of the church there has been a healthy tension between the active and contemplative traditions. The earliest monastic traditions idealized desert hermits such as Saint Anthony (251–356), who is often cited as the founder of monasticism. They were the forerunners of the great *contemplative stream*. Our minds run quickly to the great masters of this tradition such as Bernard of Clairvaux, the Rhineland mystics (e.g., Saint Hildegard or Meister Eckhart), Julian of Norwich, Saint Teresa of Avila, or Thomas Merton. This broad contemplative tradition has given the church many gifts, such as the Rule of Saint Benedict and the *lectio divina*. This is a long and wonderful tradition.

However, there were others who understood spiritual formation to occur *in* the world. This is the great *active tradition*. The mendicant orders such as Dominicans and Franciscans also renounced the world and entered into the consecrated life. However, they lived out their formation actively in the world, preaching the gospel and serving the poor.

---

[7]Frank Baker, ed., *The Works of John Wesley*, vol. 25, *Letters I, 1721–1739* (Oxford, UK: Clarendon, 1980), 616. I quote this from the 1980 edition because I agree that this famous letter was more likely written to John Clayton on March 28, 1739, rather than to James Hervey on March 20, 1739.

Saint Dominic founded the Dominicans as a preaching order. Francis of Assisi founded the Franciscans as an order to serve the poor. Wesley loved both the contemplative and active traditions, but he was drawn more powerfully to the latter. He formed his disciples in the context of actively serving in the world. Wesley understood, for example, that if you really want to be formed spiritually, you should be eager to go out into a place of pain, roll up your sleeves, and get your hands dirty serving the poor. While Wesley was deeply committed to prayer and contemplation, his vision of the church was profoundly missional. Wesley took his new preachers out to the brickyards and into the prisons. Not only was the world his parish, but for Wesley the world also is God's greatest spiritual workshop. It is on the anvil of a suffering world that God shapes and forms his disciples to understand what it means to take up their cross and follow him. Thus, the Wesleyan tradition is an active tradition; spiritual formation occurs in the context of active service in the world.

Doctrinal Clarity, Catholic Spirit

The seventh reason I am a Methodist is the wonderful way Wesley combined doctrinal clarity with a generous, warmhearted spirit toward other Christians. John Wesley's reluctance to produce any precise doctrinal formulation for the "people called Methodist," along with his "catholic spirit," have led many to wrongly conclude that he was indifferent about the core doctrines of historic Christianity. It is not unusual to hear Wesley's famous dictum taken from 2 Kings 10:15, "if thine heart is as my heart, give me thine hand," as a kind of theological blank check to endorse departures from historic Christianity, provided it is done with a warm heart. However, Wesley was fully orthodox and fully ecumenical in a way that should inspire us today. On the one hand, he was able to embrace considerable diversity among Christians who held different convictions than his on various points. On the other hand, Wesley frequently found himself embroiled in various controversies with Roman Catholics, Anglican bishops, and Calvinist thinkers. He held strong theological convictions and firmly upheld all of the historic Christian confessions. Wesley would have been dismayed at the erosion of orthodoxy in mainline churches owing to the increasing embrace of secular ideologies and a postmodern epistemology. He was both ecumenical *and* orthodox; he held firm convictions *and* had an irenic spirit and warm heart toward those with whom he disagreed. How was Wesley able to embrace both of these so ably? The key is to understand how he understood theological enquiry.

Wesley affirmed the theological unity that is necessary to our identity as Christians while allowing for broad diversity in nonessentials of the faith. Historically, this balance has been expressed through the terms *kerygma* and *adiaphora*. The word *kerygma* comes from the Greek word meaning "proclamation." It refers to the core essentials of the Christian faith as expressed, for example, in the Apostles' Creed and the Nicene Creed, as alluded to at the outset of this chapter. Wesley was firmly committed to the historic core of Christian proclamation. The word *adiaphora* comes from the Greek word *adiaphoros*, which, as used by the Stoics, meant "things indifferent." Thus, the *adiaphora* refers to those differences held by Christians which "are not sufficiently central to warrant continuing division or dispute."[8] In Wesley's day there was an assumption that Christian belief and practice should conform to the larger national identity. In other words, if someone lived in England, he or she should follow the faith and practice of the Church of England (Anglican). If someone was born in Scotland, he or she should follow the faith and practice of the Church of Scotland (Presbyterian). This meant that Christians in a particular geographic region were compelled to reach agreement not only on the broad essentials of the Christian faith (*kerygma*), but also on all the diverse particulars (*adiaphora*) of whatever national church was in place. However, Wesley forcibly rejected this territorial understanding of Christian identity. In his sermon "Catholic Spirit" he says:

> I know it is commonly supposed, that the place of our birth fixes the Church to which we ought to belong. . . . I was once a zealous maintainer of this; but I find many reasons to abate of this zeal. I fear it is attended with such difficulties as no reasonable man can get over: Not the least of which is, that if this rule had took place, there could have been no Reformation from Popery; seeing it entirely destroys the right of private judgment, on which the whole Reformation stands.[9]

[8] John Westerdale Bowker, *The Sacred Neuron: The Extraordinary New Discoveries Linking Science and Religion* (New York: Tauris, 2005), 120.
[9] *The Works of John Wesley*, 5:496 ("Catholic Spirit," 1.10).

Wesley goes on to argue that Christians should be able to dwell together in harmony even if they disagree about basic convictions such as the form of church government, the mode of baptism, the administration of the Lord's Supper, and so forth. However, he makes an important distinction between "catholic spirit" and "latitudinarianism." The latter characterizes those who wish to engage in endless speculation about the essentials of the gospel or wish to remain indifferent to holding a particular conviction. In contrast, Wesley argues that "a man of truly catholic spirit" does not have the right to set up his or her own form of religion. Rather, a Christian should be "as fixed as the sun in his [or her] judgment concerning the main branches of Christian doctrine."[10] He calls on his hearers to "go, first, and learn the first elements of the gospel of Christ, and then shall you learn to be of a truly catholic spirit."[11] Wesley's ecumenism was built on the foundation of a shared theological orthodoxy concerning the historic essentials of the Christian faith. Nevertheless, Methodists seek to take very seriously Jesus's prayer in John 17 that we "may be one" just as he and the Father are one (John 17:22).

Global Vision

The eighth reason I am a Methodist is Wesley's early appreciation for the possibility of what we know today as "global Christianity." Few have given proper recognition to the fact that Wesley is one of the leading forerunners of conceptualizing the church in its full global, rather than sectarian, dimensions. In the post-Aldersgate period, Wesley's preaching became so controversial that he was barred from the pulpits of the Church of England. Since he continued to preach in the open fields, he was charged with "trespassing" on the parishes of other ministers. He replied to this charge in a letter written in March 1739 with what has become the most famous quote of Wesley, "The world is my parish." In the letter he says, "I look upon all the world as my parish; thus far I mean, that in whatever part of it I am, I judge it meet, right and my bounden duty to declare, unto all that are willing to hear, the glad tidings of salvation."[12]

It is difficult for modern-day Christians to fully comprehend the radical nature of this statement. However, the territorial conceptions, as

---

[10]Ibid., 5:502 ("Catholic Spirit," 3.1).
[11]Ibid.
[12]Baker, *The Works of John Wesley*, 25:616.

noted earlier, were so strong that it was considered heresy to preach the gospel to those outside your parish. These territorial conceptions were one of the biggest barriers to the emergence of the Protestant missionary movement. In contrast, Wesley was ahead of his time in first conceptualizing the church in its full global dimensions and only secondarily in its particularity as, for example, Methodist Christians. Wesley asked why he should not preach the gospel in "Europe, Asia, Africa, or America," for with the apostle Paul he declared, "Woe to me if I do not preach the gospel" (1 Cor. 9:17). Wesley affirmed that he was prepared "to go to Abyssinia or China, or whithersoever it shall please God by this conviction to call me."[13] In today's "post-parish" world we may have a difficult time recognizing what a radical ecclesiology is embedded in this vision. Wesley seemed to understand that the church of Jesus Christ is indestructible since Christ is the Lord of the church and has promised to build his church. However, the indestructibility of the church is not tied to any particular institutional or geographic manifestation of it. With the dramatic rise of Christians from the Majority World, many of whom do not trace their history to the Reformation, there is a need to discover a deeper ecumenism that can unite all true Christians. Wesley anticipated the future multicultural diversity of the church and the common experience of rebirth from above that unites all Christians of every age.

Centrality of Worship

The ninth reason I am a Methodist is Methodism's great emphasis on worship. Methodists sing their theology! Wesley knew that it is not enough merely to believe and to confess the great truths of the faith. We must enter into the very presence of the triune God in worship. Music was one of the main ways early Methodists passed on the faith.

Wesley lived at a time when the standard practice of the church in worship was to sing the Psalms, often with a brief Christian doxology at the end. However, just prior to the emergence of Wesley lived a man named Isaac Watts (1674–1748). Watts is sometimes known as the father of English hymnody because of his pioneering work in introducing new compositions of worship into the church that were not directly built around a psalm or a specific scriptural paraphrase. This sparked a revival in worship that captured the life of Charles Wesley. Charles

---

[13]Ibid., 25:615.

was a gifted poet and wrote thousands of new hymns to capture the
great truths of the Christian faith and reinforce the grand metanarrative
of God's redemptive story. Hymns such as "Hark! The Herald Angels
Sing" (Christmas), "And Can It Be?" (redemption), "O for a Thousand
Tongues to Sing" (Pentecost), "Christ the Lord Is Risen Today" (Easter),
and "Love Divine, All Loves Excelling" (new creation) are recognized all
over the world as powerfully capturing the great themes of the Christian
faith. Methodism is known for excellent singing and worship. Even today,
every Methodist hymnal still reprints Wesley's original instructions for
congregational singing, which includes such classic lines as, "Beware
of singing as if you were half dead or half asleep; but lift up your voice
with strength." Methodists have taken this to heart as well as almost any
Christian group in the world.

Conclusion

Hilary of Poitiers (300–368) was one of the great defenders of the faith in
the early church. He is known as the "hammer of the Arians" because of
his vigorous opposition to their christological heresy, which had spread so
widely in his day. The Arians believed that Jesus Christ was not the eternal
second person of the triune God, but rather a being created before the
foundation of the world. However, Bishop Hilary vigorously reminded
the church that the position of Arius was not faithful to the apostolic
witness. In time, Arianism did not prevail, and the church reemerged.

In our own time, many of us have looked around and found that many
expressions of Protestant Christianity have pushed beyond the boundaries of orthodoxy and begun to seriously erode the unity of Nicaea.
Many liberal Protestants—and a few daring Roman Catholics—finally
came out in the open and, like Arius of old, denied the true deity of
Christ or the inseparable link between a truly risen Christ and the church.
Christ, they argued, must be made more reasonable for modern men
and women. Christ did not truly, bodily rise, they insisted, but arose in
the preaching of the apostles. Some boldly claimed that the Enlightenment had finally delivered the crushing blow and called for the church
to reinvent itself along lines more compatible with modernity, lest the
church have no future in a secularized world. More recently, in some of
the postmodern readings, we are called to all experience Christ in our
own way and not be bothered by the confines of some ancient apostolic

proclamation. Postmodernism urges us to live as independent islands in a sea of meaninglessness. Your autonomous opinions, they argue, are just as meaningful and valid as those who deliberated at Nicaea or who were first commissioned by the risen Lord. A hermeneutic of proclamation and faith is replaced by a hermeneutic of suspicion and doubt, and both are called equally valid. According to this scheme, theology, it seems, is really, after all, only anthropology. The church is a human construct, not a divinely ordained community. Yet, in the face of all of this, though the tempest rages for a season, the church will, once again, be reconstituted into the truth.

With the emergence of global Christianity we are witnessing many new and faithful expressions of the church from other quarters, mainly in the non-Western world, and the great unanimity of the church throughout the ages marches on because God is the one who preserves his church and its living witness to Jesus Christ. The church is constantly being reconstituted in the truth. Harvey Cox, in his book *Fire from Heaven*, observes this phenomenon, calling it, in the words of the Frenchman Gilles Kepel, "the revenge of God."[14] Indeed, every time the New Testament is opened and the gospel is proclaimed, it happens again and again throughout the world. The church, therefore, is called to persevere as the public witness of the apostolic message. We are a living community united to the risen Christ. The word *saint* never appears in the singular in the New Testament. The word for church, *ekklēsia*, denotes a public assembly, not a private cult.[15] We are a community of witnesses, and we cannot bear witness in isolation from our brothers and sisters in the faith around the world in space or the witness of the church through the ages in time. We are united to them both in worship and in witness in what the Apostles' Creed calls the communion of the saints, the *communio sanctorum*. To forsake either that worship or that witness is to cross the boundaries and to cease to be the true church.

Today, two thousand years into this great proclamation, after having weathered every storm from Gnosticism to Arianism to Protestant liberalism to the current storm of postmodernism, the true church, I remain

---

[14]Harvey Cox, *Fire from Heaven: The Rise of Pentecostal Spirituality and the Reshaping of Religion in the Twenty-First Century* (Reading, MA: Addison Wesley Longman, 1995), xvii.

[15]Gerhard Kittel, ed., *Theological Dictionary of the New Testament*, vol. 3 (Grand Rapids: Eerdmans, 1965), 501–36.

convinced, will always reemerge as the faithful witness. I say this because as I review the top nine reasons why I am a Methodist, I am painfully aware that many Methodist churches do not exhibit these great truths today. However, if we all are but stewards of a worship and a witness summoned forth by the Father through Christ in the power of the Holy Spirit, and heralded through the ages by countless millions, then our voices join the great chorus of other faithful Christians throughout the world and back through time.

In this respect, despite my deep love for Methodism, I still remain far more identified with the common evangelical witness of all true churches than with any particular outpost. As I noted at the outset of this essay, our particularity has meaning only if it is built on the great common doctrinal, experiential, and historical truths that unite all true churches together. For if we don't have doctrinal stability, we cannot have ethical stability; and if we don't have ethical stability, we don't have stability of worship; and if we don't have stability of worship, we are no longer related vitally and necessarily to the headship of Jesus Christ. Our historic boundaries become lost in a postmodern sea of autonomous self-definitions.

What a contrast to the apostle John, who in that final testimony at the end of time gives us the courage to know that in the last day the church will be preserved out of every snare, for he hears this act of worship in heaven, testifying not to another gospel or something novel, but to the apostolic proclamation: "You were slain, and with your blood you purchased men for God from every tribe and language and people and nation"; and so "to him who sits on the throne and to the Lamb be praise and honor and glory and power for ever and ever" (Rev. 5:9, 13).

Why I Am an Evangelical and a Pentecostal

Byron D. Klaus

A Pentecostal Childhood

I was born on the prairies of North Dakota and grew up in a small town of fewer than a thousand people. My earliest experiences of religious identity included the perception that my church was different from all the others in town. It was a strong Catholic community, and the seasonal processions from that church through the streets were curious to me indeed. I remember peering in the door of the Catholic Church one day and being amazed at the altar, its images of Jesus on the cross, and so many candles. One day a neighbor kid my age called me a "holy roller," and I wondered what that meant. When I found out the implication was that we rolled on floors at my church, I was left puzzled, as I had actually never seen such a thing.

Most people attended some church in our town, and it seemed they all had an opinion about the simple little white frame building toward the east end of town where my dad and mom were pastors. I grew up with this sense of being different; we had to have ready explanations for the regular snide remarks we faced. Where I gained an inner strength to deal with this "ubiquitous otherness" that many small-town Pentecostals faced was through songs that described our spiritual journey. We would sing the old Herbert T. Buffum song regularly:

> I'm going through, I'm going through,
> I'll pay the price whatever others do,

I'll take the way with the Lord's despised few,
but I'm going through, Jesus, I'm going through.[1]

Our identity as outsiders to other traditions in Christianity was implicit, and while my perspective today would certainly have much broader experiences to draw from, that "outsider" label still hovers in the background, regularly calling childhood anecdotal experiences to the surface.

Twentieth-century Pentecostalism included vibrancy among immigrant communities in rural and urban America. My parents co-pastored small German-speaking immigrant congregations while I was growing up. These ethnic enclaves certainly provided reinforcement to the "Lord's despised few" identity that we all had.

In my elementary school years, we left small-town North Dakota for a large midwestern city. The larger city also gave rise to a new experience for me: disdain from fellow Christians whose beliefs on the basic tenets of historical Christianity were the same as ours. I did not have the word *evangelical* in my vocabulary at that time, but I remember one day hearing a snide remark on the radio by a Bible teacher making a passing comment about Pentecostals. The descriptive language was graphic and startling to me. He said Pentecostals were the "last vomit of Satan." Discussion with my parents, who had much more experience in these matters, resulted in a simple but very profound response. They said that some Christians just did not "understand," and we needed to pray for them to find their personal *Pentecost*. (I found out years later that this radio speaker was simply quoting the venerable G. Campbell Morgan and his evaluation of early twentieth-century Pentecostalism.)[2]

My growing-up years in a Pentecostal church did not focus on lots of theological treatises that distinguished salient points of historic Christianity, but my theological mind was being formed in very powerful ways. The urgent eschatology that fuels the missionary heart of my denomination (the Assemblies of God) was sung into the fiber of my being. We would sing in German, "O Halleluja der Herr kommt bald," or in English,

---

[1]W. E. Warner, "Buffum, Herbert," in *Dictionary of Pentecostal and Charismatic Movements*, ed. Stanley M. Burgess and Gary B. McGee (Grand Rapids: Regency Reference Library, 1988), 101.
[2]Harvey G. Cox, *The Future of Faith* (New York: HarperCollins, 2009), 187–98. Chapter 14 is a recognition of this observation by Morgan, as it is titled "The Last Vomit of Satan and the Persistent List Makers: Pentecostals and the Age of the Spirit."

We shall see the King,
we shall see the King,
we shall see the King when he comes,
He's coming in power,
we'll hail the blessed hour,
we shall see the King when he comes.[3]

These powerful theological images were reinforced by regular preaching on the Lord's soon return. Work while it is day for "the night cometh, when no man can work" (John 9:4, KJV) was on the top list of "golden texts" to be memorized because it reinforced the mind-set of our spiritual journey. This urgency about winning the lost was undergirded by the missionaries who regularly visited our church, replete with slide presentations that depicted the urgency of the hour and the "lateness of the times." Once a month, we would take a missionary offering, and the church missions secretary would read a letter from the "regions beyond." Sometimes the person reading the letter could not even finish the report without being overcome to the point of tears about the challenges that the missionary was describing.[4]

My commitment to biblical preaching and the authority of Scripture was not rooted in a brilliant apologetic but personified in a simple song my dad had us sing before he preached. I can still hear my dad's strong voice as he belted out,

The Bible stands, though the hills may tumble;
it will firmly stand when the earth shall crumble;
I will plant my feet on its firm foundation,
    for the Bible stands.

My understanding of the authority of Scripture was further shaped by the fact that we actually saw and regularly experienced the power of the gospel. Part of the Pentecostal preaching that shaped my theological mind affirmed that the gospel has power that truly changes people's lives.

Preaching the Bible called for a response to its authority, and so "altar calls" were not just for salvation but were a place to encounter the God

---

[3] "We Shall See the King," in *Songs of Praise* (Springfield, MO: Gospel, 1935), 116.
[4] Everett A. Wilson, *Strategy of the Spirit: J. Philip Hogan and the Growth of the Assemblies of God Worldwide 1960–1990* (Cambria, UK: Paternoster, 1997), 70–88.

of the Bible who still acted to demonstrate the power of the gospel. To see alcohol or drug dependence broken at our altars was not merely a periodic and emotional experience but a life-transforming event that endured and resulted in restored families and new trajectories in life. We prayed for the sick around those altars, and divine healing was not a doctrine to be defended but a reality to be encountered. I must admit, we expected God to act, and I suppose one could say we were a bit naïve about medical verification of these miracles. All I know is that I grew up having seen people who had been diagnosed with terminal diseases by doctors. After prayer around our altars, they enjoyed full and healthy lives for decades after those medical diagnoses.

That expectant worldview of a God who intervened in the fabric of our lives was also reinforced by the "testimony meeting" where people could stand and give verbal affirmation of distinct ways that God had met their needs in everyday life. The belief that God is a God who acts on my behalf in tangible ways was specifically not described as Pentecostal, but it was clearly viewed as an expression of what we regularly described as the "full gospel." This description of the gospel could certainly carry with it "inside track" perceptions. We simply saw it as the fact that we were experiencing the *fullness* of the gospel in tangible ways and very practical dimensions of our lives.[5]

The descriptor "full gospel" also carried with it an implicit belief that the Spirit was poured out at Pentecost on both sons *and* daughters. I experienced this in my childhood years in a very simple way. My dad and mom were both ordained and served as co-pastors of the three congregations. One never knew who was going to preach Sunday morning or Sunday night or during the midweek services. The only thing that really differentiated my parents and their preaching was that my dad was more proficient at preaching in German than my mom. My mother had been a traveling evangelist before World War II who waited for my dad to return from military service before they were married. I actually did not even know that other Christian traditions had problems with ordained women until I experienced that perspective in seminary. My mom, defending her place as an ordained woman minister, never included

---

[5]Gary B. McGee, *This Gospel Shall Be Preached: A History and Theology of Assemblies of God Foreign Missions to 1959* (Springfield, MO: Gospel, 1986), 57–67; the term was actually adopted by Pentecostals from A. B. Simpson's focus on what he termed the "four-fold gospel."

any type of angry polemic. She simply said that God had called her; who was she to reject God's call? She added that there were places she went to preach that men were afraid to go or thought were beneath them. She would say there were people "perishing" simply because men would not go to those places. What was she supposed to do—let people go to hell? So she preached in cattle auction rings, mining camps, and towns that men would bypass as too small. This deep reliance on an encounter with God that inexorably alters the trajectory of our lives has been part of my life from childhood as I viewed its meaning in my dad and mom and their pastoral ministry.

An initial glimpse of my narrative reveals the roots of my faith, which I have critically evaluated over the ensuing years. My theological reflection is much more sophisticated today, but I cannot escape the formative context of my growing-up years. In one sense, my narrative reveals dimensions unique to being Pentecostal, but my guess is that many evangelicals would also resonate with much of my description as their experience as well—though experienced in another family within the spectrum of evangelical Christianity.

Are *Pentecostal* and *Charismatic* Interchangeable Terms?

Many people use the descriptors *Pentecostal* and *charismatic* interchangeably. While that may be convenient, it confuses the uniqueness of the terms historically. While there are many overlapping dimensions of these two terms, I intentionally describe myself as a Pentecostal, not a charismatic. Pentecostals are linked to global renewal movements that occurred in the late nineteenth and early twentieth centuries. While incipient Pentecostalism viewed organizations with cynicism, within several decades organizational life had begun to appear. Scores of groups emerged during this time around the world. In the United States, groups such as the Assemblies of God; International Church of the Foursquare Gospel; the International Pentecostal Holiness Church; and the Church of God, Cleveland, Tennessee, organized and today would represent the descriptor *Pentecostal*. The largest of these groups in the United States (also called classical Pentecostals) is the predominately African American Church of God in Christ.[6]

---

[6]H. V. Synan, "Classical Pentecostalism," in Burgess and McGee, *Dictionary of Pentecostal and Charismatic Movements*, 219–22.

Classical Pentecostalism is informed by five characteristic themes as an integrated structure. These historic themes include justification (God's forgiveness of sin), sanctification (freedom from the power of sin), divine healing, the second coming of Christ, and the baptism of the Holy Spirit. These five themes were common "theological winds" in the late nineteenth century when Pentecostalism was emerging. However, Pentecostalism initiated a significant shift in perspective on how God accomplishes divine purposes in the lives of people and the larger society. This change in perspective shifted God's operation in earthly affairs from historical continuity to a transcendent and instantaneous operation beyond history. The dynamic of the baptism of the Holy Spirit is not an uncommon term in the late nineteenth century, but Pentecostals infused this theme with the highlighting of *glossolalia*, demonstrating the "beyond history" dimension that is a crucial aspect of understanding Pentecostalism's larger societal impact.[7]

Charismatics are identified with renewal movements that began to appear in the late 1950s within historic churches. Catholic charismatic communities sprang up near universities such as Notre Dame, Duquesne, and the University of Michigan. Episcopalian pastors such as Dennis Bennett told of the renewing power of the Holy Spirit in their lives in books like *Nine O'Clock in the Morning*.[8] While the charismatic movement occurred largely in the Catholic and historic mainline churches, it was not as visible among more conservative evangelical groups, though Southern Baptists such as Pat Robertson, John Osteen (father of Joel Osteen), Jamie Buckingham, and Howard Conaster are notable exceptions. A personal spiritual-renewal focus would be more representative of the charismatic movement. Strategic missionary endeavor connected to an urgent eschatology would not be as obvious in the charismatic movement as among Pentecostals. The holiness roots, so noticeable in Pentecostal history, would not be so visibly present among charismatics, and the evidence of tongues connected to the baptism of the Holy Spirit

---

[7]D. William Faupel, *The Everlasting Gospel: The Significance of Eschatology in the Development of Pentecostal Theology*, Journal of Pentecostal Theology 10 (Sheffield, UK: Sheffield Academic, 1996), 85–90, 96–114; Donald W. Dayton, *Theological Roots of Pentecostalism* (Grand Rapids: Francis Asbury, 1987), 15–28.

[8]Dennis J. Bennett, *Nine O'Clock in the Morning* (South Plainfield, NJ: Bridge, 1970); see also L. Christenson, "Bennett, Dennis Joseph," in *The New International Dictionary of Pentecostal and Charismatic Movements*, rev. ed., ed. Stanley M. Burgess (Grand Rapids: Zondervan, 2002), 369–70.

would be less rigorously affirmed. Charismatics certainly participated in glossolalic activity as part of their personal renewal, but a theology of subsequence that is inherent in Pentecostal theology was not present.[9]

In the early and mid-1980s, another notable movement of the Spirit, somewhat connected to Pentecostalism, emerged. Called the Third Wave, it notably found home among evangelicals, particularly missionaries from evangelical sending agencies. Leading mission scholars such as Peter Wagner and Charles Kraft were part of this movement. Peter Wagner chronicles part of his journey from a cessationist viewpoint to full participation in a powerful spiritual revitalization in his book *Look Out! The Pentecostals Are Coming.*[10] Mission scholar Charles Kraft highlights this movement's focus on spiritual power in missionary evangelism that necessitates a further understanding of spiritual warfare in his book *Christianity with Power.*[11] His personal journey of inquiry on spiritual power related to missionary endeavor had begun in his years as a missionary in Nigeria, where he wondered why people who had become followers of Jesus under his ministry would return to their witch doctors when they were sick and in need of physical healing. These and other questions were discussed in a historic symposium in 1988 that I participated in, called the "Academic Symposium on Power Evangelism." Its proceedings were recorded in the book entitled *Wrestling with Dark Angels,* edited by Peter Wagner and Douglas Pennoyer.[12]

This Third Wave is also associated with John Wimber and the Vineyard movement that he led in Southern California. David Watson, from the United Kingdom, is another player in this movement whose charismatic experience previous to the Third Wave's emergence was a steadying force as the Third Wave developed, in both the United States and the United Kingdom.[13] Spiritual power, as an expression of the reality

---

[9]P. D. Hocken, "Charismatic Movement," in Burgess, *The New International Dictionary of Pentecostal and Charismatic Movements,* 477–519.

[10]C. Peter Wagner, *Look Out! The Pentecostals Are Coming* (Carol Stream, IL: Creation House, 1973).

[11]Charles H. Kraft, *Christianity with Power: Your Worldview and Your Experience of the Supernatural* (Ann Arbor, MI: Servant, 1989).

[12]C. Peter Wagner and F. Douglas Pennoyer, eds., *Wrestling with Dark Angels: Toward a Deeper Understanding of the Supernatural Forces in Spiritual Warfare* (Ventura, CA: Regal, 1990). See my response to Peter Wagner's early teaching on territorial spirits in *Wresting with Dark Angels,* 73–99.

[13]David C. K. Watson's influence on evangelical life in the United Kingdom can be seen in two of his books: *I Believe in the Church* (Grand Rapids: Eerdmans, 1978); and *Called and Committed* (Carol Stream, IL: Harold Shaw, 1981).

of the kingdom, is at the core of this movement.[14] The baptism of the Spirit, as understood by Pentecostals, is not as visible, and *glossolalia*, as a dimension of spiritual renewal so central to the Pentecostal movement, is not as obvious. What is very present is the belief that Christ's ministry came with power and that it is reasonable to anticipate that same power in contemporary life. If Jesus came healing and casting out demons (Mark 1:14–2:12), then he is doing the very same things today by the power of the Holy Spirit.[15]

This Third Wave was implicitly connected to mission studies globally because much of its genesis was a function of the dialogue among non-Western students in mission-studies programs who were seeking answers to their questions about handling the supernatural in strategic mission efforts. Paul Hiebert's article "The Flaw of the Excluded Middle," published in 1982, personified the tensions and discussions of the early 1980s as the Third Wave movement developed.[16] Hiebert's usage of social science and its portrayal of the ways that religion is understood provided the framework for his observation that most Westerners fail to see dimensions of spiritual reality in which a majority of the world lives on a daily basis. Because I was in my doctoral work at Fuller Seminary during this period, this expression of spiritual renewal was something I observed firsthand and participated in directly. The Hiebert article provided a wonderful set of insights for me, as it gave me clear descriptions of a familiar understanding I had affirmed of the unseen principalities and powers that did impact the lives of all human beings, whether they acknowledged them or not.

A summary of the continuing tensions between those in the crucible of this movement is seen in the faculty report at Fuller Seminary that attempted to describe and resolve the tensions that arose at the faculty level. I must admit I viewed this report as a personification of the continuing tensions I have experienced as I have attempted to navigate what it means to be a Pentecostal while simultaneously identifying wholeheartedly with the larger evangelical community. The tension is described as follows:

---

[14] John Wimber and Kevin Springer, *Power Evangelism* (New York: Harper & Row, 1986).

[15] John Wimber and Kevin Springer, *Power Healing* (San Francisco: Harper & Row, 1987), 126–66.

[16] Paul G. Hiebert, "The Flaw of the Excluded Middle," *Missiology* 10, no. 1 (January 1982): 35–47.

John Wimber, founder of the Vineyard Movement and adjunct instructor along with C. Peter Wagner and Charles Kraft, our professors, came to be linked much more closely with Fuller in the minds of the public than his busy schedule of pastoral and conference ministry warranted: his audiences and readers were tempted to impute his opinions and approaches to our faculty more readily than the faculty would support. Questions arose about the theological wisdom of conducting healing services in academic, rather than churchly, settings. Eagerness to experience the works of the Spirit and to prepare our students to minister in deed as well as word short-circuited the signals of caution that usually prevail in places like ours. In short, to borrow the language of another discipline, our engineering outran our science.[17]

The tensions described in the Fuller report demonstrate what it means to place your accent on different syllables of the same word and yet remain in the same family. That tension, though in varied forms, continues today.

I Am a Pentecostal

I am much less conscious today of the novelty of being a Pentecostal, but I am also aware that there exists an incredible lack of understanding on the part of many Christians as to who we Pentecostals really are. Our tradition is just now entering its second century, but even the most informed persons can still fixate on *glossolalia*, speaking in tongues, as the sole characteristic around which we are categorized. I must sadly admit that we Pentecostals have, all too often, contributed to that fractured understanding of our tradition. The visibility of Pentecostals in Christian media does hinder the way many Christians view Pentecostals. The mistakes made by Pentecostals are often carried out with grand style and frequently grab headlines. The self-righteous posture of some Pentecostals that conveys an insider track to God is unfortunate. I guess I would simply say that all of us have members of our own families or organizations whom we would not choose to be the sole examples by which our entire families or organizations are evaluated. The embarrassing members are part of the group, but there is more to any group or family than its most "novel" members or traits.

---

[17]Lewis B. Smedes, ed., *Ministry and the Miraculous: A Case Study at Fuller Theological Seminary* (Pasadena, CA: Fuller Theological Seminary, 1987), 15–16.

I remember this latent frustration of ongoing misunderstanding boiling to the surface in a scholarly meeting attended by a broad spectrum of Christian scholars where the focus was the contribution of Pentecostals to global mission. I still can hear a Pentecostal colleague who boldly queried how many Pentecostals there needed to be worldwide before we were taken seriously? It got pretty quiet in the room, but I must admit that I resonated with that outburst. I am part of a Christian family that is more than a curious oddity to be studied. Truth be told, we will never be understood by examinations of our doctrines alone, or even our most visible faith and practices. To understand the Pentecostal world, one needs to analyze the basic conscious and unconscious assumptions about reality and God's interaction with the created order.

Pentecostal ideological identity is really shaped by what Max Weber called "affective action."[18] To Pentecostals, the affective domain is viewed as central to the shaping of reality. To the question of causality that is critical to worldview construction, divine initiative is not just an ideal category but a powerful reality for Pentecostalism. The sacred-secular dichotomy that epitomizes modernity is rejected and replaced with an affirmation of the immediate availability of God's power and presence. We see the world through a reality construct in which God is near at hand and provides clear evidence of his powerful presence through his church.[19] Simply put, when Pentecostals approach the exegesis of biblical texts, theological reflection, or ministry activity, we do not necessarily have a Pentecostal way of doing things. Rather, we enter into those tasks, common to all Christian traditions, with a particular set of assumptions that do dynamically and directly shape the activities we initiate and participate in.[20]

My explanation in the previous paragraph may simply confirm your hunch that our faith tradition is centered in experience. *Existential*, *shallow*, and *emotional* are all terms that some would use to characterize what I have just described as central to understanding Pentecostals. Whereas emotionalism seeks to stimulate emotions as an end in itself, the Pente-

---

[18]Margaret M. Poloma, *The Assemblies of God at the Crossroads: Charisma and Institutional Dilemmas* (Knoxville: University of Tennessee Press, 1989), 5–7.
[19]Ibid., 7–9.
[20]Margaret M. Poloma and John C. Green, *The Assemblies of God: Godly Love and the Revitalization of American Pentecostalism* (New York: New York University Press, 2010), 8–10, 102–20.

costal perspective is to state that any genuine encounter with the living God brings to bear our entire being and will leave an emotional impact. I would suggest this is not emotionalism or experience-based theology but rather experience-certified theology. Belief in the availability of God's preternatural power and presence is foundational. It simply affirms a theology of God near-at-hand who gives abundant evidence of his powerful presence in the church.[21]

I recall the delight of reading Harvey Cox's groundbreaking volume *Fire from Heaven*.[22] His work in that volume affirmed that Pentecostals are not a homogenous group but, in fact, part of a faith tradition he called a "religion made to travel" that loses little in its translation from context to context.[23] He went on to provide a simple but profound explanation of my spiritual journey that frankly brought me to tears the first time I read it because someone had finally expressed what I had inherently believed and lived my entire life.

From his study of Pentecostalism globally, Cox came to describe it as restoration of spirituality that provided resolution for people, in the center of their being, to the unending struggle for a sense of destiny and significance. Cox saw this resolution as a spiritual restoration of significance and purpose to masses of people whose daily experience is one of despair, injustice, and hopelessness. He suggested that Pentecostalism was enabling a growing number of people to restore, in very concrete ways, at least three specific dimensions of basic spirituality. The first dimension he called "primal speech," which some scholars might call "ecstatic utterances" or speaking in tongues.[24] He suggested that in a world that can make people think their voices do not matter or where contrived rhetoric has emptied language of any meaning, Pentecostals participate in a "language of the heart" that is understood in heaven itself.[25]

The second dimension of recovery that Cox observes is that of "primal piety," which focuses on Pentecostalism's affirmation of the phe-

---

[21]William McDonald, "Pentecostal Theology: A Classical Viewpoint," in *Perspectives on the New Pentecostalism*, ed. Russell P. Spittler (Grand Rapids: Baker, 1976), 59–62.

[22]Harvey G. Cox, *Fire from Heaven: The Rise of Pentecostal Spirituality and the Reshaping of Religion in the Twenty-First Century* (Reading, MA: Addison-Wesley, 1995).

[23]Ibid., 102.

[24]Ibid., 82.

[25]Ibid.

nomenological dimension of human religiosity.[26] Visions and dreams, dramatic physical demonstration, and mystical experience are central to a spirituality that expects God to show up in concrete ways. This is the God who cannot be defined or contained in left-brained activity alone but is to be encountered face-to-face.

The final dimension of Cox's observation is that Pentecostal spirituality is typified by "primal hope."[27] This outlook insists that a radically new world is about to dawn. This perspective is an affirmation that the world we see is not all there is or will be. Primal hope is more of an orientation toward a future that persists despite the failure of particular events to occur. This hope is nurtured in a community in which the image of the future rule of the King is reinforced by a primal piety that participates holistically in spiritual encounter and verbalizes freely in primal speech, the language of the heart, that cannot be constrained by the particular context of tragedy or despair one may live through.[28]

Cox's writing of this volume in the mid-1990s was essentially a testimony to a growing conviction that twenty-first-century Christianity would be deeply impacted by this newer expression of Christian faith. Cox's work represents the increasing difficulty of keeping the historic lines of this spiritual renewal distinct. Even his reference to Pentecostalism as a "religion made to travel" points to the risk of defining this movement, barely a century old, in hard-and-fast terms that might overly categorize it.

The face of global Christianity has taken on the character of what Cox described in the mid-1990s. The work of David Barrett and, more recently, Todd Johnston has provided a metric testifying that the impetus that emerged in the late nineteenth and early twentieth centuries has resulted in a much broader global influence, in fact the second largest family of Christians and the largest body of Protestants.[29] This global dimension is most visibly seen in my own denomination, where the Assem-

---

[26]Ibid., 99–110.

[27]Ibid., 82.

[28]Ibid., 82–122.

[29]Todd M. Johnson, "The Demographics of Renewal," in *Spirit-Empowered Christianity in the Twenty-First Century*, ed. Vinson Synan (Lake Mary, FL: Charisma House, 2011), 55–67. Also, see Barrett and Johnson's annual demographic reports in the *International Bulletin of Missionary Research*.

blies of God numbers approximately three million in the United States and over sixty-three million globally.[30]

I Am an Evangelical

When asked whether I identify myself as an evangelical or a Pentecostal, I must admit a hesitation to answer, depending on the context of the question and who is asking. Because of my common commitment with evangelicals to historic orthodoxy, I certainly affirm cognitively my identity as an evangelical. I do so with a natural desire to align myself with what I believe are foundational biblical themes critical to historic Christian faith. But the "otherness" that has shaped my religious identity since childhood has its most painful memories rooted in frustrating encounters not with mainline, Catholic, or Orthodox persons but with evangelicals. From wholesale dismissal by those who would question Pentecostals' even being described as Christians, to those who would tolerate Pentecostals as "cousins from the fringe," I must admit continuing frustration. Even with the more respectful of evangelical colleagues, I all too often feel merely tolerated, as if I will one day come to my senses and shape up into a real evangelical.

Ultimately the tension I feel when asked about the identity of my Christian family has much more to do with an ongoing internal conversation that the years have informed. Personal struggles are real, but as a follower of Jesus, graced by God to serve in a position of influence, I must move beyond those personal speed bumps in the road. My interactions with Christians of other traditions have become, for me, a reminder of the grace of God to touch people in unique ways throughout church history. The stories of the historical intersection of God's grace and the ensuing development of Christian tradition have increasingly reminded me that we Pentecostals are only among the more recent expressions of God's grace amid humankind's quest to know God in the most meaningful ways in particular times.

---

[30] "AG U.S. Adherents, 2000–2010 Data by District and Region," Assemblies of God, accessed July 29, 2011, http://agchurches.org/Sitefiles/Default/RSS/AG.org%20TOP/AG%20Statistical%20Reports/2010%20Stats/Adher%20by%20Dist%20(Corret)%202010.pdf; "AG Worldwide Churches and Adherents, 1987–2010," Assemblies of God, accessed July 29, 2011, http://agchurches.org/Sitefiles/Default/RSS/AG.org%20TOP/AG%20Statistical%20Reports/2010%20Stats/WWAdh%20 2010.pdf.

I have come to resolve my personal tensions within the larger evangelical family by finding overarching points of connection and common ground. Even in the middle of current rhetoric about the end of evangelicalism and speculations about evangelicals' being at a crossroads, the essence of evangelicalism, as summarized by those such as British historian David Bebbington, is where I find the greatest traction.[31]

Bebbington's concise summary of the core substance of evangelicalism is instructive. He identifies the primary characteristics of evangelicalism as (1) *conversionism*, the belief that lives need to be transformed through a born-again experience and lifelong process of following Jesus; (2) *activism*, the expression and demonstration of the gospel in missionary and social reform efforts; (3) *biblicism*, a high regard for and obedience to the Bible as the ultimate authority; and (4) *crucicentrism*, an emphasis on the sacrifice of Jesus Christ on the cross as making possible the redemption of humanity.[32]

Conversionism

The *conversionist* DNA is rooted deep in Pentecostal life. As with many renewal movements in their incipient stages, fountainheads of Pentecostalism at the beginning of the twentieth century could be a bit rough around the edges.[33] To this context, where zeal could have easily sidetracked a move of God, leaders like William J. Seymour, who led the Azusa Street revival, spoke clearly about the necessary focus of spiritual renewal. Seymour simply said to those whose zeal could easily have misread God's moving at Azusa Street, "Now do not go from this meeting and talk about tongues, but try to get people saved."[34]

Conversion is a transformative encounter with God most fully explained by a power that transcends left-brained activities alone. The risks that come with conversion globally, particularly where the gospel is least accessible and most resisted, give credence to a conversion that

---

[31]David W. Bebbington, *Evangelicalism in Modern Britain: A History from the 1730s to the 1980s* (London: Unwin Hyman, 1989). In the same vein, see Mark A. Noll, *The Rise of Evangelicalism: The Age of Edwards, Whitefield and the Wesleys* (Downers Grove, IL: InterVarsity, 2002).

[32]Bebbington, *Evangelicalism in Modern Britain*, 2–17.

[33]Cecil M. Robeck, *The Azusa Street Mission and Revival: The Birth of the Global Pentecostal Movement* (Nashville: Thomas Nelson, 2006), 87–128.

[34]Grant McClung, ed., *Azusa Street and Beyond: 100 Years of Commentary on the Global Pentecostal/Charismatic Movement* (Gainesville, FL: Bridge-Logos, 2006), 1–26.

abundantly pardons and saves to the uttermost (Heb. 7:25). Conversion often results in the new believers' exclusion from their immediate social community, including family.

The Pentecostal testimony after conversion invariably contrasts the old life "in the world" and the new life "in Christ." Chilean Pentecostal pastor Juan Sepúlveda sees the goal of conversion as nothing less than a transformative work of a new creation and an implied call to discipleship.[35] While Pentecostal preaching is often criticized for its lack of theological content, it is certainly preaching directed to the needs of people, challenging a person to a transforming encounter with God. There is an implied affirmation that the Holy Spirit enables a believer to translate belief into action, faith into practices, and doctrine into daily living. Conversion that is visibly a "from-to" encounter with the living God is assumed.[36]

Activism

The *activism* component in the essential elements of evangelicalism is self-evident among Pentecostals as a demonstration of the gospel in missionary and social-reform efforts. Pentecostals have always been a missionary movement in foundation and essence. There is a firm conviction that the Spirit has been poured out in signs and wonders in order for the nations of the world to be reached before the end of the age.[37]

This activist DNA implicit in Pentecostalism was posited by the late Pentecostal historian Gary McGee and his description of the "radical strategy."[38] McGee suggested that the radical strategy was a unique pneumatological approach to mission that affirmed the need for a subsequent spiritual empowerment connecting the recipient to the continuing redemptive mission of Jesus Christ by the Holy Spirit.

McGee's observation clearly provides a picture of "activism" that is theologically reflective. The missiological grounding felt by missionary efforts in the late nineteenth century included how global missionary

---

[35]Juan Sepúlveda, "Pentecostalism as Popular Religiosity," *International Review of Mission* 78, no. 309 (January 1989): 82.

[36]Doug Peterson, "Pentecostals: Who Are They?," in *Mission as Transformation: A Theology of the Whole Gospel*, ed. Vinay Samuel and Chris Sugden (Irvine, CA: Regnum, 1999), 78–80.

[37]Allan Anderson, *Spreading Fires: The Missionary Nature of Early Pentecostalism* (Maryknoll, NY: Orbis, 2007), 294.

[38]McGee, *This Gospel Shall be Preached*, 66.

efforts could be accomplished more rapidly and effectively. There was a growing passion among mission-minded people (typified in the Student Volunteer Movement) to see the restoration of the Spirit's power. This "radical strategy" was the clear mark of fresh theological reflection among Pentecostals that informed an interactive response to the mission challenge of "how to reach the world in this generation."[39]

The conventional wisdom about Pentecostalism has tended to observe that our urgent eschatology has kept us from any type of real social impact. While American Pentecostals have suffered from the historic bifurcation between evangelism and social action that many American evangelicals experienced, an alternative picture began to emerge in the 1990s that provides clarity about the realities of global Pentecostalism. Beginning with the analysis of the growth of Pentecostalism in Latin America, sociologists asked questions about the significance of Pentecostalism as a popular social movement. David Stoll asked *Is Latin America Turning Protestant?* with a larger focus on the political implication of the growth of Pentecostals in Latin America.[40] A British sociologist, David Martin, wrote *Tongues of Fire: The Explosion of Protestants in Latin America*.[41] Those volumes frankly moved to an analysis of the implicit social activism present in the Pentecostal movement. These researchers created a more realistic vision of the social activism of Pentecostalism globally. Rather than looking at Pentecostal participation in government social programs, they began to realize that the spirituality of Pentecostalism expressed itself in a *contra mundum* response to the unjust societies where Pentecostals have seen such significant growth. The perspective of even Catholic observers was that "Pentecostals do not have a social policy, they are social policy."[42]

Current researchers such as Donald Miller and Tetsunao Yamamori are chronicling a much broader framework for research about social action. They observe that "progressive Pentecostals" are not trying to

---

[39]Byron Klaus, foreword to *Miracles, Mission, and American Pentecostalism*, by Gary B. McGee, American Society of Missiology Series 45 (Maryknoll, NY: Orbis, 2010), xiii.

[40]David Stoll, *Is Latin America Turning Protestant? The Politics of Evangelical Growth* (Berkeley, CA: University of California Press, 1990).

[41]David Martin, *Tongues of Fire: The Explosion of Protestantism in Latin America* (Cambridge, MA: Basil Blackwell, 1990).

[42]Jeffrey Gros, "Confessing the Apostolic Faith from the Perspective of the Pentecostal Churches," *Pneuma: Journal of the Society for Pentecostal Studies* 9, no. 1 (Spring 1987): 12.

reform social structures so much as they are attempting to build from the ground up an alternative social reality.[43] They posit that this "subversive" social activity is rooted in the teaching that people are made in the image of God, have dignity, are equal in God's sight, and therefore have rights regardless of their social status. Miller and Yamamori view these assumptions as fundamental to the creation of a democratic government. Their work provides alternatives to the image of Pentecostals as nonengaged socially. Their alternative picture is of a global Pentecostalism that is a wide-ranging social movement.[44]

Pentecostals clearly reflect an essential evangelical commitment to conversionism and activism. These two characteristics are intrinsically connected. To understand conversion as a transformation that has taken place is also to affirm that this conversion has considerable external implications. The supernaturalist worldview is an implicit focus for Pentecostal conversion as a visible, practical demonstration that Jesus Christ is more powerful than the spirits, power, or false gods worshiped or feared by any individual or group. Jesus's ministry makes clear that people need God's power to break their experience of captivity and receive freedom in Christ. They also need the work of the Spirit to "will and to work for his good pleasure" (Phil. 2:13). This work of God at conversion and continuing in discipleship brings intrinsic relationship with Jesus Christ. The work of conversion is about truth and the need to have a transformation of our human understanding of Jesus Christ. This work of conversion and commitment to Christ is seen in a dynamic and holistic way.[45]

Biblicism

The third characteristic at the core of evangelicalism is a high regard for and obedience to the Bible as the ultimate authority. I have already indicated that my earliest theological training on biblical authority was a song my dad regularly sang before preaching. Its simple lyrics focused on the durability of the Bible to stand regardless of the challenges and events sometimes used to tear down its efficacy. This was my earliest

---

[43]Donald E. Miller and Tetsunao Yamamori, *Global Pentecostalism: The New Face of Christian Social Engagement* (Berkeley, CA: University of California Press, 2007).

[44]Ibid., 4–5.

[45]Charles H. Kraft, "What Kind of Encounter Do We Need in Our Christian Witness?," *Evangelical Missions Quarterly* 27, no. 3 (July 1991): 258–65.

understanding of biblical authority, framed as an enduring spiritual quality in the context of life. More particular discussions of verbal and plenary inspiration, inerrancy, and so forth, while important themes, have not been the focus of my most passionate defense of the faith. It is at points like this that some of my evangelical colleagues have their greatest concerns confirmed. They will point out to me that it is because we Pentecostals have not thoroughly investigated the text with exegetical precision that we have a gap in our biblical understanding—particularly as it relates to our understanding of the baptism of the Spirit, spiritual gifts, and the power of the Spirit in ministry contexts.

Frankly, that criticism has some substance: preaching in Pentecostal churches can sometimes measure "authority" in voice volume rather than careful treatment of the text. While I acknowledge that some Pentecostal preaching is lacking in careful attention to the text, a lack that has resulted in some colorful doctrinal alternatives, I would observe that we are not the only sibling in the larger evangelical family to have seen creative license with the Bible that leads to gaps in theological precision.

In 1991, Gordon Fee, arguably the finest exegete in the Pentecostal tradition since the later part of the twentieth century, compiled a small set of essays in which he acknowledged the tension he felt as a Pentecostal New Testament scholar working at bastions of evangelical identity such as Wheaton College and Gordon-Conwell Theological Seminary. He offered his own journey as a Pentecostal in the center of evangelicalism and spoke clearly about areas of tension he felt. One of these areas was the question of religious authority, not in its ultimate but in its penultimate forms. Here he observed the potential for differing perspectives about how God communicates or reveals himself and what authoritatively mediates God and God's will to humankind. He further observed that one's understanding of authority is ultimately a matter of faith and the effort to demonstrate reasonably the validity of the type of authority we affirm. Evangelicals and all Pentecostals might affirm that our religious authority has an external source in a God who has revealed himself objectively. Together we affirm that God has revealed himself by deeds and in a Person. We view Scripture as the ultimate authority. Other forms of authority such as tradition, reason, or experience all need to be firmly authenticated by Scripture. It is in the attempt at equilibrium between penultimate forms of authority and Scripture as the primary authority that the tension lies.

It is here that I agree with Fee that the conflict can become vitriolic. I have experienced my most stressful moments as a Pentecostal because I do not enter wholeheartedly into certain evangelical battles, resulting in the perception that I am somehow less committed to the authority of Scripture and more focused on spiritual encounter/experience.[46]

William Seymour was the leader of the Azusa Street awakening that began in April 1906 in Los Angeles. While Pentecostals trace their beginning to many places globally, the Azusa Street event is arguably the most storied of these early seedbeds. Seymour was a calm and gracious son of ex-slaves whom God used in extraordinary ways to lead this wellspring of renewal. The Azusa Street mission was a place where spiritual seekers of all varieties came to reach out to God. It was at times messy; passionate spirituality was clearly in evidence. The Jim Crow attitudes of the day were evident in the reporting of this event, such as in the *Los Angeles Times*' bringing attention to "negroisms."[47] Bible-believing pastors and leaders in Los Angeles regularly sought to antagonize what was happening at the Azusa Street mission. The clear commitment to biblical authority was made by Seymour when he said: "We're measuring everything by the Word, every experience must measure up with the Bible. Some say this is going too far, but if we have lived too close to the Word, we will settle that with the Lord when we meet Him in the air."[48]

This clear statement also reveals the propensity of Pentecostals to see biblical authority as functioning in the context of the life of the church. The interaction between the "context" and "content" is dynamic. The tension between sources of authority, both ultimate and penultimate, will continue because epistemology is a philosophical category of much contention. We will have our differences, but let us not allow these differences to degenerate into battles over exegetical methods or even a quarrel over the approved set of assumptions as we enter the hermeneutical task. Pentecostals are people of the Word—the Bible stands. That has never been in question among Pentecostals.

---

[46]Gordon Fee, *Gospel and Spirit: Issues in New Testament Hermeneutics* (Peabody, MA: Hendrickson, 1991), x–xv. For more in-depth analysis of attempts to resolve these tensions, see William W. Menzies and Robert P. Menzies, *Spirit and Power: A Call to Evangelical Dialogue* (Grand Rapids: Zondervan, 2000).

[47]Robeck, *The Azusa Street Mission and Revival*, 129–86.

[48]*Apostolic Faith* 1, no. 9 (June–September 1907): 1.

Crucicentrism

The final essential quality of evangelicalism is *crucicentrism*, defined as an emphasis on the sacrifice of Jesus Christ on the cross as making possible the redemption of humanity. From the earliest statements about Christ, Pentecostals have clearly demonstrated a stress on the centrality of Jesus in the redemption of humanity. On the excitement surrounding the early days of the Azusa Street renewal, an observer of that event said:

> We may not even hold a doctrine, or seek an experience, except in Christ. Many are willing to seek power from every battery they can lay their hands on, in order to perform miracles, draw the attention and adoration of the people to themselves, thus robbing Christ of His glory and making a fair showing in the flesh. . . . We must stick to our text, Christ. He alone can save. The attention of the people must first of all and always hold to Him. A true Pentecost will produce a mighty conviction of sin, a turning to God. Believe in your own heart's hunger and go ahead with God. Don't allow the devil to rob you of a real Pentecost. Any work that exalts the Holy Ghost or the gifts above Jesus will finally land up in fanaticism. Whatever causes us to exalt and love Jesus is well and safe. The reverse will ruin all. The Holy Ghost is a great light, but focused on Jesus always for His revealing.[49]

The clear sense of Christ-centeredness present in this early statement counters accusations that Pentecostals are pneumacentric. The reality is that all followers of Jesus are called upon to keep alive Jesus's own experience of the Spirit. This close person-to-person encounter develops in that Jesus Christ initiates dialogue with us and invites a response. This is not an ideology or another "ism" but a meeting with the living person of Jesus Christ. The Jesus whom we meet is the Son of God become man who suffered for us, died, and was raised again and now leads us into the fullness of his inheritance. This intimacy with Christ enhances the depth and breadth of speaking about him and to him.[50]

In my denomination, the deepest of commitments to Christ and his work on the cross is also seen in our clearest of statements centered

---

[49]William W. Menzies, *Anointed to Serve: The Story of the Assemblies of God* (Springfield, MO: Gospel, 1971), 55.
[50]Léon Joseph Cardinal Suenens, *A New Pentecost?* (New York: Seabury, 1975), 96–97.

on what we call our four cardinal doctrines.[51] These foci all convene around Jesus as Savior, baptizer, healer, and soon-coming King. More than dogmatic statements, this so-called fourfold gospel clearly gives visibility to the work of Jesus Christ on the cross that makes possible the redemption of humanity in eschatological terms. This framework of the "foursquare gospel" was well known in the late nineteenth century, most notably connected to A. B. Simpson. Grant Wacker sees the adoption of Simpson's emphases as clear evidence of Pentecostal determination to doctrinal exactness, with christocentrism as its centerpiece. He observes that the evidence is so voluminous about clear commitment to historic doctrines of the church, "it is hard to understand how the contrary notion ever arose."[52]

This clear commitment to the work of Christ, with its plethora of eschatological implications, is seen in a heightened awareness of Christians as a community of believers displaying the powerful reality of being reconciled to God, joyfully participating in Christ's continuing redemptive mission with renewed zeal. The Spirit blows where he wills, but the concern of the Spirit is Christ with us, the "hope of glory" (Col. 1:27).

The venerable Thomas Smail puts it succinctly:

> The work of the Spirit is to draw out of Christ all that is in him for us, so that we may be the primary expression of his glory. After all this He does by grace through faith, not so that books may be written about it, but so it may be received and that the thanks of the Church may be its faithful reflection of the glory of the Lord.[53]

We're Not in Kansas Anymore

I have narrated my identification with evangelicalism as a Pentecostal with careful acknowledgment of those overwhelming areas of common passion and belief. I have also acknowledged the circuitous route that this journey has brought me through. That sometimes rocky journey also has some denominational dimensions. These can be seen in the partici-

---

[51]"Our Core Doctrines," Assemblies of God, accessed July 28, 2011, http://ag.org/top/beliefs /our_core_doctrines/salvation; "Assemblies of God Fundamental Truths," Assemblies of God, accessed July 28, 2011, http://agchurches.org/Sitefiles/Default/RSS/AG.org%20TOP/Fundamen tal%20Truths%20(cond).pdf.

[52]Grant Wacker, *Heaven Below: Early Pentecostals and American Culture* (Cambridge, MA: Harvard University Press, 2001), 77.

[53]Thomas A. Smail, *Reflected Glory* (Grand Rapids: Eerdmans, 1975), 128.

pation the Assemblies of God have had with the National Association of Evangelicals (NAE). As an ordained minister with the Assemblies of God (USA), I think it is interesting to note that we are now the largest denominational group in the NAE. That is true today, but might not have been conceived of back in the late 1930s and early 1940s when outspoken fundamentalists tried to capture the leadership of evangelicalism and failed. The response of Carl McIntire to this event is telling as he berates the NAE for allowing Pentecostals to participate. McIntire said:

> Tongues is one of the great signs of the apostasy. As true Protestant denominations turn from the faith and it gets darker, the Devil comes more into the open. . . . The dominance of the "tongues" groups in the NAE "denominations" and their compromise in regard to the Federal Council will not, we believe, commend this organization to those who desire to see a standard lifted in behalf of the historic Christian faith.[54]

We have come a long way since those days, but it would be best for all of us to at least acknowledge the path we have walked together and be honest enough not merely to smile as if there have not been potholes along the way. Compare McIntire's observations with more recent statements by evangelical leaders like Rich Mouw, who said, "During the past century, Pentecostalism has gone from a 'wrong side of the tracks' movement to the most influential reality in global Christianity."[55] Mouw's observation is given fuller development by Canadian biblical scholar Roger Stronstad, who said:

> In the development of Protestant theology, the Reformed tradition has emphasized the activity of the Spirit in initiation-conversion, the Wesleyan tradition has subsequently emphasized the activity of the Spirit in holiness or sanctification, and the Pentecostal tradition has finally emphasized the charismatic activity of the Spirit in worship and service. It is the sad lesson of church history and contemporary experience that the charismatic activity of the Holy Spirit cannot flourish in a climate which is hostile or indifferent to this dimension of activity of the Spirit. Thus, Luke's charismatic theology challenges the Reformed and the

---

[54]Carl McIntire, "Editorial," *Christian Beacon* (April 27, 1944): 8.
[55]Richard J. Mouw, endorsement of *An Eyewitness Remembers the Century of the Holy Spirit*, by Vinson Synan (Grand Rapids: Chosen, 2010), 1.

Wesley traditions to add the activity of the Spirit to their initiation-conversion and holiness experience of the Spirit.[56]

The years have a way of giving perspective to what once seemed to be insurmountable conflict. The painful memories of past skirmishes really are sometimes not easily forgotten by participants. We may not be in Kansas anymore, but twenty-first-century challenges to the common themes held firmly by the evangelical family should yield solidarity, not further tension.

Reaching Forward

Revelation 21:3–6 is framed from the vantage point of the future. Its perspective juxtaposes our current experience with the lens of eternity. The central figure in this passage is Jesus, who has entered into our time from the future and demonstrated that the future and its victory can now show up in the most unlikely places. The ministry of Jesus shows that no place can escape the future as incurable diseases are healed, demonic strongholds are shattered, and those left by the wayside are given hope that was previously inconceivable. This word the Revelator writes is first heard by those who were in the minority, persecuted religiously, and marginalized both politically and socially. The message of the Revelator made sense to these early hearers and readers. In the middle of insurmountable odds in the first century, God demonstrates that he is as good as his Word. Believers are told to write it down, count on it, and live by it.

It is in the twenty-first century that these ancient words of the Revelator speak to us. By whatever moniker we call ourselves as followers of Jesus, we are in a battle. For many folks in our nation, the word *evangelical* speaks of tyranny, bigotry, and all they want the world to be free of. Affirming the core qualities of evangelicalism that I have reflected on in this essay seems to elicit increasingly vitriolic public responses. From the satire of media gurus to the imagery of John Lennon's classic song "Imagine," we are not as welcome in the public arena as we sometimes suppose. Truth be told, we will have to seek unity around a clarified understanding of ourselves as evangelicals.

[56]Roger Stronstad, *The Charismatic Theology of St. Luke* (Peabody, MA: Hendrickson, 1984), 83.

We will have to commit to a *conversionism* that joins the proper pathways of initiation into the faith with a spirituality that commits to a long obedience in the same direction. Triumphalism will need to be tempered with humility that affirms that the faithful following of Jesus is "not by might nor by power, but by the Spirit of God" (Zech. 4:6). Smiles and styles as the substance of our call to the transformed life are no longer adequate. Suffering in massive quantities is already the experience of the majority of followers of Jesus in the world today. Conversionism that ignores what it means to thrive in contexts of opposition will surely atrophy.

We will have to commit ourselves to an *activism* in which evangelism involves actually looking people in the eye and engaging them relationally over a period of time. The far reaches of virtual reality may be both ubiquitous and unexplored, but the word *friend* is not in need of an overhaul that excuses followers of Jesus from the messiness of face-to-face human existence. Our activism may, in the name of Christ, need to champion worthy interventions in the obvious tragedies that the tears, mourning, and death pictured by the Revelator bring our way. Let us still affirm that the greatest problem facing humanity is alienation from God.

Our *biblicism* will need to include efforts to reclaim and reinvigorate our creeds by thorough and conceptual frameworks that capture the hearts of people set adrift by human self-destruction, which reveals our lostness. The Bible's authority needs not only a conceptual defense; it needs those who would align with the moniker *evangelical* to see this authoritative revelation as God's lens through which we navigate the world of tears, mourning, pain, and death. It is truly a lamp unto our feet and light unto our path (Ps. 119:105).

Our *crucicentrism* will need to be clothed by the Lord in the power of the Holy Spirit so that we will be powerfully enabled to give the world a dynamic testimony of the central truth of Christianity, namely, that Jesus is alive and is drawing all humanity to himself. We express our commitment to the centrality of Christ's redemptive work in a context where there is expanding competition for whose explanation of the world will carry the day. Robert Webber has observed that in this marketplace of who gets to narrate the world, there are two front-runners.[57] The

---

[57]Robert E. Webber, *Who Gets to Narrate the World? Contending for the Christian Story in an Age of Rivals* (Downers Grove, IL: InterVarsity, 2008).

first is a radical secular humanism, which wants to offer a world rid of any notion of God. This ranges from the aggressive posture posited by proponents such as Sam Harris and Richard Dawkins to the folks who suggest that a religious system *sans* God is a worthy pursuit.[58] Webber believes that the other leader in this global competition is radical Islam, which affirms the forceful removal of all opponents to the inevitability of Allah's rule over created order.[59] Webber's view of our contemporary experience is synthesized in the following:

> We live in a crucial time of history, a time when our faith will be increasingly tested by the enemies of God's true narrative. The powers and principalities still actively oppose the Lord of history and seek to distort and destroy his truth. *Who gets to narrate the world?* is not a mere academic question. If Christians are to witness to God's mission to restore the world, to recover the Garden, to establish once again the communion of God's creatures within the communion and fellowship of the triune God, then we must know the narrative, proclaim it and live it—to the death if necessary.[60]

That narration of the world is at the heart of what followers of Jesus are called to pursue passionately. The essence of evangelicalism, which I have experienced as a Pentecostal, can rise to the challenge that Webber describes for us. The prayer of Jesus in John 17:21 need not be a lofty theme for discussion only—it may be the linchpin that allows the *evangelical* narration to be heard.

Lesslie Newbigin summarizes the crux of the matter for all members of the evangelical family when he says: "How is it possible that people should come to believe that the power which has the last word in human affairs is represented by a man hanging on a cross? I am suggesting that the only answer, the only hermeneutic of the gospel, is a congregation of men and women who believe it and live by it."[61]

---

[58]Sam Harris, *The End of Faith: Religion, Terror, and the Future of Reason* (New York: Norton, 2004); Richard Dawkins, *The God Delusion* (New York: Houghton Mifflin, 2008). See also www. TED.com for fascinating perspectives from top thinkers around the themes of technology, entertainment, and design.

[59]Webber, *Who Gets to Narrate the World?*, 100–113.

[60]Ibid., 132–33.

[61]Lesslie Newbigin, *The Gospel in a Pluralistic Society* (Grand Rapids: Eerdmans, 1989), 227–32.

8

Why I Am an Evangelical and a Presbyterian

Bryan Chapell

I began this essay thirty-five years ago. I had just completed a course in Presbyterian church government taught by a godly professor using a classic Presbyterian textbook. My classmates seemed convinced. Yet despite all the careful analysis of biblical history and original texts, I was not. I could not ignore the arguments based on silence, the appeal to exegetical methods we had criticized in others, the ready conclusions that left other possibilities unconsidered, and—most disconcerting—the apparent willingness to assume that wise saints of other church traditions had for millennia simply misunderstood what was supposedly obvious to us in a late-twentieth-century classroom of an evangelical seminary representing a small, North American, largely white, middle-class denomination.

My first response was to draft a rebuttal—youthful and unwise in expression—that utilized many of the analytical and exegetical tools that had been taught to me by the very professor who was now defending Presbyterian ways. I still have the paper, but I never turned it in, never convinced anyone (but myself) of its gravity, and never left the Presbyterian ranks whose adherents continue to unfurl the arguments that left me unconvinced decades ago. Some of my Presbyterian friends reading this are now thinking, "I always knew there was something wrong with him." But others are asking, "Then, why did you stay, and why have you given such sweat, tears, and blood for a church whose foundations you consider biblically suspect?" The answer is that I do not consider those foundations suspect at all and have come to appreciate their biblical rootedness all the more, but for reasons not fully identified in that long-ago class. In the following pages, I shall attempt to spell out some of those reasons.

Personal Experience

Why am I Presbyterian? I would never argue for a church's validity based upon personal experience, but I would not be honest if I claimed that my life's course had nothing to do with my becoming Presbyterian. Were I raised in parts of Africa where the major expressions of Christianity are Anglican, Pentecostal, and Roman Catholic, I doubt that Presbyterianism would have been my choice. Still, my coming to Presbyterian convictions was not simply a matter of refusing to veer from familiar paths or to wrestle with Scripture.

Church Beginnings

My father is a sincere and able lay preacher in a small Baptist denomination. I grew up immersed in congregational life and thought. However, the independent church we attended on occasions when my father's church did not meet was pastored by a Presbyterian minister who treated my family with great kindness, as did a number of that church's lay leaders. So when my father's job put us in a location distant from his church, the recommendation of these caring believers landed us in a Presbyterian church for a season. Years later, when I was wrestling with career choices, the seminary president I had met during this season of Presbyterian associations graciously provided for my theological education, even though I was honest about not considering myself "one of the frozen chosen," otherwise known as Presbyterians.

Spiritual Considerations

These personalities and paths are not the basis of my Presbyterianism, but they contribute to the tapestry of my life that Presbyterians identify as *providence*—God's working all things together for his good purposes. In the providence of these early life circumstances, I would not yet find all that I needed to become a committed Presbyterian, but I did become convinced that a Bible-believing Presbyterian church had members who genuinely demonstrated the fruit of the Spirit (Gal. 5:22–23). While this was not a sufficient reason to become Presbyterian, such a discovery was necessary for me to be willing to consider whether the Presbyterian church was a true branch of the vine that is Christ's visible church throughout the world (John 15:1–5).

Evangelical Convictions

Above any Presbyterian distinction are my evangelical convictions. I need to know that a church's people believe Jesus is their Savior from sin and are living for him before I will consider being a part of that church (Rom. 3:25–26; 10:9). It is simple for me: the church is the body of Christ (Col. 1:24). If a group identifying itself as the church does not evidence his presence through humble dependence upon his means of grace (Word, sacraments, and prayer) and faithful obedience to his commands, then Jesus is not really honored there and that gathering of people is not really a church. But where Christ is loved and lived, there really is a church, even if it may be different in expression from my tradition or preference (Eph. 4:4–6, 12, 16). No single church, or denomination, is the full expression of Christ's body on earth (Eph. 1:22–23), but knowing that these Bible-believing Presbyterians evidenced Christ's reality among them encouraged my initial associations.

Scriptural Commitments

My willingness to consider Presbyterianism ultimately hinged on the church's willingness to be ruled by Scripture. I had the dual blessings of being raised with the simple understanding that the Bible is true and being so taught by men and women too intelligent not to address sophisticated challenges to that understanding. As a consequence, I was not sorely tempted in high school or college by arguments against the trustworthiness of Scripture. I had already seen that those who pick and choose their way through teachings of the Bible ultimately create a book reflective of their own thought rather than revelatory of God's. They inevitably are manipulated by the human perspectives in vogue instead of being led by God's Word.

As a result of these experiences and observations, I recognized that the veracity of the Word is a combination of the credibility of its reasonable interpretation and the willingness of the hearer to submit to its authority. As a believer, I wanted to be guided by God's Word, and I recognized in the Bible-believing Presbyterians with whom I began to associate a similar desire with a willingness to address the hard questions about the Bible. These dual commitments won my respect, and ultimately my loyalty. I was particularly impressed that the Presbyterians were careful to formulate their doctrines based on the teaching of Scripture (rather than on church tradition), and at the same time were willing to say that the only infallible rule of faith and practice is the Bible instead of their formulations.[1] They were willing to be informed by their history, but ruled only by Scripture.[2] That struck me as both intelligent and humble.

Historic Roots

Reformed

Those who categorize churches identify Presbyterians as descending from covenants of solidarity signed by elders (the Greek word for elder is *presbyteros*) of the church in 1638 and 1643 to resist a monarch's attempts to control the Protestant church in Scotland. In the next decade, those efforts also resulted in the production of the Westminster Confession of Faith in England, which became the doctrinal standard for Presbyterian churches throughout Great Britain and elsewhere. I appreciate this history because it reminds me that my church is not a modern novelty, or an innovation of American culture, or the experiment of a few friends who are gathering together because they do not like their parents' church. When I am associating with an organization whose teachings have eternal consequences, I would like for it to have some historical rootedness—to evidence that it has passed the test of time.

But the test of time would be a problem for me if my Presbyterian heritage did not begin until the seventeenth century. If that were true, then I would be forced to contend that the Lord did not birth a biblically orthodox church until more than a thousand years after the resurrection of Jesus. Of course, this would also mean that my church was "new" in the 1600s, even if it is not so now. My evangelical commitment to biblical Christianity—and my consequent need to believe that my church is anchored to something more steadfast than a passing trend in English history—is met by the understanding that Presbyterians are the product of a larger movement known as the Reformation.

---

[1] Westminster Confession of Faith (hereafter WCF) 1.2; 1.5.
[2] WCF 1.4; 1.10.

The claim of Reformers such as Jan Hus, Martin Luther, John Calvin, Ulrich Zwingli, and John Knox in the centuries surrounding the development of Presbyterianism was that they were restoring the original distinctives of Christianity. By the seventeenth century, social and political trends had led to the secularization of much of the Roman Catholic Church, which was dominant in those portions of the world that had become Christian. Thus, when reactive movements in many nations led to the founding of new churches, the leaders of these "Reformed" churches argued not for new theologies but for old ones.

Apostolic

In modern parlance, the Reformers wanted to be "retro," to return to the foundational distinctives of apostolic (original) Christianity. We still repeat the Apostles' Creed in Presbyterian churches because we believe that we are maintaining the original teaching of the New Testament church. Yet, to establish that their beliefs were truly apostolic, the Reformers had to counter the claim of the Roman Catholic Church that it was the true apostolic church because its leader, the pope, was a successor of the apostle Peter (whom Roman Catholics contend Christ made head of the church).

The way that the Reformers answered the Roman Catholic claim was by testing their ideas against the teaching of Scripture. They believed, as I do, that the truly apostolic church is the one whose doctrines conform to apostolic teaching. Instead of identifying the ancient church by human successors elected by contemporary leaders in Rome, the Reformers said that the ancient church was the one whose teaching was rooted in the Scriptures inspired by God.

The Reformers adopted the principle of *sola Scriptura* (Scripture alone) as the basis for their beliefs to indicate that they wanted their church to be rooted in the ancient church of apostolic origin. This principle meant that the Reformers would always seek to discern the original intent of the biblical authors as the basis for their duty and doctrine. By making Scripture the foundation of their church, the Reformers not only distinguished themselves from the authority of popes and councils who had contradicted (even excommunicated) one another, but also identified the One who provided the Word as the Head of the church.[3] Since the apostle Paul said that the church is built on the foundation of the apostles and prophets with Christ Jesus himself being the chief cornerstone (Eph. 2:20), making the Bible their ultimate authority was also the Reformers' acknowledgment that Christ was the supreme and perpetual Head of their church—just as he was for the apostles.

Catholic

Since Jesus gave the Scriptures by his Holy Spirit, making the Bible the only infallible rule of faith and practice for the church enthrones Christ as the ultimate authority for the church. Instead of choosing a man to be the "Vicar of Christ on Earth" (as the pope has been designated by Catholic tradition) or making our judgments and/or traditions the standards of the church, the Reformers believed Christ remains the Head of his church as we heed the instruction of the Word that his Spirit gave. In addition, they taught that as we yield to his Word in what we believe and do, we are perpetually bound to Christ and to the true church so yielded in all ages in all places. In this sense, Presbyterians are convinced that we not only are rooted in the church that is ancient in origin, but also are united with churches throughout time and throughout the world that are faithful to Christ. By being Scripture-bound, Presbyterians believe we are rooted in the apostolic church, are under the authority of Christ, and are united to the church catholic (i.e., universal).[4]

This perspective that Presbyterians are Reformed in heritage and catholic in status allows me to appreciate the distinctives of my church without needing to invalidate the integrity of all other churches. I can still advocate aspects of my church that I think are prudent and important for advancing the purposes of Christ without believing those distinguishing features of my church are essential features of every church of Christ.[5]

True

There are essentials that mark any true church of Christ: the Word of God rightly preached, the sacraments rightly administered, and church

---

[3]WCF 8.1.

[4]WCF 25.

[5]L. Roy Taylor, "Presbyterianism," in *Who Runs the Church? Four Views on Church Government*, Counterpoints Series, ed. Paul E. Engle and Steven B. Cowan (Grand Rapids: Zondervan, 2004), 96.

discipline rightly practiced. These "marks of the church" identified by the Reformers were not meant to exclude aspects of worship and mission that should also be occurring in all churches. Rather, the marks of the church are what distinguish a church from other religious gatherings.[6] The Reformers understood that without these special marks that relate to biblical preaching, sacraments, and discipline, people could well gather for fellowship, worship, inspiration, education, and mission efforts and still not possess all that is needed for the spiritual nurture and protection of God's people. In other words, a high school Bible study or a street rescue mission may do wonderful work for God and still not do all that is necessary to be a church. The wisdom of this observation early on led me to consider whether historic Presbyterianism possessed the marks of a true church.

For the Word to be rightly preached, the church must provide for the proclamation of biblical truth without contradicting or compromising it in instruction or conduct. In order for the sacraments to be rightly administered, Scripture must regulate what the church believes and does regarding the ordinances of initiation into and communion with the body of Christ. In order for discipline to be rightly enforced (enabling both the right preaching of the Word and the right administration of the sacraments), the church must protect the testimony of the church and the spiritual health of its members by faithfully, fairly, and charitably helping members to turn from sin and to God (e.g., 1 Cor. 5:13; Gal. 6:1; 2 Thess. 3:14). Faithfulness and protection of the flock require not only the biblical discipline of those within its ranks, but also the discipline to separate from unbelief that would threaten gospel faithfulness (2 Cor. 6:17).[7] In light of Christ's call for the unity of the visible church that he knew would be imperfect (John 17), biblical separation should never be lightly considered. But in light of Christ's call to gospel loyalty, the church leaders must occasionally be willing to sacrifice fellowship when the truth of the gospel is being compromised beyond reasonable repair.

I soon recognized that the kind of Presbyterian churches I was exploring possessed all of these marks (though I initially struggled with one of the sacraments, as I will explain later) and thus warranted further exploration. However, with little additional study, I also recognized that

---

[6]WCF 25.4; 29.8.

[7]J. Barton Payne, *What Is a Reformed Presbyterian?* (Lookout Mountain, GA: Mandate, 1974), 12–13.

it is more than possible for churches that call themselves Presbyterian not to bear these marks, and for churches that are not Presbyterian to bear them. Faithfulness to Christ, not heritage and title, marks a true church. Thus, I am a Presbyterian not because of any church label (and *not* because I consider no other churches true bodies of Christ), but because the Presbyterian churches I love have historically borne these validating marks of true churches in addition to holding other important scriptural commitments.

Biblical Doctrine

Grace to Humanity

No scriptural commitment carries more weight than Christianity's essential claim that, in contrast to all other religions' teachings that persons must somehow reach to their god(s) to claim spiritual benefits, our God reaches to us to bestow his blessings. We are rescued from the wrath of God and the eternal consequences of our sin not by our efforts or merits, but solely by the mercy of God. He sent his Son to live a life of humility and suffer a death of humiliation upon a cross in order to pay the penalty we deserve for our sin. As a consequence, all who depend upon Jesus will never have to pay the spiritual penalty that he paid in our behalf. Presbyterianism not only affirms this essential message of the grace of God but also applies it to every dimension of life.

At its core, the message of grace is not simply that God pardons wrongdoing, but rather that he supplies the holiness he requires. Since a holy God cannot abide sin, he must provide a way for sinful people to come to him—to be as holy as he is. As is the case in most Protestant denominations, Presbyterians affirm that God provides this grace by justifying (declaring without the guilt of sin) those sinners who put their faith in him (Rom. 3:21–26). But Presbyterians expand the dimensions of grace by noting every aspect of human need that requires God's help according to Scripture.

The Bible says that apart from the work of God's Spirit no one can or would trust in Jesus's sacrifice in their behalf (John 3:3). We both inherit the sin nature of our first parents and personally transgress God's law (Rom. 5:12). As a consequence we are dead in our sin and unable to respond to him (Eph. 2:1–2). Though we are always at liberty to love and obey God, unless he sends new life into our hearts by his Spirit, we are hardened to his love and resistant to his ways (Rom. 8:10–11). God must send his Spirit to regenerate hearts of stone and make them beat for him (Ezek. 11:19). He requires hearts that love him, but he must provide in us the new hearts that can or will. Presbyterians identify this provision of new hearts as the grace of *regeneration*.

These hearts that beat for God must trust in Jesus for their rescue from the consequences of sin. But in order for us to trust in the saving work of Jesus, he must have come and must have had witnesses to his work; and we must have the minds to understand his work, and must also have the willingness to depend upon his work. Where do all these necessary components of faith come from? They are all supplied by God in whom "we live and move and have our being" (Acts 17:28). Thus, the faith that God requires of us, he provides too. Faith is a gift of God (Eph. 2:8–9). God provides his Son to take the penalty our sin required, as well as providing the faith required for trust in him (Rom. 3:24, 26). This is the grace of *justification*.

Because Christ's work makes holy those who trust in him, we become as holy as he and spiritually united to him (Rom. 12:1–2; Gal. 2:20). Thus we are no longer considered aliens of heaven, but rather members of God's household and siblings of Christ (Eph. 2:19). Instead of living as enemies of a holy God, we are reconciled to him and at peace with him (Rom. 5:1–11). Instead of being counted with the outcasts of heaven, we are numbered among the heavenly Father's children and called his precious treasure (Rom. 8:15; 1 John 3:1). He provides the relationship his love requires. This is the grace of *adoption*.

Now all that occurs in our lives is arranged for our ultimate good (Rom. 8:28). Not a hair can fall from our head without the approval of God, and there is a hedge about us that nothing can enter except for the purposes of our eternal good. Nothing can separate us from his love—not even our own sin and doubt (Rom. 8:29–30, 38–39). Because he promises to work all things together for the good of his children, God will not allow any of us to sin to the point of his rejection or to draw one breath beyond belief. To allow such things that would not work for our eternal good would be to break his Word—which he cannot do. Though we may face many difficulties in this life and endure many failures that shake our personal assurance of his love, in fact his affection never wavers and his protection never slackens (Rom. 8:35–36). God will protect and preserve his relationship with his children forever. He provides the bonds to himself that his promise requires. This is the grace of *perseverance* that endures until the grace of *glorification*, when we eternally abide in the glory of his nature and provision.

From life's conception to heaven's reception God nourishes and secures the souls of his people (John 10:28–29). Thus even the life that we live for him is enabled by him. Each breath drawn, each thought grasped, the will bolstered, the resolve strengthened, the resistance raised, and the good accomplished are all by his Spirit (John 15:5; Phil. 4:13). He provides all the resources we need for the work that we do for him (Phil. 4:19). The holiness he requires, he also provides—for today as well as for eternity (1 John 5:4–5). This is the grace of *sanctification*—the work we do for him as he works his will in us (Phil. 2:12–13).

Over time, I grew to understand that the grace God provides for sanctification is one of the most precious doctrines of Scripture, and a key distinction of historic Presbyterianism. While most Protestant churches are clear about the grace of justification, they often seem to imply that sanctification—because it is a maturing process in which our efforts and wills are engaged—is entirely a product of human grit, rather than a gift of God. The consequence of such thought is that personal evaluation of one's own righteous performance becomes the basis of determining present status with God. The prideful think they have done well enough, and the pessimistic despair. Both err in determining their status based upon their accomplishments.

The Presbyterian emphasis upon God's grace providing all that we need for life with God shifts the focus of sanctification from human performance to divine provision. We are holy not because of what we do, but because of what Christ has done and is doing in our behalf. Through our union with Christ, believers are immediately and forever holy, pleasing, and perfect to God (Rom. 12:1; Heb. 10:14). Though we strive to progress in holy living to show our thanksgiving for our Lord's love, we rest in the knowledge that we already and perpetually are accepted as holy in God's sight. In fact, we strive best when we are most rested. Instead of wrestling for approval, we respond to the assurance of God's acceptance with the joy that is our strength (Neh. 8:10). As a consequence, love and thanksgiving become the great motivations of the Christian life (Matt.

22:37; John 14:15; Phil. 4:6). Pride and despair are annulled. We live for God not to establish our holy status but to reflect it (Eph. 5:8).

Grace provides not only the motivation but also the power that enables our progress in holy living. The power that sin has over us is a direct consequence of our love for it. If sin did not attract us, it would have no power over us. Thus, the way that God counters the power of sin is by filling our hearts with a greater love. His Word assures us that all believers are robed with the righteousness of Christ and share his identity (Isa. 61:10; Gal. 2:20; 3:26–27). This means we are as precious to the Father as is Jesus. Knowing that we are so loved causes us to love God and live for him (John 14:15; 1 John 4:19). Thus, to enable us to overcome our love for sin and to empower our service to him, God designs his work and Word to fill us with a greater love. He reveals his gracious character in works of covenant, atonement, and mercy throughout Scripture. These are intended to fill us with a compelling love for him that drives out love for the things of the world (Titus 2:12). Thus the grace of God motivates and enables the holiness his Word requires from us even as that same grace provides the mercy needed to atone for the holiness lacking in us.

Glory to God

The preceding words about the grace of God may occasionally seem puzzling because they push away from assigning merit to human striving (which many consider the essence of great faith) and lean toward glorifying God for every spiritual privilege we enjoy. This tension is intentional. The goodness of Presbyterianism is that it humbly affirms the mysteries of God's love while always bowing to his majesty (Job 42:3; Ps. 22:27–28). You cannot be in Presbyterian circles long without hearing about the "sovereignty of God"—a phrase conveying that our infinitely wise and powerful God controls all things (2 Chron. 20:6; Matt. 10:29–39). Presbyterians talk about God's being sovereign (or King) over all things so that we will give him proper glory for all that he does or enables us to do (Psalm 29). We realize that what will always give our lives purpose and meaning—even in the midst of great difficulty—is making our chief delight that of bringing glory to the One who made us, loves us, maintains our world, and secures our eternity.[8]

---

[8]"Man's chief end is to glorify God, and to enjoy him forever" (Westminster Shorter Catechism 1).

Comments about God's sovereignty can get a harsh edge as minds determined to defend Scripture's claim of God's absolute rule marshal their arguments against those more concerned about human autonomy. Presbyterians can sometimes even make the "doctrines of grace" (the phrase used to capture God's fatherly provision for all that pertains to our salvation) seem heartless. Too often the harsh tones result from those trying too hard to resolve all the logical knots inevitably woven into our explanations of the sovereignty of God, rather than bowing before the glory of One who rescues us from our sin for reasons and in ways that are beyond our explanation.

Mystery surrounds God's sovereignty because the glories of his lordship exceed our logic (Rom. 11:33). Human reasoning cannot untangle the logical dilemmas of a God who—to be true to his own nature—must both propel his creatures down the path of his predetermined purposes and yet judge their actions. If God predestines the course of all, then he appears unjust in his condemnation of any—particularly if he controls human thoughts and actions (Job 38:36; Ps. 68:35; Rom. 11:8). And, of course, he must control the thoughts and actions of the unregenerate, or he is not sovereign over all. But if to rescue our conception of his justice we say that he is not in charge of the thoughts and actions of the unregenerate whom he judges—or the choices of the regenerate whom he saves—then we have denied that he is in sovereign control of all things. No human theology has yet determined how to reconcile the justice and omnipotence of God without ejecting some quality of divinity established in Scripture.

The Bible is not blind to the conundrums of grace. The apostle Paul even asks the justice question he knows his critics will pose in objection to his statements about God's absolute sovereignty: "Why does he still find fault? For who can resist his will?" (Rom. 9:19). Paul's answer is not to deny God's sovereignty but to affirm our limitations: "But who are you, O man, to answer back to God? Will what is molded say to its molder, 'Why have you made me like this?'" (Rom. 9:20). The apostle indicates only that the master potter intended some vessels for destruction in order to make the riches of his glory known to those he beforehand prepared for glory (Rom. 9:21–23). The reasoning does not sit well with a culture that idolizes the liberty and autonomy of everyone's choices, but the apostle is not writing for everyone. He is writing so that those who are saved by the mercy of God alone are not tempted to pride by their accomplishments or to despair by their failures. Affirmation of God's sovereignty leads his people always to glorify him for their salvation, rather than to base their destiny on the measure of their own merits—or to fear their destiny based on the same (Rom. 9:15–16; Eph. 2:4–5).

The apostle wants God's people to know that *God* saves them. This is the strength of Presbyterianism that simply takes the biblical texts as they are given in order to make sure that we honor God above all. The theological system of Calvin or Augustine that is generally associated with Presbyterianism (and often identified with the term *predestination*) is really nothing more than an affirmation of the Bible's statements about God's sovereignty. To those who say, "But this makes God seem unfair," we should be willing to say, "Yes, at the level of considering how God judges those whose lives and hearts he controls, there is an apparent unfairness. But there is a counter unfairness in that God shows mercy to those he regenerates and draws to himself, despite their being undeserving" (Rom. 5:15–19). For those concerned about the fairness of the judgment of an absolutely sovereign God, we can also agree with the Presbyterian apologists of past centuries that God doesn't have to be merciful to anyone because all were represented in Adam's sin, *and* all have sinned and fallen short of God's glory (Rom. 3:23). So God's willingness to save anyone is more than fair and the evidence of his grace.

Humility before Scripture

But as true as these responses are, they do not solve all the justice/sovereignty issues the Bible itself raises about God's predestinating judgment and mercy. For example, the Bible regularly acknowledges that those who should be judged for their actions are only those who can be accountable for their actions (e.g., Acts 17:30; Rom. 4:15; 5:13; 7:7; 1 Tim. 1:13). So we have difficulty reconciling the judgment of those whose ears have not been made able to hear the gospel with God's holding them accountable for believing it. Even if we say the unregenerate are accountable because they were justly represented in Adam, we still have trouble reconciling either the justice or the sovereignty of God with Adam's sin. If God is absolutely sovereign, then he is ultimately responsible for Adam's sin. Sensing this problem, the Westminster divines wrote, "Our first parents . . . [were] left to the freedom of their own will."[9] But if Adam had free will, then how was God in sovereign control of all his creature's actions; and if God were not in control of all Adam's actions, then how was the Creator still sovereign over all things? The questions do not simply apply to the past. Ultimately we are led to ask, If God was still sovereign while Adam had free will, then why cannot God still be sovereign and grant us the same kind of free will Adam had?

The human-responsibility and divine-sovereignty questions can tie our minds in knots that human logic cannot unravel. I confess that I spent a lot of my early theological energies as a teen, college student, and seminarian trying to untie these knots—or trying to show others the knots they were unwilling to address. But slowly and patiently the Holy Spirit worked to humble me and to convince me that the ultimate goal of scriptural studies is not discovering the solution to every logical dilemma of biblical faith. It is more important to remember for whom the Bible was written as we consider its claims of God's sovereign activities in our salvation. The Bible was written for believers, not unbelievers. As a consequence, the prophets and apostles apparently thought it was better to assure believers of God's sovereign care than to defend God's justice to unbelievers. When assured of God's sovereign provision of salvation, believers would know that all the glory for their salvation should be his, and all his strength for their sanctification would be theirs. Rejoicing in his provision they would rightly honor and love him (fulfilling the Great Commandment); and relying upon the assurance of his unwavering love, they would be equipped for doing his work without doubt or despair (fulfilling the Great Commission).

The strength of the heartiest Presbyterianism is that it is brave enough to affirm what Scripture says and meek enough to be silent when Scripture is silent. We should not try to remove the mysteries of God's sovereignty that necessarily remain until we are with the Lord. The apostle Paul wrote for a reason, "Oh, the depth of the riches and wisdom and knowledge of God! How unsearchable are his judgments and how inscrutable his ways!" (Rom. 11:33). And Calvin, whose theology Presbyterians are sometimes so anxious to believe explains everything about divine sovereignty, actually comes to the end of his logic regarding predestination before bursting into a similar doxology: "For it is not right for man unrestrainedly to search

---

[9]WCF 9.2; WSC 13.

out things that the Lord has willed to be hid in himself. . . . Understand then that through this [doctrine] he should also fill us with wonder."[10]

Does the Bible deny that there is any human responsibility for trusting God or any human accountability for obeying him? The answer is definitely no. The apostles and prophets call all persons to repentance and faith (Acts 17:30). Christ calls his followers to obey him (Matt. 28:20). The Bible does not allow us to say, "God is in control, so I have no responsibility." To the contrary, Scripture's perspective is that we should trust and obey because God is in control (2 Thess. 1:8–12). Historic Presbyterianism maintains the tension between divine sovereignty and human responsibility by affirming each without trying to reconcile the two. In doing so, Presbyterians simply bow before Scripture's truths, rather than making them bend to the standards of human reason. The reason we must do so is that maintaining the glory of God in our salvation promotes the love for God required for our obedience.

Precisely because we are responsible for obeying God, we need the motivation and ability to serve him. God provides our ability to honor him by informing us of his laws in Scripture and by giving us the power to obey through his indwelling Spirit. The motivation—the willingness—to obey comes from love for God that is stimulated by our apprehension of his love for us (John 14:15; 1 John 4:19). Our understanding of the sovereignty of God is the ultimate source of this love. At its heart, the doctrine of divine sovereignty is the affirmation of God's fatherly care that makes us want to embrace and honor him. When we know that he chose us before we were conceived, loved us before we could acknowledge him, claimed us through no merit of our own, gave his Son for us despite our sin, grants his mercy to us despite our rebellion, holds us when we fall, shepherds us when we stray, fathers us when we rebel, remains faithful despite our unfaithfulness, maintains his care despite our waywardness, pursues us when we flee him, delights in us though we doubt him, perseveres in his love when we forget, and glorifies us though we fail and forsake him—when we know all these dimensions of divine sovereignty, we love God. Such love adores its object, and such adoration results in loving service that is the glory of God in the Christian life.

---

[10]John Calvin, *Institutes of the Christian Religion*, ed. John T. McNeill, trans. Ford Lewis Battles (Philadelphia: Westminster, 1960), 3.21.1.

Some will say that by denying man's free will to choose to believe in Christ as one's Savior apart from God's regenerating and enabling Spirit, Presbyterianism precludes human ability to love God. After all, they reason, puppets cannot truly love even if they respond to the will of their maker. We answer that Presbyterians do not deny human responsibility or free will. We understand that a God who would punish for the actions he causes could not be loved. So we affirm that God acts in such a way as to do no violence to the will of the creature in order to maintain his righteous judgment, but we do not attempt to explain how this is so.[11] Presbyterians do not deny the mysteries of divine sovereignty or human responsibility revealed in Scripture. We confess the points at which our human explanations fail, but emphasize God's sovereignty over human autonomy in order to give our Lord the glory his Word requires (Pss. 96:3; 108:5).

Mission in the World

While the preceding discussion of God's sovereignty has focused upon his preeminent role in our salvation, there is another implication of God's pervasive rule that is important for those who identify themselves as Presbyterian and Reformed in perspective. Often the term *Reformed* is narrowly used to describe a system of doctrine relating to the priority of God's work in our salvation. It has been important to me, however, to recognize that the term has a wider meaning for those well versed in the origin of that system. Key to being Reformed is the understanding that our God is "King over all" (Ps. 47:2). This certainly means that he initiates and accomplishes the work of salvation in our hearts, but it also means that his authority extends to every dimension of our lives.

We have no warrant to draw a line between the spiritual and the material world in order to limit his authority to one. God is not bound by our secular-sacred divides. He not only is the author and finisher of our salvation, but is also the Creator and sustainer of all things made, the one whose glory is declared by heaven and earth, the one whose image all humanity bears, the one whose Spirit indwells all who are regenerate, the one whose glory is the object of all our exertions and entertainments, and the advocate of all who seek him. In my youth, Presbyterian minister

---

[11] WCF 3.1; 9.1.

Francis Schaeffer powerfully proclaimed this understanding of the wide domain of our divine King as "the Lordship of Christ over the whole of life."[12] The phrase reminded Christians of their right and responsibility to honor their Savior in every aspiration, sphere, endeavor, and relationship of life.

Schaeffer taught that the church is not the only place to honor Christ. We honor him in how we steward the resources of his creation, sacrifice for the good of all made in his image (especially those with worldly disadvantage), lovingly co-labor for the gospel with all who truly bear his name, employ the talents he has bestowed to honor him in whatever field (business, arts, entertainment, media, education, industry, etc.) he calls us to serve his interests, honor our responsibilities in our homes, and trust him to accomplish our good when earthly circumstances give no cause for doing so. Every Christian in every profession or avenue of life is called to serve God's purposes of redeeming the world for his glory. Every such calling is sacred. There are no secondary callings and no little people—all are ennobled by their role in the holy purposes of God's grand design.[13]

Leaders of the Reformation sought to capture the importance of honoring God in every area of life by preaching about the "priesthood of believers." The phrase indicated that every legitimate profession is a holy calling to honor God with the gifts and opportunities he has provided. Martin Luther famously argued that the plough boy was as called as the priest to honor God. This declaration that all believers are priests of God's glory not only dignifies every profession as a sacred calling, but also makes every believer responsible for advancing God's kingdom in his or her arena of relationships and responsibilities. In more recent times, those who are Reformed in theology have advanced this thought to inspire the present generation with the understanding that God is using his people to fulfill his mission on earth.

All of Scripture describes this divine mission of redemption. God did not abandon his creation when it was corrupted by the sin of humanity. In the earliest pages of Scripture, God promised to redeem this fallen world by the provision of his Son (Gen. 3:15). The rest of Scripture unfolds the

---

[12]Francis Schaeffer, *The Complete Works of Francis Schaeffer: A Christian Worldview*, vol. 2 (Westchester, IL: Crossway Books, 1982), 375–76.

[13]See Francis Schaeffer, *No Little People* (Westchester, IL: Crossway Books, 2003).

plan and places every person, event, and instruction within the context of God's mission to redeem his people and restore his world by the work of his Son. But when the Son came to redeem, he told us that his mission would not be entirely fulfilled by his sacrifice for our sin. He rose and sent his Spirit to empower his body (the church) to continue his redeeming purposes (John 16:7–15; Rom. 12:5–8; 1 Cor. 12:27). This means that we have the great privilege of being participants in God's plan to renew the world for his glory.

Understanding that we are part of God's plan and participants in his mission has made those who are Reformed, Calvinistic, and Presbyterian major contributors to the world's missionary movements. Those who contend that a commitment to God's sovereign election of his people destroys missionary zeal fail to recognize that confidence that we are God's instruments inspires and sustains mission efforts even in the face of great opposition and pain. John Calvin's efforts resulted in over three thousand new churches in France and neighboring nations despite great persecution. The great missionary movements of Western history were led by those Calvinistic in conviction (some Presbyterian, some not), such as William Carey, David Livingstone, and David Brainerd. And great movements of today are being led by Calvinists such as John Piper and Tim Keller, as well as Presbyterians in Korea, Brazil, and other Majority World nations. The Presbyterian denomination of which I am a member presently has more missionaries than at any time in Presbyterian history despite the secularization and opposition of our culture. Such zeal comes not only from loyalty to the Great Commission but also from confidence in our role in God's great plan of redemption.

We are not simply observers of the divine plan; we are part of the plan. Christ has declared that his church is the most powerful change agent in the world and those in her ranks have eternal purpose despite their earthly challenges. Though it faces opposition, persecution, insignificance, schism, betrayal, or apparent insignificance, the church will endure beyond all secular powers and prevail over all spiritual enemies.

> The Church shall never perish!
> Her dear Lord to defend,
> To guide, sustain, and cherish,
> Is with her to the end;
> Though there be those who hate her,

And false sons in her pale,
Against both foe or traitor
She ever shall prevail.[14]

Biblical Organization

As we consider the mission of the church, we need to consider how the church should be organized to fulfill its purposes in a manner consistent with biblical doctrine and purpose. Much of what I have written above about Presbyterian beliefs could also be associated with a cadre of other denominations that are Reformed in their doctrines of salvation, Scripture, and mission. So I now need to describe the distinctive features of Presbyterian organization that also make me glad to associate with this particular branch of Christ's church.

This task leads me back to the discussion that opened this chapter. Significant aspects of Presbyterian government have frequently been defended with biblical proof-texting of a kind that we would criticize in others. For example, some have taken the Greek term *cheirotoneō* (a combination of words meaning "hand" and "stretch out") in Acts 14:23 to indicate that officers were always elected by a congregation's showing of hands in the New Testament church. This would support the Presbyterian practice of church members electing their officers. But if we were in a class on exegetical fallacies, a faithful professor would quickly point out that combining root words does not always provide the meaning of a present word. Combining the meaning of *butter* and *fly* does not tell us what a butterfly is.

The word *cheirotoneō* may mean "elect" (it does in some ancient literature outside the Bible), but it could also mean "select," "appoint," or "ordain." The context of Acts 14:23 only references what Paul and Barnabas were doing (i.e., preaching, making disciples, strengthening and encouraging the church). Thus, the text does *not* specifically say that the *church* elected or appointed elders, but says that Paul and Barnabas did. This does not necessarily mean that the church failed to have an election (perhaps the church elected those whom Paul and Barnabas later ordained), but the verse does not *prove* that a general election occurred. And even if the elders were elected or appointed in the towns of Acts 14,

---

[14]Samuel J. Stone, "The Church's One Foundation," in *Lyra Fidelium: Twelve Hymns of the Twelve Articles of the Apostles' Creed* (London: Parker, 1866).

that one-time mention of what happened there does not necessarily mean all church leaders everywhere should always be appointed in that way. A single example does not a pattern make—a description is not necessarily an imperative. Perhaps this was only the practice when an apostle was present. But noting that there was an apostle present could create other considerations not frequently mentioned. For example, the apostles cast lots to determine Matthias's office. And if they stretched out their hands to do so, maybe casting lots was the method being referenced in Acts 14:23. In the absence of further description, what one presumes to be the case can largely determine how one will interpret the text.

My intention in the preceding two paragraphs is not to cast doubt on all features of Presbyterian government, but to indicate that my loyalties to Presbyterian polity are often based on prudent application of general scriptural principles, rather than on specific practices established by isolated proof texts. Such texts will often show that our present practices are a plausible or reasonable application of biblical principles for church government without necessarily proving that all differing practices are wrong, or that this practice is always right.

Presbyterians who do not understand that prudence in a given situation may be more appropriate than citing proof texts will not only unfairly condemn other denominations' polity, but also needlessly censure fellow Presbyterians. For example, it is fruitless and divisive to try to determine by proof texts whether a minister should be a member of a congregation or a presbytery, or whether the office of elder is of one or two classes, or whether elders should rotate or be perpetually in office, or whether church mission should be done by permanent agencies or temporary committees. Such determinations must be made, but our churches would be far healthier if we understood that our decisions regarding such matters have been made (or will have to be made) on the basis of the general principles of biblical wisdom applied in the context of particular circumstances, rather than on the basis of specific practices that can be extracted from proof texts and applied with certainty to all circumstances. In my ordination vows I say that I believe my church's practices are "in conformity with the general principles of biblical polity." I do not say that all these practices are specifically mentioned or required in Scripture. I approve of what I believe is consistent with Scripture, conforming to the following general principles that are undeniably biblical.

Mutual Accountability

Presbyterians believe that just as members of the church should be accountable to one another for their beliefs and practices, so should churches. We are fallen creatures whose hearts are deceptive, whose minds are limited, and whose perspectives can become clouded. As a consequence, we are frequently admonished in Scripture to be in submission to one another (Rom. 12:10; 1 Cor. 16:14–16; Eph. 5:21; Phil. 2:2–4; 1 Thess. 5:12–13; Heb. 13:17; 1 Pet. 2:13–3:9; 5:5). What is characteristic of us individually will also be true of us collectively. Churches, too, can be deceived, limited in understanding and clouded in perspective. Therefore, it seems prudent for churches also to have some means to be in submission to one another.[15] Presbyterians provide for this mutual accountability through regional gatherings (called presbyteries) of local church elders, and through occasional gatherings of presbyteries to make decisions about the doctrine, mission, and leadership of their churches.

This general principle of mutual accountability seems to have been the reason leaders of separate churches decided to gather to deal with a widespread problem in Acts 15. I recognize that some will argue that the ensuing Jerusalem Council was either an error (though Scripture does not say so) or unique (in that it was convened with apostolic authority and participation). However, the apostle Paul does not hesitate to apply the same general principle of mutual submission among churches when he calls for particular behaviors because they are practiced "in all the churches" (1 Cor. 7:17; 14:33; cf. 1 Tim. 3:15). Paul and other apostles also address their letters to both specific churches and groups of churches, expecting those churches to act in concert, and expecting their letters to be read by more churches who would do the same (e.g., 1 Cor. 16:19; 2 Cor. 1:1; Gal. 1:2; Col. 4:16).

The apostles write their letters with the obvious expectation that churches will *not* act autonomously. This is not simply because of the apostles' authority. They also write with the basic understanding that churches will act in concert because they are all united to Christ. In his farewell prayer, Jesus prayed for the new community that would be established after his departure. He prayed that "they may be one even as we [heavenly Father and Son] are one, I in them and you in me, that they

---

[15]Robert C. Cannada and W. Jack Williamson, *The Historic Polity of the PCA* (Greenville, SC: A Press, 1997), 5.

may become perfectly one, so that the world may know that you sent me and loved them even as you loved me" (John 17:22–23). This essential union should be the grounding principle upon which Presbyterians unite their efforts and hold each other accountable for biblical faithfulness.[16] We can reasonably cite verses that show that gatherings of Christian leaders occurred in the New Testament church, but each citation will have unique characteristics that will enable some to claim its features are not now applicable. What is always applicable is the principle of mutual submission that the Presbyterian form of government well addresses through its connectional leadership.

Biblical Leadership

SCRIPTURAL

Presbyterians structure their local church leadership according to offices identified in Scripture: elders and deacons. It seems reasonable to me that the Lord would tell us the basic aspects of leadership that he desired for his church, and it makes sense that the requirements in Scripture call for leaders who are godly, wise, informed, and experienced. Old Testament parallels and New Testament instruction make it clear that elders meeting these qualifications should govern the spiritual affairs of the local church (1 Tim. 3:1–7; Titus 1:5–9). Deacons have a stewardship role that is less defined but requires spiritual maturity and seems to focus upon the mercy ministries and material needs of the congregation (cf. Acts 6; Rom.12:8; 1 Cor. 12:28; 1 Tim. 3:8–13). Each office possesses functions vital to protecting and propagating the church's witness of the gospel.

SHARED

Presbyterians differ from Episcopal and some Congregational forms of government by advocating the plurality and parity of elders in the local church. The New Testament consistently demonstrates that more than one elder served each local congregation (Acts 11:30; 15:2, 4, 22–23; 16:4; 20:17; 21:18; 1 Tim. 5:17; Titus 1:5; James 5:14). Again, wise and godly persons can find logical reasons to say that this consistent pattern is not universally applicable. For example, the plural reference to elders in Paul's letter to Timothy may occur because the church at Ephesus

---

[16]Sean Michael Lucas, *On Being Presbyterian: Our Beliefs, Practices, and Stories* (Phillipsburg, NJ: P&R, 2006), 70.

likely included many congregations, as we have previously seen. And it is possible that each of these congregations had only one elder. Still, it seems unlikely that so many references to elders in the plural would occur if they were limited to one per congregation.

Yet what ultimately guides my thought is not the biblical examples. They cannot be universalized without accompanying biblical instruction (again, an example does not necessarily make an imperative in Scripture). More important than the individual examples is our understanding of the fallenness of all humanity. Because we are limited in perspective and vulnerable in heart, the church is healthier and safer with more than one person to guide it. I am not as convinced of the necessity of the plurality of elders by biblical examples as I am by the pervasive biblical teaching of the depravity of man.

As to the question of whether there should be parity (i.e., equal status and authority) among elders in a local church, my thoughts are mixed. The old debate about whether there is a separate office of bishop in the New Testament seems readily resolved to me by those verses where elder and bishop are identified as the same thing for different language groups (Acts 20:17, 28; 1 Pet. 5:1, 2). Thus, I do not perceive there to be a hierarchy defined by differing titles. However, Paul does write to Timothy, "Let the elders who rule well be considered worthy of double honor, especially those who labor in preaching and teaching" (1 Tim. 5:17). Distinctions of honor seem to be possible on the basis of distinguished exercise of wisdom and authority, as well as on the basis of preaching and teaching. We ordinarily interpret this to mean that preachers have a right to be paid (as opposed to elders who merely exercise authoritative wisdom, i.e., ruling elders), but it seems reasonable to assume that godly and experienced men will rise in the esteem of the church. And though they do not have a separate office applied to them by scriptural warrant, they may well have greater respect appropriately granted to them by reason of the positive regard in which they are held throughout the church.

The regard that grants certain individuals greater sway in the church may be a blessing or a curse. A blessing if the regard is stewarded for good; and a curse if the status is used for personal advantage. For these reasons I appreciate the Presbyterian system whose plurality and parity of elders provides checks and balances in the decision-making processes of the church. Shared governance allows for those held in high esteem to be well regarded, but also to be readily resisted if their efforts begin to turn the church from gospel faithfulness.

REPRESENTATIVE

Already I have discussed some of the conundrums surrounding verses used to describe how elders were elected or selected for their tasks. Helpful to my thought is the description of the way leaders were chosen for service in Acts 6. When the apostles were being consumed with decisions regarding provision for the material needs of widows, the Twelve "summoned the full number of the disciples and said, '. . . Brothers, pick out from among you seven men of good repute, full of the Spirit and of wisdom, whom we will appoint to this duty'"(Acts 6:2–3). Though the apostles had the authority to appoint whomever they wished to aid them, the Twelve gave the "full number of the disciples" the privilege of selecting leaders for the task at hand.

We are not told the details of the selection process, but the general principle of giving people say regarding those who will have authority over them in the church seems clear. The truths behind this principle have already been presented among the distinctives of Presbyterian doctrine: the image of God in every person and the priesthood of believers. I would have trouble arguing conclusively from the biblical evidence that every church officer today should be elected by a general vote in the church. Given the culture of the apostles' time, I would wonder who was allowed to vote: men, women, slaves, children? Diving into the details of the examples Scripture gives is unlikely to provide precedence for the particulars of all our present procedures. Nevertheless, the general principles relating to human dignity and value that are evident and relevant substantiate the appropriateness of the representative government in historic Presbyterianism.

Cooperative Ministry

An additional principle evident in the apostles' instruction for the church at Jerusalem to choose those who could be appointed for helping with the distributions to widows is the necessity of cooperative ministry. No one and no one group can do all that is required for the advancement of the gospel. The varieties of gifts that bless individual churches are broadened and their effectiveness is multiplied when churches connect their efforts. The apostles used gathered wisdom when they convened the Jerusalem Council (Acts 15).

Paul used gathered resources when he collected from the churches of Asia Minor and Greece for the destitute in Jerusalem (Acts 11; 2 Corinthians 9). The Asian and Greek churches themselves had previously benefited from the mission efforts of the church at Antioch (Acts 13:1–3; 15:40). And the church at Antioch had benefited from the mission efforts of the church in Jerusalem (Acts 11:22–24).

Presbyterians value such connectionalism both for what it promotes and for what it protects. By our support of one another we provide more coordinated talent and resources for the promotion of the gospel than any single church could supply. In addition, our connectionalism provides for the broader church to examine the teaching and credentials of the leadership of individual churches that might otherwise be led spiritually astray by strong, mistaken, or defective leaders. The prime example of Presbyterianism's connectional protection is our mutual commitment to the Westminster Confession of Faith. While believing that Scripture is the final authority for all doctrinal decisions, the Westminster Assembly, consisting mainly though not exclusively of Presbyterians, banded together to create the confession as a trustworthy summary of what the Scriptures teach. By using this document as a good-faith expression of the system of doctrine taught in the Scriptures, we hold each other accountable for biblical faith and protect the church from doctrinal erosion.[17]

Confessional Humility

The connectionalism that supports mutual mission efforts and sustains doctrinal faithfulness is ultimately a reflection of a biblical characteristic that true gospel ministry always requires: humility. We unite with one another in confession that we cannot do all of the ministry God requires in isolation from one another. And we hold each other accountable for orthodox expression of the gospel, confessing that every individual is vulnerable to pride, rebellion, and error. Our connectionalism should not be so much a basis for condemning those who do not agree with us as a reminder of our constant need for the grace of God to do his will. Apart from him we can do nothing (John 15:5). All pride of accomplishment and doctrine should vanish in our acknowledgment of our need for others.

---

[17]Presbyterian Church in America, *Book of Church Order*, 21-4 and 21-5.

In this same vein of humility, I should add that I do not think Presbyterians must contend that every other form of church government is abhorrent to God. We typically divide the forms of church government into three categories: Congregational, Episcopal, and Presbyterian. In broad strokes of explanation, Congregational churches view each local church as an autonomous body without central or hierarchical control; Episcopal churches are governed by a hierarchy with higher powers in the hands of the ranks of bishops; and Presbyterian churches are governed through representative bodies elected by members of the church.

These broad strokes of explanation are problematic for at least two reasons: first, they do not describe the corporation-like structures in Western culture that have become increasingly typical of actual church operations; second, they do not reflect the nuanced practices within each separate form of government that enable denominations to function with the strengths of the other forms of government they claim to reject. For example, the Southern Baptists' zeal for the autonomy of local congregations does not keep them from cooperative mission efforts that actually make them more connectional than many Presbyterian churches and more hierarchical than some Episcopal ones. In addition, modern denominations of Episcopal convictions have increasingly given congregations representative powers at all levels of decision making. And, finally, Presbyterians—despite their protestations against hierarchies—as noted above, undeniably have informal "bishops" and ranks of ministerial power. All these anomalies of polity simply indicate that human nature, common sense, business necessity, and biblical principles create certain commonalities of practice among organizations that are faithfully seeking to fulfill God's calling. While I believe Presbyterian polity most nearly reflects the biblical principles of church government, I do not believe that I must declare all other denominations unfaithful because they do not mirror mine.

Biblical Worship

Regulated

The humility with which we make our confession before the church should reflect the humility with which we offer our worship to God. Presbyterians have historically reflected this ethic by holding to the "regulative principle of worship." The Westminster Confession defines this principle: "The acceptable way of worshipping the true God is instituted by himself, and so limited by his own revealed will, that he may not be worshipped according to the imaginations and devices of men . . . or any other way not prescribed in the holy Scripture" (WCF 21.1). A common way of expressing this principle is that Christians are to worship God only as he has instructed, and whatever he does not prescribe in his Word is prohibited. The principle sounds simple, but it creates innumerable questions about particular worship practices and styles. Does the Bible really say what tunes to sing, clothes to wear, prayers to include, liturgies to follow, bulletins to use (or not), sermons to preach, or sacraments to offer? The answer is yes to some of these questions and no to others. The key to answering lies in separating the abiding principles of worship from the incidental applications of them in biblical times and in ours.

Rivers of ink have flowed as scholars (including me)[18] have tried to distinguish the true "elements" of worship from incidental "circumstances."[19] Still, as hard as application of the regulative principle remains, I like it. The principle forces us to look to God's Word, rather than to human innovation, for acceptable worship. The reason this is so important is that if innovation were the mark of our best worship, then we would be forever trying to please God with our novelty and forever doubting that we had been creative enough to satisfy the Creator. By finding our worship guidelines in Scripture, we can focus our worship on bringing glory to God rather than on distinguishing ourselves.

Inevitably unbridled innovation leads to excess, error, and doubt. But mindless ritual, rote repetition, and unbending traditions deaden the worship of those made in the image of the infinitely creative Creator. Humility before God requires both that we bow before all the instruction of his Word and that we offer him all the beauty we can muster from the talents he has granted (1 Cor. 12:4–7; 14:12; Eph. 4:8). We can become the lords of our worship by creating either new elements the Scriptures do not approve or new restrictions the Scriptures do not prescribe. Either alternative makes God's honor subject to the hubris of human choices. Thus, seeking to regulate worship within the boundaries that Scripture

---

[18]Bryan Chapell, *Christ-Centered Worship: Letting the Gospel Shape Our Practice* (Grand Rapids: Baker, 2009).
[19]WCF 1.6.

marks and seeking to honor God with the creativity he models are compatible goals held in balance by Presbyterian worship.

Covenantal

Because the priorities of Presbyterian worship are established by God so that we can commune with him, our worship reflects the covenantal nature of the gospel. In a covenant, God sovereignly initiates and maintains the administration of his grace to his people (e.g., Gen 9:12; 15:17–21; 17:7). Since God in his Word tells us how we may relate to him and enjoy his grace, all aspects of biblical worship reflect his covenantal love.

The sacraments of Communion and baptism especially make God's covenant relationship with his people evident in worship. Both were provided by God to exhibit and extend the blessings of his grace to his people. I did not understand this in my early experience with Presbyterians. I had previously understood both sacraments to be memorials to Christ in which we participated to show our faithfulness to him. I had to grow in understanding that the Lord's Supper enables God's people to feast upon the present realities of his grace as well as memorialize its past provision. I also came to understand fairly readily that baptism is a ceremonial cleansing where the amount of water is not a priority (study of the Greek word for baptism in Heb. 9:10 was especially helpful in this). But I did not understand infant baptism. Why should someone be baptized prior to the ability to express faith? Two matters helped me first to accept infant baptism and then to love it.

The first aid in accepting infant baptism was a study of the word *seal* in Scripture. I had always thought of the sacraments as being a way we promise God that we will be faithful to him. That was why we had to be old enough to express our faith in order to receive baptism. However, the apostle Paul says that the Old Testament sacrament of circumcision was a "sign and seal" of Abraham's righteousness (see Rom. 4:11). The purification rite was a *sign* representing the purity that characterized Abraham as a consequence of the righteousness credited to him on the basis of his faith. But the rite was also a *seal* (a mark such as a signet ring makes to visibly represent the pledge of its owner to fulfill the promises expressed within a document). Circumcision ultimately was representative not of Abraham's faithfulness to God, but of God's faithfulness to Abraham. The Old Testament sacrament physically represented God's pledge that he would fulfill the promises of his covenant according to the spiritual conditions that he established. That is why God told Abraham, immediately after his expression of faith, to circumcise all the males in his household. Not all would yet have shared his faith, but as members of Abraham's household they would all have the privilege of receiving God's pledge that when the condition of the covenant (faith in Abraham's God) was met, the promises would apply.

The second aid in my embracing infant baptism was a study of Colossians 2. Having studied the significance of the Old Testament sacrament, I was then encouraged to study the verses where Paul identifies baptism as the New Testament parallel of circumcision (Col. 2:11–12). No more would the covenant sign require the shedding of blood (since Christ's blood had been shed once for all). Instead, the covenant sign of purification with water would indicate the cleansing Christ's blood accomplishes for all who believe in him. But because this sacrament was also a seal as well as a sign, it too would represent God's pledge that the promises of the covenant would apply to those who met its conditions. The sacrament did not have to be attached to the time the conditions were met because it was a pledge of what God would do, not a sign of what the recipient had done.

I had been trained by my Baptist upbringing to look for the Bible verse that commanded believers to baptize their children. But Presbyterians taught me to look for something different: the verse that prohibits believers from baptizing their children. For two thousand years believing parents had the privilege of providing God's physical pledge of his spiritual faithfulness to their children. Now with the great expansion of grace in Christ Jesus, why would they think that the covenant seal was being restricted and removed from their households? If baptism was the new sign of covenant inclusion, believers would expect continuity with the precedent of two millennia and would naturally administer the sacrament to their children, unless there was a specific prohibition. Not only is there no such prohibition, but there are instead multiple examples of baptisms being administered to entire households. In fact, except for the baptism of the Ethiopian eunuch (who could have no household) every New Testament baptism described in detail after Christ's resurrection includes believers *and* their households.

Missional

God's provision for families made Presbyterian worship particularly precious to me as he provided my own family. I was further refreshed and inspired by worship when I recognized that it was God's means of celebrating and extending his own family. Edmund Clowney introduced me to the concept of "doxological evangelism."[20] He said that if God's people worship with enthusiastic, respectful, and grateful praise for God's grace, then their joy will anticipate the culminating praise of God at the end of this age.[21] The church's worship ushers forward the benefits of the kingdom for God's people. In addition, such joy will be a magnet to lost and hurting people. These ends not only explain why worship is so important to God that he regulates its practice; they also remind me why I so rejoice in the biblical worship upon which Presbyterians insist.

I am not Presbyterian because all such churches echo such glorious praise. But I am committed to such churches because their Presbyterian principles encourage them to reach for the glory of biblical worship, and their convictions enable many to grasp it. Ultimately, this is the reason I associate with my church. I recognize that, though all Presbyterians are sinfully flawed in their representation of the gospel of grace, their biblical commitments always provide them hope of reflecting their Savior better. They limp along the path to biblical faithfulness, but they are on the right path. So I am happy to limp along with them, looking toward the Savior whose glorious grace makes the journey possible.

Final Thoughts

As I observe what I have written above, I recognize that I have not written a *formal* analysis or defense of the beliefs and practices of the Presbyterian church. Neither have I tried to survey the various branches and brands of those calling themselves Presbyterian—some of which have wandered far from the convictions of our forefathers. My simple effort has been to be true to my assignment: reflecting on why I as an evangelical have chosen to associate with my particular Presbyterian church. Faithfulness

---

[20]See Edmund Clowney, "The Singing Savior," *Moody Monthly*, July–August 1979, 42; also Tim Keller's reflections on Clowney's work in *Worship by the Book*, ed. D. A. Carson (Grand Rapids: Zondervan, 2002), 218–19.

[21]Edmund P. Clowney, "Kingdom Evangelism," in *The Pastor-Evangelist*, ed. Roger S. Greenway (Phillipsburg, NJ: Presbyterian and Reformed, 1987), 15–31.

to this assignment has led me to identify those features of Bible-believing Presbyterianism most dear to me in the context of the providences of my own life experience. I recognize that others will have different contexts and reasons for their decisions, and there are certainly other important features of Presbyterian conviction that deserve much additional comment in other contexts. Still, I am appreciative of this opportunity to relate my love for my church, and I pray that these thoughts may encourage others while recommitting me to seek the glory of Christ in the life of his church.

9

Denominationalism

HISTORICAL DEVELOPMENTS, CONTEMPORARY CHALLENGES, AND GLOBAL OPPORTUNITIES

David S. Dockery

As a prisoner for the Lord, then, I urge you to live a life worthy of the calling you have received. Be completely humble and gentle; be patient, bearing with one another in love. Make every effort to keep the unity of the Spirit through the bond of peace. There is one body and one Spirit—just as you are called to one hope when you were called—one Lord, one faith, one baptism; one God and Father of all, who is over all and through all and in all. (Eph. 4:1–6, NIV1984)

Most people today think that denominationalism is on the decline. Some things about that decline may be good; other aspects may not be. The question is this: If the denominational structures that have carried Protestant Christianity since the sixteenth century are on the decline, what will carry the Christian faith forward into the twenty-first century? How are we going to respond to the changes all around us? Before rushing to answer that question, we need to take a glimpse at denominational history to see where these different traditions originated. In doing so, we will try to connect the links of history to see how we arrived at this point today.

In the 1987 publication by neurologist Oliver Sacks called *The Man Who Mistook His Wife for a Hat*, Dr. Sacks wrote about patients with a neurological illness characterized by profound amnesia, a syndrome that describes those who do not know what they are doing at any given time or why they wander around in a state of profound disorientation. In losing their memories these people have lost themselves. I fear that American Christianity is on the verge of losing its hope and its identity in a similar disorientation. The problem for many is not so much doubt but a loss of memory. The history of Christianity is best understood as a chain of memory, and we need to reconnect some aspects of that chain.

An In-House Conversation

Going back to the eighteenth century, at the time of the First Great Awakening there was already a movement toward a nondenominational identity. A forerunner in that particular century of what is happening in our day was George Whitefield, the great preacher of the First Awakening. While preaching a sermon in 1740 in Philadelphia, Whitefield, who was known for his theatrics, called out:

> "Father Abraham, Whom have you in heaven? Any Episcopalians?"
> "No!"
> "Any Presbyterians?"
> "No!"
> "Any Independents or Seceders, New Sides or Old Sides, any Methodists?"
> "No! No! No!"
> "Whom have you there, then, Father Abraham?"
> "We don't know those names here! All who have come are Christians—believers in Christ, men who have overcome by the blood of the Lamb and the word of his testimony . . ."
> "Then . . . God help us all, to forget having names and become Christians in deed and truth."[1]

This statement by Whitefield is very similar to the statement of one of the key editors of the volumes known as *The Fundamentals*, in which R. A. Torrey a century ago described himself as an "Episcopresbygationalaptist." C. S. Lewis, in describing denominational issues, said that our divisions should never be discussed except in the presence of those who have already come to believe that there is one God, and that Jesus

---

[1]George Whitefield, quoted in William Warren Sweet, *The Story of Religion in America* (New York: Harper and Brothers, 1939), 142.

Christ is his only Son. Therefore, the discussions in this chapter are best understood as in-house family conversations.

History of Denominationalism

The idea of denominations, a term that comes from the Latin word meaning "to name," is a negative concept for some people. Granted that there is no biblical mandate to establish denominations; they have, nevertheless, been important for the history of Christianity as the structures and organization that carry forward the work of those who come together around shared beliefs and practices. Denominations have historically provided accountability, connections, coherence, structure, and organization to carry out work to support churches, benevolent work, missions, and educational institutions.

In the history of Christianity there have been three major branches of the church: Roman Catholicism, Eastern Orthodoxy, and Protestantism. The contributors to this volume come from this third tradition, the Protestant tradition, which finds its beginning in 1517 with the posting of the Ninety-Five Theses, penned by Martin Luther.

We all know that there are more than three groups within Christianity. There are hundreds, even thousands, of different denominations. Let us take a quick look at how these various movements developed.

Early Church

Certainly the early church was more unified than we are today, particularly as it came together following the great councils of the fourth and fifth centuries. There were four major councils from Nicaea in 325 to Chalcedon in 451, and bishops gave strong leadership and organization to promote a sense of unity in the church. But by 1054 there was a major and public break between the East and the West, between Orthodoxy and Roman Catholicism, that had been brewing for some time, particularly over the use of icons and the infallibility of the pope. Protestantism is best understood as a further break from Catholicism.

The Reformation

We can trace the birth of Protestantism to a monk with a mallet who had no intention of starting a new denomination; yet that is exactly what happened when Martin Luther nailed the Ninety-Five Theses to the Wittenberg church door. From that initiative, denominations began to proliferate. As this movement began in Germany in the early part of the sixteenth century, something very similar was taking place across the border in Switzerland with Ulrich Zwingli. Before long Luther and Zwingli came together to see if they could agree and unify the two movements referred to as the German Reformation and the Swiss Reformation. They were able to agree on a number of points such as the Holy Trinity, who Jesus Christ is, and the nature of salvation. Significant differences were uncovered, however, over the understanding of the Lord's Supper, and the groups went their separate ways. From this fracture came the proliferation of break-off groups, not only groups following Luther, Zwingli, and the Swiss Anabaptists, but also groups following John Calvin and others. A "third way" group developed in England, which we know as the Church of England or Anglicans. While there was general agreement among all of these groups on the central truths of the Christian faith, they were not able to agree on key details, and new movements were spawned around their disagreements.

From these various movements concern soon arose regarding the growing fragmentation of the body of Christ. Phillip Melanchthon and Martin Bucer (a follower of Luther and teacher of Calvin, respectively) began to raise questions about this proliferating fragmentation. Fresh calls for unity were issued, reminding others of their shared confession of the Nicene Creed, "We believe in one holy catholic and apostolic Church." But these calls went largely unheeded.

Seventeenth Century: Expanding Denominational Differences

If these new movements began to take off during the sixteenth century in the Protestant Reformation, they went into an accelerated pace in the seventeenth century as the Puritans sought to purify the churches with a focus on preaching and experiential Christianity, or what they called experimental religion.

From the Puritans or the Separatists came other offshoots: Baptists, Congregationalists, Presbyterians, and Quakers. By the seventeenth century the church family tree looked something like this: The apostolic church developed from New Testament times to 1054, with Catholicism going in one direction and Orthodoxy in another, Lutheran and Reformed groups heading in different directions, and Anglicanism developing as a third way. The branch groups that developed from within Anglicanism moved in multiple directions.

Eighteenth Century: Awakenings

The eighteenth century saw the Awakenings springing forth in Europe and the United States. From these movements came the Wesleyans, or the Methodists, influenced by John and Charles Wesley, who preached thousands of sermons and hymns, many of which hymns we still sing today. John Wesley was an organizational genius, and his emphasis on methods to extend the gospel and strengthen the church led to the use of the term *Methodists*.

Nineteenth Century: Revivalism

In the early part of the nineteenth century there were great revivals, such as the Cane Ridge revivals in Kentucky, led by Barton Stone and Alexander Campbell, who started what is referred to as the Restorationist Movement, which produced the Churches of Christ and the Disciples of Christ. The Holiness Movement was also a break-off renewal movement, and now the denominational picture looked even more complicated. Each group attempted to purify what had come before, with the Restorationists doing an end run around all of the others, seeking to return to the New Testament ideal. They claimed that they did not come from Catholics or Lutherans or Anglicans or the Reformed, but that their roots could be traced to something more pure, the New Testament itself.

Twentieth Century: The Holy Spirit and Sign Gifts

In the twentieth century there was yet another new movement: the Pentecostals, who trace their origins to Topeka, Kansas (though something quite similar took place about the same time in the Azusa Street revivals in Southern California). This sectarian group was not accepted by any denomination in the early years of the twentieth century, but now they are the fastest-growing movement in American Christianity and the world.

We find ourselves at the beginning of the twenty-first century. The Pentecostals have evolved from the Holiness Movement, and the ongoing emphasis upon distinctives within and among denominations has not been balanced by an appreciation of commonalities.

Denominational Distinctives

Though all denominations are more complex than their most prominent features, certain distinctives stand out. Roman Catholics emphasize
sacrament and tradition. The Orthodox highlight liturgy and mystery.
Lutherans center on Word and faith. Presbyterians cling to the sovereignty
of God and covenant theology. Anglicans focus on worship as formu-
lated in the Book of Common Prayer. Baptists place their priorities on
Scripture, conversion, and baptism. The Quakers appeal to the inner life,
while Methodists proclaim a heartfelt religion and spiritual disciplines.
Holiness movements stress piety and separatism. Restorationists trace
their roots back to the New Testament church, and Pentecostals proclaim
the power and manifestation of the Spirit.

So many different groups, so many distinctions. Can we say that these
are all true to the words in Ephesians 4 that proclaim there is "one Lord,
one faith, one baptism"? Literally there are dozens of varieties of each of
these major groups, resulting in the thousands of denominations in this
country and around the world. Some have given up on how to figure out
these things, weary with the questions about our history and heritage.

So Many Denominations

The First Great Awakening, with George Whitefield leading the way, provided a step toward a generic evangelicalism that came to prominence in
the twentieth century. An important book by H. Richard Niebuhr in the
early part of the century confirmed for many the problem of "so many
denominations." This verdict reflects the overriding thinking today that
denominationalism as a whole is a failure; some go so far as to say that
it is sinful, divisive, and harmful. Most acknowledge that fragmentation,
especially unnecessary fragmentation, is not good. But we must recognize
that Niebuhr's words "denominationalism represents the moral failure of
Christianity" represented a focus more on the sociological differences and
ethnic identities within each denomination than on doctrinal differences.[2]

THEOLOGICAL DIFFERENCES

Theological differences are often thought to help people understand and
define denominations. But theological issues like Calvinism and Armin-
ianism are not the only way to view denominational developments. Some

---

[2]See Richard H. Niebuhr, *The Social Sources of Denominationalism* (New York: World, 1929).

doctrinal emphases, it is true, are very difficult to bridge. Perhaps it is better to understand denominational differences not by asking who is a Calvinist and who is an Arminian, or who is a premillennialist and who is not, but rather by discerning our differences from the vantage point of church polity, how churches are organized, how they structure and govern themselves.

DENOMINATIONAL POLITY

History reveals that Presbyterians, Anglicans, and Baptists alike have maintained some kind of Calvinist heritage, yet they are quite different in the ways they govern the church (or churches). (And yes, there are Arminian Baptists and Presbyterians as well.) We think of Episcopalians or Anglicans as those who emphasize governance from the top down, in a hierarchal structure. Presbyterians have a synod with external authority, as well as elders who are part of the church and who rule and lead from within. Congregationalists and Baptists, with their emphasis on voluntarism and the priesthood of believers, have developed something more akin to a bottom-up approach to leadership. Polity certainly seems to be a preferred way of understanding how these denominational differences came about, as well as how they continue.

LITURGICAL PRACTICE

Another way to understand the development of denominations is through the window of liturgy and worship. Roman Catholics understood the Lord's Supper in one way with their approach to transubstantiation, while Lutherans responded by saying, "No, the elements are not supernaturally changed into the body and blood of Christ, but he is 'in and under' the bread and cup." The Presbyterians answered by saying, "No, there's the spiritual presence of Christ, but not in the same way that Lutherans had described it." Many Baptists responded by saying that the Supper is primarily a remembrance looking back to the death of Christ. The Quakers countered by saying no to all of these perspectives, thus not celebrating the sacraments or the ordinances at all.

The primary differences between denominations continue to be over church organization and ordinances or sacraments—questions about how we should understand baptism, who dips or dunks, and whether a drop or a dab is enough water to qualify as a real baptism. Whether we understand denominationalism from the vantage point of organizational structure, sociological movements, theological emphases, polity, or worship, there are huge visible differences among those who name the name of Christ.

A SOCIOLOGICAL PERSPECTIVE

Others have suggested the sociological window as the best vantage point for understanding denominational life, observing that there are three major churches: the church in the East (or Orthodoxy), the church at Rome (or Roman Catholicism), and the church in England (or Anglicanism). Every other group, so it is maintained, is understood as a renewal sectarian group that has broken off from one of these. Lutherans broke from the church of Rome, Baptists broke from the Church of England, and on and on the story is repeated.

But often the demise of the Spirit's work seems to begin when these break-off groups, so-called purifying groups or renewal movements, become denominational structures themselves. When these movements progress from outcast sectarian groups to responsible denominations within society, the emphasis seems to shift to concerns regarding structure, resulting in bureaucratic tendencies and often taking away from the work of the Spirit.

Jaroslav Pelikan has keenly observed that there is always a struggle between the work of structure, which is necessary to carry forward the work of Christianity, and the movement of the Spirit. Too much emphasis on the Spirit on one side or too much structure on the other can create error in either direction.[3] We have pointed to the beginning of denominationalism by going back to the seventeenth century. From that point we can see the proliferation of denominations that grew out of and from within Protestantism through the movements of Puritanism and Pietism, bringing about new initiatives that arose from within these so-called renewal movements, all seemingly in search of a purer and truer form of New Testament Christianity.

Denominationalism through American Eyes

Denominationalism, like evangelicalism as most of us know it, is primarily an American phenomenon: not because America is the only place where denominations proliferate, but because the freedoms in our coun-

[3]See Jaroslav Pelikan, *Spirit versus Structure: Luther and the Institutions of the Church* (New York: Harper & Row, 1968).

try have enabled denominations to expand, flourish, and break off from those from which they were birthed. Now we find ourselves with so many denominations that it is almost impossible to keep up with them all.

Unfortunately—and I say this with caution—I believe this development has resulted more in the Americanization of Christianity than the Christianization of America. Because of this we need to think in a fresh way about denominations. We need to think anew about the structure that will be able to carry forth the Christian movement in the twenty-first century. Looking back to the time of the Revolutionary War in the eighteenth century, there were only three major denominations in this country. About 75 percent of the population were Congregationalists, Presbyterians, or Episcopalians. But by 1850, less than 20 percent of the population belonged to one of these "big three." By then there were two new kids on the block: the Methodists and the Baptists. Particularly with growth in the South and in the Midwest, the Methodists and the Baptists outpaced all the other groups in terms of numerical growth. The Methodists grew from merely a handful of people at the time of the Revolutionary War to the largest denomination in America by the time of the Civil War.

This does not take into account ethnic groups and others who came along in the eighteenth, nineteenth, and twentieth centuries. African American churches were founded by George Lyle and Andrew Bryan, with the first African American church in Savannah, Georgia. The focus on freedom, pilgrimage, and hope characterized both their songs and their sermons. From this initial work has come a great movement within African American churches, as well as other immigrant churches, many of which have remained largely non-English speaking even into the twenty-first century.

The charismatic movement of the twentieth century now has full sway among growing sectors of people. The songs currently sung in so many praise and worship services can be traced back to the participatory worship emphasis among charismatics. This small group which was birthed in Topeka, Kansas, and Southern California in the early 1900s has now spread worldwide. William Seymour could not have imagined what would happen with the Pentecostal and charismatic movements that began a century ago as sectarian outcast groups who were looked down upon by all other denominations. Now these groups, as previously mentioned, are the only ones in the entire country, and perhaps in the world, that are consistently growing—the Assemblies of God in particular.

The Birth of American Evangelicalism

The twentieth-century divisions paved the way for the birth of evangelicalism as we now know it. It is to the development of American evangelicalism that we now turn our attention.

The Rise of Liberalism

The twentieth century began as a time of social and cultural turmoil, massive immigration, urban growth, and a shift toward an industrialized economy. Every aspect of society and culture was influenced by these trends, even the religious world. And people began to ask whether the Christian faith as believers had known and practiced it was still relevant to this changing cultural context. The Enlightenment and evolutionary thought, along with these trends, resulted in the rise of theological liberalism. Liberalism had a strong foothold in the United States as the nineteenth century gave way to the twentieth.

Influential shapers of liberalism included Friedrich Schleiermacher, Horace Bushnell, and Walter Rauschenbusch, among others. Schleiermacher, with his book *On Religion: Speeches to Its Cultured Despisers*, called for a way in which the Christian faith could be heard afresh in a culture influenced by the Enlightenment, and he sought to adapt the Christian faith to this changing culture. Bushnell suggested that we need to focus on nurture rather than conversion. Rauschenbusch, a Baptist theologian, emphasized the social application and the social witness of the gospel, which eventually began to substitute for the gospel itself, resulting in what has become known as the "social gospel."

And so these three influential shapers altered the Christian faith in their attempts to adapt it to the changing context of the culture and society at the beginning of the twentieth century. Their serious academic work was popularized by three great preachers during this time, Harry Emerson Fosdick, Henry Ward Beecher, and Phillips Brooks, in key pulpits in the New York and Boston areas. Their sermons were echoed over and over again; they were masterful orators who could speak clearly, confidently, and prophetically. In 1922 Fosdick stood in his pulpit and suggested in a sermon titled "Shall the Fundamentalists Win?" that it was time for the end of fundamentalism. He answered his own question with a resounding no! It was time for the triumph of liberalism in the churches, a view boldly affirmed in 1926 by the editors of *The Christian Century*.

These popularizers brought about changes in the churches that could be characterized as the adaptation of faith to the times. Such changes were more than attempts to show the relevance of the Christian faith or communicate it in a way that it could be heard afresh; instead, they transformed the message of the Christian faith itself. The result was a lost connection with the great history of Christian doctrine, a disconnect with the "Great Tradition."

Their naturalistic perspectives about the world tended to dominate. Creative communicators brought skeptical views of the supernatural, particularly as it related to the reality of the miraculous, and elevated reason above revelation and the importance of experience over tradition. Now all of these things are characteristic of classical liberalism, but we would be wrong to relegate them to the last century, for we see similar ideas resurfacing today.

Orthodoxy, Fundamentals, and Fundamentalism

Liberalism was challenged by orthodox Christians. The best response to liberalism came from the great Presbyterian thinker J. Gresham Machen. In his 1923 book *Christianity and Liberalism*,[4] he suggested that liberalism is not a form of Christianity. He brilliantly contended that Christianity and liberalism are really two different religions. Machen's work was masterful, articulate, and generally well received. It resulted in a revival of orthodox thinking. Many people found new ways to articulate their faith in the face of the changing culture and the rise of liberalism.

The claim that liberalism is not a form of Christianity, but rather another religion altogether, found followers in the churches. Machen argued that liberalism is empty, a claim echoed by H. Richard Niebuhr, who poignantly insisted that liberalism's basic message is, "A God without wrath brought men without sin into a kingdom without judgment through the ministrations of a Christ without a cross." But Machen's informed theological reply to liberalism was not the only response.

People in various regions of the country offered a more reactionary approach to liberalism, resulting in a fiery fundamentalism. Unlike the articulate, well-reasoned, orthodox critique by Machen, these reactionary approaches, best exemplified in the southern fundamentalist J. Frank

---

[4] J. Gresham Machen, *Christianity and Liberalism* (Grand Rapids: Eerdmans, 1923).

Norris, known as the "Texas Tornado," took no prisoners in advancing their movement. This fierce fundamentalism went beyond a defense of historical orthodoxy in *The Fundamentals*, as they were well articulated in the set of books by that name.[5] These volumes offered reasoned and persuasive biblical and theological arguments from a wide range of contributors, including British thinkers such as J. Edwin Orr, Southern Baptists such as E. Y. Mullins, and the more well-known evangelical and fundamentalist leaders of the time. But the movement calling for an orthodox Christianity turned in a different direction when Norris and others redirected it from a commitment to the fundamentals to "fundamentalism," which changed the whole nature of things. Fundamentalism became reactionary, separatistic, and legalistic.

At this time, near the end of the nineteenth century and the beginning of the twentieth, prophetic conferences came on the scene that called for a commitment to what they believed to be the foundational issues of the Christian faith, including the truthfulness of Scripture, the deity of Christ, the virgin birth, the substitutionary atonement, the importance of Christ's bodily resurrection, and a belief in miracles. The list, however, became longer and longer as the fundamentalists gained influence in the churches. Soon, it included commitment to dispensationalism, separatism, and withdrawal from the denominations, which started the decline away from the denominational entities and the important structures that had carried Christianity forward, particularly from the sixteenth through the nineteenth centuries.

Fundamentalism became hard-line, harsh, and isolationist, resulting in additional fragmentation. Splits in denominations occurred, particularly in the north among Presbyterians and Baptists. There were numerous Presbyterian groups and hundreds, even thousands, of independent Baptist churches that began to spring up all across America, as well as Bible churches and other nondenominational groups. They also started new mission groups and Bible colleges, resulting in informal networks loosely related to one another. These new networks began to take the place of denominations. A need for some sort of structure, formal or informal, became apparent. So fundamentalism grew out of the controversies of the early twentieth century.

---

[5] R. A. Torrey and A. C. Dixon, eds., *The Fundamentals: A Testimony to the Truth*, 12 vols. (Los Angeles: Bible Institute of Los Angeles, 1910–1915).

Twentieth-Century American (and British) Evangelicalism

Around the time of World War II (the 1930s and 1940s), many began to question whether fundamentalism had fallen off the rails on one side, very much as liberalism had fallen off the rails on the other. Several people joined together under the leadership of Billy Graham, Harold Ockenga, and Carl F. H. Henry, all of whom were calling for a renewed commitment to historical orthodoxy, or what was being called "the new evangelicalism," with connections to aspects of revivalism, Pietism, Puritanism, and the Reformation.

In Carl Henry's masterful 1947 work, *The Uneasy Conscience of Modern Fundamentalism*, he called for three primary changes within fundamentalism: (1) Christianity cannot be anti-intellectual, but calls for serious engagement with the Christian intellectual tradition, including the academy and the culture; (2) Christianity cannot be only otherworldly, nor can it only focus on this world either, for there must be a balance; and (3) particularly, evangelicalism must not be separatistic and legalistic.[6]

Ockenga, commenting on Henry's work, claimed that the fundamentalists had lost the ability to do theological triage. They could no longer prioritize what was important as opposed as to what was preferential. Therefore, Ockenga said that fundamentalists could not distinguish the importance of the deity of Christ from opposition to card playing. Building on the three pillars of Henry's argument in *The Uneasy Conscience of Modern Fundamentalism*, the new evangelicalism appealed to a transdenominational, gospel-centered, historical orthodoxy, an appeal echoed in Britain by the likes of John Stott, J. I. Packer, and F. F. Bruce.

New Affinity Groups: Transdenominational Evangelical Networks

The first days of the National Association of Evangelicals, which began in 1942, pulled evangelicals together into new networks, new alliances, and new ways of relating to one another, at the same time siphoning energy away from historical denominational entities. While people largely stayed within denominations, many had one foot in and another foot planted outside them. Most denominations, including the Southern Bap-

---

[6]See Carl F. H. Henry, *The Uneasy Conscience of Modern Fundamentalism* (Grand Rapids: Eerdmans, 1947).

tist Convention, were quite divided over whether this new evangelicalism was helpful or hurtful.

As in the time of the Awakenings and revivals, evangelicalism primarily worked around denominational structures rather than through them, creating new entrepreneurial networks that were doing things differently than the way the denominations had done them before. It therefore seems best to understand the development of historical evangelicalism over the last seventy years not only in terms of David Bebbington's fourfold description of traditional beliefs—the truthfulness of the Bible, the uniqueness of the gospel, the necessity of conversion, and the importance of service and missions—but also in terms of people identifying (at least in part) with these transdenominational movements, special-purpose groups (as Robert Wuthnow calls them), or connecting networks.[7] These new interlocking networks, more than denominations, have formed and framed the center of evangelicalism in the United States over the past seventy years.

TOWARD RESTRUCTURING

As Wuthnow emphasized in his book *The Restructuring of American Religion*, this shift toward transdenominational movements is the biggest change in Christianity since the Reformation.[8] It is the biggest change because no longer do people identify with kindred spirits in vertical alignments, as Lutherans, Anglicans, Presbyterians, Methodists, or Baptists. Instead they identify more by other connections and monikers such as fundamentalists, conservatives, evangelicals, moderates, and liberals. Thus liberal Anglicans and liberal Methodists have more in common than liberal Anglicans and conservative Anglicans; evangelical Baptists and evangelical Presbyterians more than liberal Baptists and evangelical Baptists. With this shift we have the restructuring of American religion along horizontal lines rather than vertical ones, which has changed the entire way in which the structure of Christianity is understood, especially when compared with the denominational developments of the past four centuries.

---

[7]David W. Bebbington, *Evangelicalism in Modern Britain: A History from the 1730s to the 1980s* (London: Unwin Hyman, 1989).

[8]Robert Wuthnow, *The Restructuring of American Religion: Society and Faith Since World War II* (Princeton: Princeton University Press, 1988).

Wuthnow also has observed that the rise of special-purpose groups, sometimes called parachurch movements, has had a large impact on the shape of these horizontal networks. Parachurch organizations, evangelistic and missionary agencies, relief and social organizations, publishers, broadcasters, schools, colleges, and seminaries have created new networks and coalitions. If you look at a directory of the National Association of Evangelicals, all of these groups basically form the index or the lineup of the organization. These are the various groups that join this loosely connected coalition called the evangelical world.

THE INFLUENCE OF D. L. MOODY AND BILLY GRAHAM
But just as during the Awakenings, when George Whitfield took the first step in a transdenominational direction, so in the nineteenth century D. L. Moody particularly popularized parachurch movements. Moody was an entrepreneurial activist who wanted to connect the dots in any direction he could to advance the gospel. The movements Moody started were blessed and expanded by Billy Graham in the twentieth century, leading to the growth of these organizations. In this process the organizations themselves became more important than historical denominational structures. So with the rise of these special-purpose groups, the blessings of Graham, the decline of liberalism, and the mainline denominations' becoming untethered from their heritage, there developed new movements—not new denominations—into which the evangelicals poured their energy and their lives: parachurch groups such as Youth for Christ, World Vision, Young Life, Campus Crusade, the Navigators, Prison Fellowship, *Christianity Today*, and thousands of others.

If someone were asked, "What is the connection between Rick Warren, Chuck Colson, Carl F. H. Henry, Harold Lindsell, and Billy Graham?" the answer might not be obvious, but all had or currently have their church membership in a Southern Baptist church. Yet hardly anyone first thinks of these visible leaders as Southern Baptists. Their identity comes from a particular parachurch group, a social network, an organization, rather than a denomination. Historically we identify Lutheranism with Martin Luther, Presbyterianism with John Knox, Anglicanism with Thomas Cranmer, Methodism with John Wesley, and the Baptist movement with William Carey. Throughout history Christian leaders have connected with a denominational identity, but in the twentieth century, Christian leaders—at least in the evangelical world—have often been more identified with a parachurch organization, or to use Wuthnow's term, a special-purpose group, which has changed the entire way we think about the importance of denominations.

Networks, Denominations, and a Theology of the Church

The evangelical movement is largely understood as a grassroots ecumenism that holds people together because of like beliefs and like structures. While evangelical theologians have done a magnificent job of focusing on the truthfulness of Scripture, hermeneutics, the doctrine of revelation, and the importance of the gospel, for the most part evangelicals have not done a good job of articulating a theology of the church. That weakness has led to an ambiguous understanding of how churches relate to one another and how they relate to structures within and outside of denominations, creating this uneasy marriage between the church and the parachurch movements. This observation is one of the reasons that many believe ecclesiology will be the doctrinal focus of the first decades of the twenty-first century.

Over the past twenty-five years there has been a slight shift. The networks have started to move away from parachurch organizations as a base and more toward church structures. The shift started in California, largely with Calvary Chapel, which arose out of the Jesus Movement, then moved to the Willow Creek and Saddleback networks with Bill Hybels and Rick Warren. And so that generation birthed the next generation, with all kinds of new networks we know today as Acts 29, the Emergent Village, Desiring God, 9 Marks, the Gospel Coalition, and others like Together for the Gospel and Together for Adoption.

Now we find ourselves in the second decade of the twenty-first century, with major changes in the way people think about denominations and denominationalism. In 1955, when Will Herberg wrote his classic volume *Protestant, Catholic, Jew*, one in twenty-five church-going Americans tended to change denominations over a lifetime.[9] In 1985, one in three Americans changed denominations during their lifetime. By 2011 that number was more than one in two, or about 60 percent, which means most will change denominations somewhere along the way in the twenty-first century. We have seen not only a decline in denominational loyalty, but

---

[9]Will Herberg, *Protestant, Catholic, Jew: An Essay in American Religious Sociology* (New York: Doubleday, 1955).

also an increase in the number of people who identify more with a special-purpose group or a parachurch group than with a particular denomination.

Denominational Rivalry and Geographical Perspectives

These shifts have changed the way we perceive the importance of denominations, resulting in additional challenges to the denominational diversity we have observed. The rivalry between denominations has changed. We now find ourselves in a new pluralistic context. However, we cannot ignore the importance of geography, the importance of place. New movements and groups have developed as the country has migrated westward over the past one hundred years. One of the reasons there seems to be conflict in almost every group and every denomination in America is that there is nowhere else for people to move in the continental United States. Thus, we see the rise of new global opportunities. Certainly geography has shifted, but the generalizations about geographical presence and denominational influence still hold. Roman Catholics continue to have great sway in New England, Lutherans are most prevalent in the upper Midwest, Baptists are a majority in the South, and the Dutch Reformed are represented throughout other portions of the Midwest.

Perhaps even more important than geographical regions is the kind of city or town or place where one resides. Great differences in the understanding of denominational importance exist in metropolitan areas and cities versus rural areas or towns. Suburban areas are where megachurches have tended to thrive. Surprisingly, over 50 percent of all churchgoing Americans attend less than 12 percent of all churches. The megachurches in the suburbs now shape large aspects of Christianity. They tend to be generic, which means that the denominational label means much less than it did in previous generations.

Nancy Ammerman, a sociologist at Boston University, acknowledges this trend by pointing to the responses to denominationalism on the West Coast and in the Northeast, where about 30 percent of people respond positively to denominational identity, as opposed to 70 percent in the South. Such comparisons are even more exaggerated from rural to urban areas: 84 percent of people who live in rural areas persist in thinking that denominational identity is important, as opposed to less than half who reside in an urban or suburban setting. One more important point regarding place: most churches can still be found in rural areas, while most people live in urban and suburban areas, another reason for the ongoing decline of denominations. So in addition to the influence of postmodernism and the other great changes and challenges around us, the shifts in population and perceptions regarding denominational importance are hard to calculate, particularly in metropolitan areas on the East and West coasts.[10]

From Mainline to Sideline

Most of the mainline denominations have sadly lost their way. Some have become disconnected from their heritage, and even more so from Scripture and the great Christian tradition. And some today are clearly not only postdenominational but also on their way toward becoming post-Christian as their conversations focus on issues of inclusiveness and universalism, sexuality, and interreligious spirituality.

Denominationalism and Evangelicalism: Questions about the Future

So what does this say about the future of denominationalism? I want to say that while denominationalism is in decline, denominations still matter; certainly some sense of structure matters. I have appealed in this chapter to Jaroslav Pelikan's important book *Structure versus Spirit*, in which he maintains that Christianity needs structure in order to carry forward the Christian message. Yet if we focus too much on structure, we wind up leaning precariously toward bureaucracy. If we focus too much on the Spirit, we tilt toward an amorphous Christianity. So there must remain some place, some future for denominationalism or for structures, even as we recognize the importance of variety in an expanding pluralistic context.

Denominational Conviction and Cooperation

Perhaps more important for the twenty-first century than the future of denominations will be the role of networks. Networks fit well Wuthnow's descriptions regarding groupings and structure. Networks seem to be replacing denominations for many people, at least for the short term, and may be the most significant change in the religious landscape for

---

[10]Nancy Ammerman, ed., *Everyday Religion: Observing Modern Religious Lives* (New York: Oxford, 2006).

the twenty-first century. While there will be a place for denominations, and denominations that thrive will remain convictionally connected to Scripture, the gospel, and their tradition, they will explore ways to partner with affinity groups and networks, moving out of their insularity while seeking to understand better the changing global context of our day. Learning to work afresh in cooperative ways will also be important. Denominations must no longer see themselves as rivals with either the networks or other denominations, but must look instead for commonalities while working together with special-purpose groups. Conviction and cooperation, boundaries and bridges, structure and the work of the Holy Spirit will all be necessary to move forward in a dynamic and constructive way in coming years. All of these concerns must be held together in balance without our ignoring or overemphasizing any.

A Global Perspective

We find ourselves in the global context of the twenty-first century. And it presents us with what I believe is a new opportunity, one in which we will face great challenge and great change, but also have reason for great hope. If we look around us and all we see are trends and signs such as secularism, the new atheism, the new liberalism, and the various fundamentalist reactions, we will likely become discouraged. When we hear talk of the decline of Christian America and an embattled evangelicalism whose young people are characterized by what Christian Smith has called "moralistic therapeutic deism," we can easily get pulled off track.[11] But I would like to suggest that it is time for us to move the conversation in a more hopeful direction.

Without losing our heritage and the key distinctives that have shaped the Christian tradition, we no longer need to look solely to the Western hemisphere for the future of Christian faith. It is time for us to think more globally. And it is imperative that we do so. In 1900, 80 percent of the Christians in the world lived in Europe and America. But in 2000, 60 percent of the Christians in the world were found in Asia, Africa, and Latin America—an immense change. We must turn our attention away from intramural and denominational squabbles at home in order

---

[11]Christian Smith, *Soul Searching: The Religious and Spiritual Lives of American Teenagers* (Oxford: Oxford University Press, 2005); Smith, *Souls in Transition: The Religious and Spiritual Lives of Emerging Adults* (Oxford: Oxford University Press, 2009).

to see what God is doing literally around the world through the work of his Spirit.[12]

During the twentieth century, Africa was transformed from a continent that was 10 percent Christian in 1900 to one that was 46 percent Christian in 2000. It is astonishing to see what God is doing there. There are now more Christians on the continent of Africa than there are citizens in the United States of America. Over the last one hundred years Christianity has grown from 10 million professing believers in Africa to over 360 million. And by 2025, the most conservative estimates are that if these trends continue, in Africa there will be over 630 million believers, in Latin America around 640 million, and in Asia around 500 million.[13]

At that point, the typical Christian will be a woman living in a Nigerian village or a Brazilian city, contrasted with the typical Christian of 1900: a man living in a Midwestern town in the United States. What an incredible change in both the growth and the center of Christianity. Let us not miss the fact that these same kinds of directional influences are present in America as well, for wherever denominations here are growing, they are growing largely among Asian Americans, Hispanic Americans, and African Americans. God's Spirit is moving around the globe, and it is time for us to look in different ways with new eyes and fresh viewpoints in this country and around the world rather than with the old lenses we have employed in the past. While we continue to struggle with Enlightenment and post-Enlightenment issues, our brothers and sisters in Africa face the challenges of the demonic and of intense persecution from Islam on a daily basis. As we look at them and at their world, they seem much more closely identified with apostolic Christianity than almost anything we know from experience.

Toward Hopefulness and Renewal

But please hear this word: we must realize that our struggles are not against fellow Christ-followers, but rather against demons, secularism, and unbelief. What is at stake if we do not take our eyes off the intramural squabbles that seem to characterize most denominations is not only a loss of the unity within the Christian movement, but also a loss of the

---

[12]See Philip Jenkins, *The Next Christendom: The Coming of Global Christianity* (New York: Oxford, 2002).

[13]Ibid.

mission focus of the Christian movement in the West. What we need is a fresh commitment to biblical orthodoxy, a historic Christianity, a faithful transgenerational, transcontinental, and multiethnic movement that stands or falls on first-order issues.

Without forsaking our denominational distinctives, we are called to a commitment to gospel commonalities that are more important than and precede those distinctives: things such as a commitment to the divine nature and authority of God's written Word, the deity and humanity of Jesus Christ, a heartfelt confession of the Holy Trinity, the uniqueness of the gospel message, the enabling work of God's Spirit, salvation by grace through faith alone, the importance of the church and the people of God who are both gathered and scattered, the hope of Christ's return, and the sacredness of life and family. In the twenty-first-century church we must learn to disagree graciously over our differences. We will likely not find ways to agree on a wide variety of secondary and tertiary issues. We must find ways to connect and re-create contexts of belonging for the multiple generations and various ethnic groups within the body of Christ.

A Plea for Denominational Faithfulness

We are drawn back to our question, what then do we do with denominations and their distinctives? I still maintain that denominational structures can be helpful, guiding, informative, connecting, cohering, and even essential for us. If, for instance, you decide that baptizing your infant children is more important than waiting for them to be baptized after a faith commitment as a mature young person or adult, then you will be more at home with Presbyterians than with Baptists. If you decide that going to war is not faithful to the biblical tradition, then you likely will find a place of belonging with Anabaptists or Mennonites. We must recognize that we will have to find places of belonging around these common beliefs and practices, because in our local expressions of Christianity we will find it difficult to ignore these key secondary matters. Yet we must be willing for those things truly to be secondary matters for the sake of a common mission to fulfill the Great Commission in this generation.

What is also needed for our day is the reclamation of a model of dynamic orthodoxy. The orthodox tradition must be recovered, one that is in conversation with the great history of the church, the great intellectual tradition that traces its way from Nicaea to Chalcedon, from Augustine to Bernard, to Luther and Calvin, to Wesley, the Pietists, and the revivals, resulting in what J. I. Packer and Thomas Oden have called "the one faith" that has been believed by all God's people in all places at all times.

A recommitment to such a confessional integrity will help us recover a call to the unity of the Christian faith in accord with the Nicene affirmation that the church is one, holy, universal, and apostolic. All of us in this changing twenty-first-century world must recommit ourselves afresh to the oneness and the universality of the church. This recommitment must also be supported by the right sort of virtues: a oneness that calls for humility and gentleness, patience, forbearance of one another, a love and diligence to preserve the unity of the Spirit in the bond of peace. We trust that God will help us to do so. Along with these things will be a global perspective that includes a renewed dedication to racial reconciliation in our country, looking forward to a day in which the great multitude from every nation, all tribes and all people groups and tongues, shall stand before the Lamb as proclaimed and promised in Revelation 7:9.

Trinitarian Christians, Gospel-Centered Missions, the Church, and the Future of Denominationalism

So do denominations still matter? Yes! I believe they do matter and they will continue to matter, but if, and only if, they remain connected to Scripture and to the orthodox tradition. We need conviction and boundaries, but we also will need a spirit of cooperation to build bridges. We need to understand that our various denominational heritages and distinctives do matter, but more importantly what is needed today is a fresh kind of transgenerational and transcontinental approach to the Christian faith. We need a new spirit of mutual respect and humility to serve together with those with whom we might have differences of conviction on less important matters.

It is possible, yes it is very possible, to hold hands with brothers and sisters who disagree on secondary and tertiary matters of theology and work together for the common good to extend the work of the gospel and the kingdom of God on this earth, partnerships that will pull us out of our inward focus. That is particularly the case where we can work together with Trinitarian Christians from across the board in social action, cultural engagement, and matters involving the public square, including religious freedom, marriage, sexuality, and beginning- and ending-of-life issues. We can do evangelism and missions with gospel-centered people of various denominational stripes.

Please, however, hear this: we will do congregational life with those who share common beliefs—not only with those who agree on primary matters of faith, but with those who share commonalities regarding polity as well. And if this is true, and if we can do more together than alone, and if we need accountability and connections for our work, which I wholeheartedly believe, then denominational structures that reflect the attributes we have described and connect the work of these congregations will serve us well in days ahead, and there can be a most hopeful future for denominations that remain faithful to the gospel.

We can trust God to bring a fresh wind of his Spirit; to bring renewal to our theological convictions and to our work of evangelism and missions; to revive our education and service so that we can relate to one another in love and humility and thereby inspire true fellowship and community; and yes, to bring new life to Christians, churches, and denominations as well. We pray not only for a new commitment to confessional, convictional, and courageous orthodoxy as modeled by many global church leaders, but also for a genuine orthopraxy that can be seen by a watching world, a world particularly in the West that stands on the verge of completely giving up on the Christian faith.

Let us join together in asking God to grant us a renewed commitment to the gospel, the church, and the truthfulness of Scripture, bringing about a renewed spirit of cooperation for the good of God's people around the globe. Let's work together to advance the gospel and trust God to bring forth fruit from our labors, resulting in renewal to churches, partnerships with networks and structures, and faithfulness to our denominations and their efforts to make known God's kingdom on earth and the eternal glory of our great God.[14]

---

[14]Portions of this chapter previously appeared in David S. Dockery, ed., *Southern Baptists, Evangelicals, and the Future of Denominationalism* (Nashville: B&H, 2011).

Bibliography

Sources for Denominational Distinctives

Buschart, W. David. *Exploring Protestant Traditions: An Invitation to Theological Hospitality*. Downers Grove, IL: IVP Academic, 2006.

Campbell, Ted. *Christian Confessions: A Historical Introduction*. Louisville, KY: Westminster John Knox, 1996.

Mead, Frank S., Samuel S. Hill, and Craig D. Atwood. *Handbook of Denominations in the United States*. 13th ed. Nashville: Abingdon, 2010.

Sources for Evangelical Unity in the Church

George, Timothy, and John Woodbridge. *The Mark of Jesus: Loving in a Way the World Can See*. Chicago: Moody, 2005.

Packer, J. I., and Thomas Oden. *One Faith: The Evangelical Consensus*. Downers Grove, IL: InterVarsity, 2004.

Phillips, Richard D., Philip G. Ryken, and Mark E. Dever. *The Church: One, Holy, Catholic and Apostolic*. Phillipsburg, NJ: P&R, 2004.

Sources for Evangelical History and Thought

McGrath, Alister. *Evangelicalism and the Future of Christianity*. Downers Grove, IL: InterVarsity, 1995.

Noll, Mark. *American Evangelical Christianity: An Introduction*. Oxford: Blackwell, 2001.

Sweeney, Douglas. *The American Evangelical Story*. Grand Rapids: Baker Academic, 2005.

Sources for Anglican History and Thought

Bray, Gerald. *The Faith We Confess: An Exposition of the Thirty-Nine Articles*. London: Latimer Trust, 2009.

Chapman, Mark. *Anglican Theology*. New York: T&T Clark, 2012.

Sykes, Stephen, and John Booty. *The Study of Anglicanism*. Philadelphia: Fortress, 1988.

Sources for Baptist History and Thought

Bebbington, David. *Baptists through the Centuries: A History of a Global People*. Waco, TX: Baylor University Press, 2010.

George, Timothy. *Baptists: A Brief History*. Nashville: B&H, forthcoming.

Hammett, John. *Biblical Foundations for Baptist Churches: A Contemporary Ecclesiology*. Grand Rapids: Kregel, 2005.

Sources for Lutheran History and Thought

Gritsch, Eric W. *Fortress Introduction to Lutheranism*. Minneapolis: Augsburg Fortress, 1994.

Lagerquist, L. DeAne. *The Lutherans*. Westport, CT: Greenwood, 1999.

Nelson, E. Clifford, ed. *The Lutherans in North America*. Rev. ed. Philadelphia: Fortress, 1980.

Sources for Methodist History and Thought

Heitzenrater, Richard P. *Wesley and the People Called Methodists*. Nashville: Abingdon, 1995.

Hempton, David. *Methodism: Empire of the Spirit*. New Haven, CT: Yale University Press, 2005.

Rack, Henry D. *Reasonable Enthusiast: John Wesley and the Rise of Methodism*. London: Epworth, 1989.

Sources for Pentecostal History and Thought

Karkkaninen, Veli-Matti, ed. *The Spirit in the World: Emerging Pentecostal Theologies in Global Contexts*. Grand Rapids: Eerdmans, 2009.

Macchia, Frank. *Baptized in the Spirit: A Global Pentecostal Theology*. Grand Rapids: Zondervan, 2006.

Miller, Donald, and Tetsunao Yamamori. *Global Pentecostalism: The New Face of Christian Social Engagement*. Berkeley: University of California Press, 2007.

Sources for Presbyterian History and Thought

Hart, D. G., and John R. Muether. *Seeking a Better Country: 300 Years of American Presbyterianism*. Phillipsburg, NJ: P&R, 2007.

Lucas, Sean Michael. *On Being Presbyterian: Our Beliefs, Practices, and Stories*. Phillipsburg, NJ: P&R, 2006.

Waters, Guy Prentiss. *How Jesus Runs the Church*. Phillipsburg, NJ: P&R, 2011.

Contributors

Gerald L. Bray (DLitt, University of Paris-Sorbonne), Research Professor of Divinity, Beeson Divinity School

Bryan Chapell (PhD, Southern Illinois University), President Emeritus and Adjunct Professor of Practical Theology, Covenant Theological Seminary

Anthony L. Chute (PhD, Trinity Evangelical Divinity School), Associate Dean and Associate Professor of Church History, California Baptist University

David S. Dockery (PhD, University of Texas-Arlington), President and University Professor of Christian Thought and Tradition, Union University

Timothy F. George (ThD, Harvard University), Founding Dean and Professor of Divinity, Beeson Divinity School

Byron D. Klaus (DMin, Fuller Theological Seminary), President and Professor of Intercultural Leadership Studies, Assemblies of God Theological Seminary

Christopher W. Morgan (PhD, Mid-America Baptist Theological Seminary), Dean and Professor of Theology, California Baptist University

Robert A. Peterson (PhD, Drew University), Professor of Systematic Theology, Covenant Theological Seminary

Douglas A. Sweeney (PhD, Vanderbilt University), Professor of Church History and the History of Christian Thought, Trinity Evangelical Divinity School

Timothy C. Tennent (PhD, University of Edinburgh), President and Professor of World Christianity, Asbury Theological Seminary

General Index

Scripture Index

THEOLOGY IN COMMUNITY

FIRST-RATE EVANGELICAL SCHOLARS
TAKE A MULTIDISCIPLINARY APPROACH
TO KEY CHRISTIAN DOCTRINES

Edited by CHRISTOPHER W. MORGAN
and ROBERT A. PETERSON

READ THE WHOLE SERIES:

The Deity of Christ
The Glory of God
Suffering and the Goodness of God
The Kingdom of God
Fallen: A Theology of Sin

For more information visit www.crossway.org.